Women in the Informal Sector and Poverty Reduction in Morocco

The city of Fez as a case study

Africa in Development

Volume 16

Souad Belhorma

Women in the Informal Sector and Poverty Reduction in Morocco

The city of Fez as a case study

PETER LANG
Oxford · Bern · Berlin · Bruxelles · New York · Wien

Bibliographic information published by Die Deutsche Nationalbibliothek.
Die Deutsche Nationalbibliothek lists this publication in the Deutsche Nationalbibliografie; detailed bibliographic data is available on the Internet at http://dnb.d-nb.de.

A catalogue record for this book is available from the British Library.

Library of Congress Control Number:
A CIP catalog record for this book has been applied for at the Library of Congress.

ISSN 1662-1212
ISBN 978-1-78997-158-3 (print) • ISBN 978-1-78997-159-0 (ePDF)
ISBN 978-1-78997-160-6 (ePub) • ISBN 978-1-78997-161-3 (mobi)

Hochfeldstrasse 32, CH-3012 Bern, Switzerland
info@peterlang.com, www.peterlang.com, www.peterlang.net

This publication has been peer reviewed.

Printed in Germany

I dedicate this book to my lovely parents. A special feeling of gratitude is to my father Mohamed Belhorma and my mother Houria Benjelloun Andaloussi whose words of encouragement are ringing in my ears.

To my brother and sisters for their very special encouragement. To my dearest nephews Yasser, Ghali and Ryad for the special moments of happiness. To my husband Abdelhamid Azzedine for his time and consideration.

I also dedicate this book to my professors Dr. Souad Slaoui, Dr. Sadiqi Fatima and Dr. Mohammed Moubtassim among others who have supported me throughout the academic process.

I dedicate this book to everyone who helped me in one way or another.

Contents

Figures

Tables

Preface

The present book aims to study the participation of women in the informal sector and the extent to which their contribution through self-employment helped in the household poverty reduction in the city of Fez. The study is based on a mixed-method approach, where data are collected using both quantitative and qualitative research methods. It also uses descriptive statistical and ethnographic analysis of the data obtained from questionnaires and interviews, which are convergent in nature in order to reach logical conclusions. The results show a high participation rate, statistically significant, of women in the city of Fez who work in the sectors of the informal economy. These unregulated work activities can be considered as an important tool to create job opportunities for many women living in difficult social and economic conditions. Because of the pressure on the inadequate living budget, the study reveals that most respondents effectively contribute to the financial expenses of the family, where they struggle to secure a source of livelihood as well as an increase in the productivity, thus their income. Therefore, they attempt to reduce poverty and maintain the survival of and the unity within the family. Moreover, the study reveals that women's participation in political and civil life is almost non-existent due to many reasons such as social and cultural obstacles as well as the patriarchal society that prevent their effective participation. It also increases their reluctance of engaging in political and social work. The research also shows that many of the women surveyed in the field research are facing many obstacles and difficulties, which negatively affect both their performance of economic activities and limit the development of their economic and social situation. Despite this, and through women's opinions and ambitions, most of them insist on challenging these barriers and obstacles with determination and a strong desire to express their aspirations and hope for a better future.

Acknowledgments

I am most grateful for the help and support I have received. I believe the following people should enjoy recognition for offering their time and their assistance.

I owe unending thanks to Dr. Souad Slaoui. I am very grateful for her continuous support and energy that were invested in all parts of the book. Special thanks equally go to Dr. Fatima Sadiqi for believing in me, providing me with academic support, and encouragement. My acknowledgments are also extended to Dr. Mohammed Moubtassim for his assistance and for providing me with a perfect working environment.

My deepest gratitude is extended to my female interviewees and respondents. I hope this book can be as constructive for their individual situation, as their stories and experiences have been for my personal development. My thanks are extended to all the heads of the cooperatives and the professional associations in the city of Fez who openly received me. My gratitude also goes to all the members of those institutions for sharing their views on informal employment and poverty issues.

On a more personal note, my deepest gratitude is extended to my strongest supporters. Words cannot convey how truly blessed I feel to have my parents as my greatest supporters. I value their principle in life about their children's education above everything. I dedicate this book to them as a fruit of their unconditional love, support, sacrifice and guidance, without which my academic achievements so far would have been virtually impossible. I would also like to acknowledge the enduring support and encouragement of my unique brother and sisters as they have been accompanying me during this process from inception to completion.

I acknowledge the invaluable contribution of my husband. His unwavering support, unfailing optimism and belief in my work have helped me to overcome even the hardest periods during the process of writing this work.

Abbreviations

ADFM	Association Démocratique des Femmes Marocaines
BAJ	Barnamej Al Aoulaouiyat Al Ijtimaia/Social Priority Program
ESPOD	Association Point de Départ
GDP	Gross Domestic Product
ILO	International Labor Office
IPU	Informal Production Units
NGO	Non-Governmental Organizations
NPA	National Plan of Action
PANIFD	Plan of Action for the Integration of Women in Development
PJD	Justice and Development Party
PME	Petites et Moyennes Entreprises
PMI	Petites et Moyennes Industries
SAP	Structural Adjustment Program
SPSS	Statistical Package for Social Sciences
UNDP	United Nations Development Program
UNIFEM	United Nations Development Funds for Women

Introduction

Over the past few decades, a wave of reforms sparked throughout Morocco as a result of the preoccupation in most government agendas, public debates, civil-society activism and feminist thoughts. In reality, the purpose of the changes is to make incredible progress in terms of enhancing the status of women and their inclusion in development. In this respect, a number of initiatives and laws have been advanced and reformed. These include the National Plan of Action for the Integration of Women in Development, the amendment of the Family Status code, the participation in the political field, the change of the labor code, the reform of the constitutional law, to name but a few.[1]

In addition to the cultural, legal and political changes, women's economic rights have been boosted by a genuine reform of the labor code. This new law puts into practice rules to fight gender-based discrimination in places of work. It also aims to reduce sex differentials in the workplace. This extends to employment opportunities, salaries, working hours, recognition and penalization of sexual harassment in workplaces. These changes are significant tools to promote the status of Moroccan women, to better their lives, and to bring them from the margins to the centers. Therefore, these efforts have tried considerably to help create the transition from paper to action, such that the reforms have made a significant influence on women all across the country.

It follows from what have been stated above that Morocco aspires to uplift the situation of its female segments of society. However, a number of impediments hinder the application of the labor code which are of socio-economic, cultural and patriarchal nature. According to the 2013 national

1 For further information, see Fatima, Sadiqi. *Women, Gender and Language in Morocco*. Leiden: Brill, 2003. See also Zakia, Salime. *Between Feminism and Islam: Human Rights and Sharia Law in Morocco*. Minneapolis: University of Minnesota Press, 2011.

survey published by Haut Commissariat au Plan (High Commission for Planning), the female segment of the Moroccan society comprised 22.3% of the total active population in 2012. Moreover, the percentage of the feminization of unemployment increased from 25.7% in 2000 to 29.1% in 2012.[2] Similarly, Belarbi argues that the salaried female workers in Morocco are fully discriminated against in the workplace while they are simultaneously supposed to fulfill their traditional gender-based roles.[3] Equally important, Meknassi examines the types of jobs women perform in the labor market in Morocco. He finds out that they occupy soft jobs, which he describes as subaltern functions.[4] These studies generally describe the formal form of employment, but they lack quantitative and qualitative data on the informal sector of employment. However, scholars who conducted research on the work of women in the informal economy are not numerous. For example, Cairoli investigates the evolution of the Moroccan industry sector, which allowed the creation of job opportunities to women, especially in the city of Fez.[5] In this respect, Schaefer's study in rural areas is about the examination of the work of women weavers in villages who opt for seasonal activities in order to generate incomes to help the survival of their families.[6] Concerning the category of self-employed, Biadillah provides a prominent study about their situation as employees.[7]

2 Direction de la Statisque. *La Femme Marocaine en Chiffres: Tendences d'Evolution des Charactéristiques Démographiques et Socioprofessionnelles*. Rabat: Haut Commissariat au Plan, 2013.

3 See Belarbi, Aicha. 'Salariat Féminin et Division Sexuelle du Travail dans la Famille: Cas de la Femme Fonctionnaire.' In Fatima Mernissi, ed. *Femmes Partagées: Famille-Travail*. Casablanca: Le Fennec, 1988.

4 Rachid, Meknassi Filali. *Femmes et Travail*. Casablanca : Editions Fennec, 1994.

5 Laeitia, Cairoli M. 'Garment Factory Workers in the City of Fez.' *The Middle East Journal*, Vol. 53, No. 1 (1999).

6 See Susan, Schaefer Davis. 'Women Weavers OnLine: Rural Moroccan Women on the Internet.' In *Gender Technology and Development*. New Delhi: Sage Publications, Vol. 8, No. 1 (2004).

7 Maryem, Biadillah. *Women in the Moroccan Economy: Employees, Self-Employed*. Ifran: Al-Akhawayn University Press, 2002.

In this respect, though it is doubtless that the informal sector plays an important role in the creation of job opportunities to many rural and urban people, to my knowledge, there is a scarcity of academic research on the relationship between gender, informality of employment and poverty reduction in Morocco with particular reference to the city of Fez. Therefore, the present book tends to focus on investigating the contribution of women's work in the informal sector in reducing household poverty in the city of Fez using self-employed activities as a case study.

The informal economy represents a universal reality.[8] Its division in different contexts is the focus of an increasing body of literature.[9] In the recent decades, for instance, one of the main interests of researchers and policy makers among developing economies is the incorporation of women in the development process mainly through their participation in the labor market. In this respect, efforts are directed to the examination of women's situation in the labor market and the different motivational aspects behind their decision to work. Because of the various discriminatory practices, hindrances and the repercussions on women's work, this issue increasingly becomes a subject matter of many researchers. Thus, much labor literature and research have been devoted to the understanding of the gender inequalities and various theories were innovated such as the human capital,[10] occupational sex

8 Manuel, Castells and Alejandro Portes. 'World Underneath: The Origins, Dynamics, and Effects of the Informal Economy.' In Portes, Alejandro, Manuel Castells and Lauren Benton, eds. *The Informal Economy: Studies in Advanced and Less Developed Countries*. Baltimore, MD: Johns Hopkins University Press, 1989.

9 See Keith, Hart. 'Informal Income Opportunities and Urban Employment in Ghana.' *The Journal of Modern African Studies*, Vol. 11, N. 1 (1973): 61–89; Salem. V, Sethuraman. 'The Urban Informal Sector: Concepts, Measurement and Policy.' *International Labour Review*, Vol. 114, No. 1 (January 1976): 69–81; Michele, Hoyman. 'Female Participation in the Informal Economy: A Neglected Issue.' *Annals of the American Academy of Political and Social Science*, No. 493 (1987): 64–82.

10 See Gary, Becker. 'Human Capital, Effort, and the Sexual Division of Labor.' *Journal of Labor and Economics*, Vol. 3, No. 1 (1985).

segregation[11] as well as dual labor markets,[12] which are used to approach and interpret such inequalities.

Conversely, much attention in the literature was addressed to specific formal workers and activities.[13] Indeed, few studies are about workers and occupations practiced in the informal sector, which are not official and are outside labor laws and regulations. However, data derived from the literature on different countries show that the informal segments of work have a crucial role in creating job opportunities. In other words, informal workers represent an important proportion of the workforce. Additionally, studies revealed that women constitute a major portion of workers in the informal sector such as family workers, home-based workers and self-employed.[14]

In Morocco, the informal sector seems to be a crucial weapon fighting against unemployment of many individuals in different regions of the country. This means that the informal sector accounts for considerable and growing share of employment in Morocco. In other words, men and women, both in urban and rural areas, depend on informal activities for their livelihoods. Available statistics indicate that the contribution of the informal sector to the total GDP is 17%.[15] The number of informal units

11 See Jude Browne. *Sex Segregation and Inequality in the Modern Labor Market*. Bristol: Policy Press, 2006; also see William T. Bielby and James N. Baron. 'A Woman's Place is with other Women. Sex Segregation within Organizations.' In Barbara F. Reskin, ed. *Sex Segregation in the Workplace*. Washington, DC: National Academy Press, 1984.

12 Peter B. Doeringer and Michael J. Piore. *Internal Labor Markets and Manpower Analysis*, Lexington MA: Heath, 1971.

13 See Guerraoui, op. cit; Belarbi, op. cit; Meknassi, op. cit.

14 For a detailed discussion of these issues, see Standing, Guy. 'Global Feminization through Flexible Labor.' *World Development*, Vol. 17, No. 7 (1989): 1077–1095. Also see Tokman, Victor E. 'Policies for a Heterogeneous Informal Sector in Latin America.' *World Development*, Vol. 17, No. 7 (1989): 1067–1076; Sylvia Chant. *Women Headed Households. Diversity and Dynamics in the Developing World*, London: Palgrave Macmillan Press, 1997a; Sylvia Chant. 'Women-headed Households: Poorest of the Poor? Perspectives from Mexico, Costa Rica and the Philippines.' *IDS Bulletin*. Vol. 28, No. 3 (1997b): 26–48; Hoyman, op. cit.

15 Direction de la Statistique. *Enquête National sur le Secteur Informel, 1999/2000*, Rabat: Haut Commissariat au Plan, 2003: 19.

located in urban areas accounts for 69.8% and one of 10 units are headed by women.[16] Despite the fact that the informal sector plays a crucial role in creating employment opportunities for many individuals and developing the economy, however, to my knowledge, there is a scarcity of information about its contribution and particularly women's employment for poverty reduction in the city of Fez. The absence of the basic information of this nature resulted into the increase of efforts in the development of the formal sector, namely by most policy makers and practitioners in development. They have additionally focused on women's status within the formal sector in terms of providing certain regulations and rights examining it with the informal sector. Hence, the development of the informal sector has often been slow.

The motivational aspects of the present investigation stem from the growing interest in the informal sector, and the implications of gender inequality in the informal employment. Although investigations on the Moroccan case show interest in women's participation in the agriculture or in the formal sector, the informal sector has not gained much attention to provide statistical documentation and careful analysis. Thus, the aim is to consider this gap by examining the presence of women in the shadow economy and by exploring their contribution to the national economy. Hence, the objectives of this study are as follows:

- To assess the profiles of women in the informal sector activities in the city of Fez, which will be done through the examination of their socio-demographic and professional characteristics. It will also deal with their main motives and reasons to end up working in self-employed activities.
- To make a situation analysis of the contribution of women's work in the informal sector to reduce poverty in their households in this region of Morocco.
- To identify the linkages between working as self-employed and emancipation of women through their participation in political and social activism in Fez.

16 Direction de la Statistique. *Enquête National sur le Secteur Informel 2006–2007*. Rabat: Haut Commissariat au Plan, 2007.

- To discover the main difficulties impeding the development of women in the self-employed activities in the informal sector and identify the various perspectives for the development of their businesses in Fez.

The main research question that the book seeks to address is does the participation of Moroccan women as self-employed workers in the informal sector help them to reduce poverty in their households and contribute to their emancipation? This question subsumes under it other sub-questions stated as follows:

- What types of women are engaged in the informal sector?
- How does the participation of women in the shadow activities contribute to the household poverty reduction?
- To what extent does the participation of women in the informal sector activities enable them to get involved in political and social activism?
- What are the main challenges facing up this category of self-employed women?

In this respect, the following hypotheses are stipulated to answer the above research questions:

1. The lower the socio-demographic and professional characteristics of women is, the greater the chances they will end up working in an informal activity in its self-employed form is, since it represents an important source of absorbing labor force and creating employment opportunities for women.
2. The higher women's engagement in self-employed activities in the informal sector is, the greater the chances that their work will lead to household poverty reduction are.
3. Women's deep involvement in the informal economic activities will not allow them to be active in political and community based activities, but that will enable them to evaluate themselves more favorably, anticipate greater psychological and emotional well-being, and feel empowered to gain their goals, which are based on respect, power, and self-esteem.

4. Women who choose to work in the informal segments of the labor market to ensure a financial survival source are likely to encounter different constraints and problems, especially that their work will enable them to gain social and economic independence from the male dominance in the household and from the collective male control of the social system.

Concerning the scope of the study, the present research undertakes a survey on the employment of women in the informal segments of work in the city of Fez. Specifically, the study focuses on the informal activities practiced by women as self-employed workers. It is of great importance to mention at this stage that the investigation and the data presented are by no means comprehensive. This means that the survey excludes agriculture from the measurement of the informal sector, and it focuses mainly on the urban informal sector in its self employment form.

In regard to the significance of the study, the importance lies in finding the correlations between the variables of gender, informality, and poverty reduction in the city of Fez. It is hoped to be an additional contribution to the already existing literature about the issues under investigation. In fact, there are different views on the role of the informal sector. On the one hand, this sector is a source of job creation for women and a means of income generation whereby women are able to secure a source of living, which enables them to contribute financially to the household and reduce its poverty. However, women are confronted with discriminating practices and obstacles, which hinder their full emancipation.

Furthermore, through the present study, there is an attempt to contribute to the literature written about women's participation in informal labor force and poverty reduction. To my knowledge, no research has been specifically conducted in the city of Fez on this particular subject. Thus, the results of this research can be of some importance for policy makers and stakeholders. They may help them to better design their policies and intervention strategies focusing on the development of the informal sector as well as on the promotion of women as its primary workforce. Most importantly, the significance of the present study is related to the role of the informal sector as a job creator for many women. Indeed, it is about its provision of all the means women made use of in order to contribute to the national economy, to the survival of the family and to household poverty reduction. In what follows, a detailed description of the organization of the book is given.

The present book encompasses six chapters supported by a general introduction and conclusion. The first chapter tries to set both the theoretical foundations and the conceptual framework for the research. It is divided into two main sections. The first one provides a general overview of the development of the concept of the informal sector across time, tracing its origins, changes and development in different types of studies both in the Western and the Moroccan contexts. The second one shifts to a presentation of the literature related to poverty, especially in its relation to gender and informal employment.

The second chapter is a detailed discussion of the research methodology. It is made up of two sections. Firstly, it starts with a detailed description of the data collection procedure and fieldwork. It focuses on a discussion of the sample frame used in the study. It is followed by an explanation of the main research instruments of data collection used in this research: these are questionnaires and interviews developed by the researcher drawing both on the literature review and on personal experiences and ideas. Likewise, this section contains an overview of the way the fieldwork of the study is organized. Secondly, this chapter provides the main methods of processing and analyzing quantitative and qualitative data. Finally, the last section provides the main problems and limitations encountered during the research process.

The third chapter takes charge of presenting the analysis of the empirical results of both the quantitative and qualitative data. Like the previous chapters, this one is divided into two sections. The first one starts with an analysis of the profiles of women working as informal self-employed in the city of Fez. It tries, on the one hand, to examine their socio-demographic characteristics such as the age group, the educational attainment, the marital status among others. It discusses, on the other hand, the professional characteristics of this category of workers. For example, the nature and the type of economic activities, the employment status, the location of the activity inside or outside the home, to name but a few. Then the focus is oriented in the second section towards the examination of the main reasons and motives that push women to end up working as self-employed in various informal economic activities and sectors.

The fourth chapter is another step in the core of the book. It continues to explore the contribution of women who are working as self-employed in the expenses of their daily lives as well as in poverty reduction within the household. It starts with an analysis of the main economic characteristics of women's work in informal activities and the way of marketing goods and services. The second section shows how the informal sector allows women to secure a source of income helping them to contribute to the needs of the family. Similarly, it examines how women make use of their income and how they make personal savings.

The fifth chapter contributes to the discussion of women's work in the informal sector and the various means of emancipation. It starts with a discussion of the participation of women informal workers in political and community based activism. In particular, it refers to their political participation, cooperative involvement as well as associative activism. The second section tends to discuss the participation of women in shadow segments of work and the private sphere responsibilities, their perceptions of housework as well as the various ways to reconciliate between work and domestic labor.

Likewise, the sixth chapter contains two sections. The first one explores the chief obstacles and constraints that women face in the unobserved economy in its self-employment form. The second section unfolds the core perspectives and potentials for women in the informal economy within the given constraints.

CHAPTER 1

Theoretical and Conceptual Framework

ABSTRACT

The purpose of the present chapter is to provide an overview of the main studies carried out on the correlation between the informal sector, poverty and gender issues. The first section addresses the emergence, the characteristics, and the development of the informal sector in both the Western and the Moroccan contexts. The second section reviews the concepts of poverty and the informal sector from economic and social perspectives with a purpose to provide an alternative to gender approach.

Informal Sector in Western and Moroccan Contexts

It is of paramount significance for the purposes of the present research to consider how various studies approach the concept of the informal sector in order to emphasize that the informal employment is only one form of job creation. The dispute over whether the informal sector is considered as a creator of income opportunities for women or stall economic growth is rife with debates in the informal sector literature, which gives birth to a diversity of perspectives from which four have been selected to be reviewed in this work. The present debate will focus on the following: the dualist, the structuralist, the legalist and the feminist views respectively.

To start with, the dualist theorists consider the urban informal sector of the economy as a transitory phenomenon during the economic crisis that will disappear with the development of the economy. In this respect, the dualist theory has developed a perspective based on the dichotomous status of legitimate and illegitimate income opportunities.

However, many scholars consider the marginal activities as distinct from the formal activities,[1] which are the main sources of income opportunities that motivate many migrants to urban areas dislocated from agriculture. They are obliged to seek sources of survival in the unofficial economy within which transactions occur outside regulations, where access is easier and the earnings are lower and unprotected.[2] This obliges many sub-proletariats to combine different sources of income and duplicate their economic activities to secure a livelihood.[3] Therefore, the informal sector is regarded as a refuge for many workers. This segment within the low productivity sector is often characterized by its low levels of human capital and socio-economic status.[4]

As far as the Structuralists' view is concerned, it refutes the notion of the dualist nature of economic activities by which individuals would find employment in the informal sector. Viewed from this perspective, the structure of the relationship between the controlled and the uncontrolled activities by the state regulations is made the main focus of this school of thought.[5] More particularly, the Structuralists consider economic informality in terms of its relationship to economic formality. That is to say, they characterize informal phenomena as income-earning activities, which are unregulated by the state in contexts where similar activities are regulated.[6] Moreover, the structuralist theory expands the debate about the unofficial sector to advocate the availability of two main exploitative relationships.

1 Hart, op. cit.; ILO, *Employment, Incomes and Equality: A Strategy for Increasing Productive Employment in Kenya*. Geneva: International Labour Office, 1972; Sethuraman, op. cit.

2 Hart, , op. cit.; ILO, , op. cit.

3 Hart, , op. cit., 78.

4 Michael Todaro. 'A Model of Labor Migration and Urban Unemployment in Less Developed Countries.' *American Economic Review*. No. 59 (1969): 138–148.

5 See Caroline Moser. 'The Informal Sector Revisited: Viability and Vulnerability in Urban Development.' *Regional. Development Dialogue*, Vol. 5 (1984): 135–178; also see 'Informal Sector or Petty Commodity Production: Dualism or Independence in Urban Development.' *World Development*, Vol. 6, No. 9 (1978): 1041–1064. Castells and Portes, op. cit.

6 See Castels and Portes, op. cit.

On the one hand, there is an emphasis on the idea that the informal sector simply represents an extension of the production activities of large firms. On the other hand, this sector subsidizes the formal economy by providing cheap products to the labor force. By so doing, they enable large firms to pay extremely low wages. In contrast to the dualist model, the structuralist maintains the co-existence, connection and interdependence between modes and forms of production.[7] Thus, there exists more of a continuum between the formal and the informal economy.[8]

The main concern of the Legalists' approach is to relate the informal sector to the illegally practiced activities. Indeed, they operate either partly or fully outside the state regulations. Its workers consist of individuals who take the risk of operating their economic activities informally out of choice and not out of necessity. This means that the choice made by the entrepreneurial class, as a group of the informal workforce, is justified by their own decision to avoid costs, time and efforts of formally regulating their work and converting it into legally recognized units.[9] Hence, workers in the unofficial sector will continue to perform their activities illegally as long as the government does not reduce the costs and change the procedures of moving from an informal to a formal sector.

As the informal sector has grown, scholars have begun to explore the variations within its workers. Perhaps the most significant set of variations is the study of the gender dimension within the informal sector activities. For instance, Peterson and Lewis referred to the study of MacEwen,[10] who observed that research on the informal sector is mostly limited to the examination of the men's activities regardless of those practiced by women.[11] Within the same context, the two scholars made reference to

7 See Moser, op. cit; Castells and Portes, op. cit.

8 Castells and Portes, op. cit.

9 See Hernando De Soto. *The Other Path: The Economic Answer to Terrorism*. New York: Harper Collins, 1989.

10 Scott, MacEwen. 'Informal Sector or Female Sector? Gender Bias in Urban Labour Market Models'. In Elson, D. *Male Bias in the Development Process*. Manchester: Manchester University Press, 1995.

11 See Janice Peterson and Margaret Lewis. *The Elgar Companion to Feminist Economics*. Gloucester: Edward Elgar Publishing, 1999: 473.

Mazumdar[12] who merely tackled the issue of women and informal sector while defining its major characteristics (e.g. low opportunity cost). It follows from the above discussion that women, according to Peterson and Lewis, who chose to operate in the informal sector were not assumed as squandering their time spent either in household activities or leisure activities to do informal work. Their productive work was indeed conceived to lack value.[13]

A different line of reasoning has been developed by the feminist economists who attribute women's participation in the informal sector to different factors. For instance, Peterson and Lewis argued that the remarkable presence of women in the informal work can be taken as an evidence for the gender-based discrimination deeply rooted in the mainstream economies.[14] This means that women's participation in the informal segments to generate more income opportunities has become visible. Moreover, the recognition of their financial contribution to the household income becomes known due to its important input to the development of the household, family and society. However, their participation in economic production challenges the traditional view of the male figure as the main breadwinner and the head of the household.[15] It has clearly been noticed that the contribution of women's income has relatively been more valued than did men's income on the family in general and children in particular.[16]

Accordingly, stakeholders and policy makers started to debate the significance of women's earnings as a double-edge promoting means. In fact, women's income opportunities help the improvement of their welfare within the family and society. By way of illustration, women's income is a means to promote, on the one hand, the welfare of children in the case

12 Dipack Mazumdar. 'The Theory of Urban Underemployment in Less Developed Countries. World Bank Staff Working Paper.' *World Bank*, No. 198 (1975): 1–39.

13 See Peterson and Lewis, op. cit.

14 Peterson and Lewis, 474.

15 See Chapter 4.

16 See Nancy, Folbre. 'Hearts and Spades: Paradigms of Household Economics.' *World Development*, Vol. 14, No. 2, 1986.

of married women informal workers, and on the other hand, it contributes to the economic development of the country as a whole. Therefore, the informal work helps women shift from the margins to the center. As Peterson and Lewis further note, a debate has developed among feminist economists to examine women's work in informal segments of the economy because of the *revolutionary* thinking about women and development.[17]

On the one hand, the feminist economists confirmed pragmatically some acceptance to the dualist perspective to informal work. For instance, the feminist version of the dualist view accepts that women perform informal economic activities because they lack other work opportunities in other sectors.[18] In other words, they consider women's work in the informal sector because they lack alternative income generating opportunities and that the sector is a source of benefit to them if they perform economic activities in the care economy. Nevertheless, this view cannot be applicable and relevant to other contexts.

On the other hand, the structuralists developed a challenging perspective to the feminist dualist view regarding the informal sector. Their main concern is to highlight the importance of women's intense participation in the most vulnerable sector of the economy.[19] The view of the structuralist feminist economists emphasizes the issue that the informal sector is inferior to the formal sector. They stress on the fact that foregrounding a development strategy based on the informal enterprise will not have a great impact on women as it ignores certain prerequisites. A case in point is the example of those women's enterprises, which have low levels of human capital and backward knowledge technology level.[20]

I may venture to say that the structuralist feminist view on the informal sector is relevant since it stresses the relevance of the vulnerable conditions of women in their informal work. At the same time, the dualist aspect of the feminist approach can be considered relatively positive as it views the informal sector as a beneficial sector of employment opportunities to

17 For further discussion on this issue, see Peterson and Lewis, op. cit., 474–475.

18 Peterson and Lewis, 475.

19 See Moser, 1978 op. cit; Moser, 1984, op. cit; MacEwen, op. cit.

20 See Peterson and Lewis, op. cit.

women. These latter are also active in the economy while they refer to the obstacles they may face based on their gender in having a decent work.

All these theoretical views and feminist perceptions of the informal sector led me to go back to the debate about the concept of informality which neglects the contribution of women's activities to the economy. Following the two feminist views regarding the informal sector and women as informal workers, I address several issues: does the informal sectoral placement has any implications on women's financial contribution to the household income? If the easy entrance to the informal employment is a source of job creation, then what is its impact on the reduction of poverty? Does women's entrance to the informal sector indicate tangible consequences to them and their families? Such questions remain key elements in this research that will trace their responses through an investigation of urban self-employed workers within the informal sector and an examination of their contribution to the reduction of poverty in the city of Fez.

Informal Sector in Western Thoughts

Since its discovery in 1970s, scholars have continually revised the meaning of the informal sector.[21] In fact, the term triggers many interpretations and confusions in variance with how people view it. Various scientific debates and political discussions developed due to the deferring or unsatisfactory definitions of the term.[22] However, exclusion represents a common characteristic of this sector of the economy. It is excluded from official registration, from record in the national accounting system and the statistical coverage, from traditional trade unionism and social security as well as

21 The following is a small selection of terms, which are either used in this paper synonymously or interchangeably for different areas: underground economy, illicit work, informal sector, irregular sector, leisure economy, alternative economy, black economy, hidden economy, unofficial economy, parallel economy, shadow economy, unobserved economy, unrecorded economy, invisible economy.

22 See for example, Hart, 1973; Ferman & Ferman, 1973; Gutmann, 1977; Guillermo, et al., 2007.

Gross Domestic Product estimates.[23] The present sub-section attempts to provide an overview of three elements. First, it provides different attempts to define the informal sector. Second, it offers a lens at the different characteristics of the informal sector. Third, it examines the linkages between formal and informal sectors.

Definitions of the Informal Sector

Many researchers name the informal sector using different labels. It has been referred to as the irregular economy,[24] the subterranean economy,[25] the underground economy,[26] the black economy,[27] the shadow economy,[28] and the informal economy.[29] Relatively, they represent different labels in academic writings to describe a phenomenon that appears in the conventional

23 At this point of the paper, it is interesting to point out that this literature review excludes criminal activities, which are part of the underground economy although the later is a subset of the general informal economy. Meeting the objective of this book, the criminal activities are excluded from the definition. Therefore, the term of the informal economy/informal sector is used to refer to those enterprises and economic activities operating outside regulations (taxation, business practices, and labor market regulations) and it is not engaged in criminal activities.

24 Patricia Ferman and Louis Ferman. 'The Structural Underpinning of the Irregular Economy.' *Poverty and Human Resources Abstracts*. Vol. 8, (1973): 3–17.

25 Peter, Gutmann. 'The Subterranean Economy.' *Financial Analysis Journal*, Vol. 33, No. 6 (November-December, 1977): 26–34.

26 Carl P. Simon and Ann D. Witte. *Beating the System – The Underground Economy*. Boston, MA: Auburn House Publishing Company, 1982. Also see Joel, Houston. 'The Underground Economy: a Troubling Issue for Policymakers.' *Business Review Federal Reserve Bank of Philadelphia* (September-October, 1987): 3–12.

27 Dilnot, A., and Morris, C. 'What we Know about the Black Economy in the United Kingdom?' *Fiscal Studies*, No. 2 (March 1981): 163–179.

28 Bruno S. Frey, Hannelore Weck, and Werner W. Pommerehne. 'Has the Shadow Economy Grown in Germany? An Exploratory Study.' *Review of World Economics*, No. 118 (1982): 499–524. See Cassel, Dieter, and Cichy, Ernst Ulrich. 'Explaining the Growing Shadow Economy in East and West: a Comparative Systems Approach.' *Comparative Economic Studies*, Vol. 28, No. 1 (1986): 20–41.

29 Kevin F. McCrohan, and Timothy F. Surgrue. 'An Empirical Analysis of Informal Markets Participation.' *Social Science Quarterly*, Vol. 79, No. 1 (March 1998): 212–226.

statistical analysis of economies. This multiplicity of terms proves that there is a huge debate on what the informal sector is. The main source behind this diversity is undoubtedly related to the wide range of disciplines and specialties interested in the phenomenon such as economics, politics, law, anthropology, sociology, psychology, etc. This multitude of approaches and theoretical perspectives has a mission to theorize.

One of the earliest scholars who studied the informal sector is Keith Hart. His definition of the concept postulates a dualist model of income opportunities of the urban labor force. It is based largely on distinguishing between two forms of employment: wage-employment and self-employment. Hart's use of the concept of informality applies to individuals operating their economic activities in a self-employed manner to secure a livelihood due to the lack of employment opportunities in the formal sector. Moser wrote:

> Hart's Dualist model of informal and formal sectors was based on a distinction between wage-earning and self-employment, with the key variable being the degree of rationalization of work, in other words, whether or not labor was recruited on a permanent and regular basis for fixed reward. (Moser, 1978: 1052)

This means that the distinction between the two sectors of the economy is a clear cut, self-evident and unproblematic division.[30]

The famous report of the International Labor Office[31] about the employment mission in Kenya[32] has adopted the concept as a major category to analyze the labor market in the developing countries. It defines the informal sector as an urban 'way of doing things,' whose enterprises are characterized by the recognition of employment as a source to generate income, which is crystallized by its informal nature.

During the early 1980s, Sethuraman redefined the informal sector on the basis of a description about how the target group is identified. This target group falls into two general categories, which he describes as follows:

30 Jaafar Aksikas. 'Prisoners of Globalization: Marginality, Community and the New Informal Economy in Morocco.' Mediteranean Politics, Vol. 12, No. 2 (2007): 252.

31 ILO, 1972, op. cit.

32 It is considered the first of a series of reports.

(a) Those that are characterized by the income level of the individuals concerned or by the variables that depend on the income level (e.g. access to housing or other urban services, adequate food, etc.);
(b) Those that are based on the variables which determine the individual's income (e.g. personal characteristics, occupational characteristics, employment status, labor market characteristics, characteristics of the activities or enterprises on which he depends). (Sethuraman, 1976: 74)

Sethuraman's line of argument emphasizes the interest in improving the livelihood's conditions of the individual. It is based on the determinants of the income level. Accordingly, the emphasis must be placed on the category (b). He justified this by the fact that as long as an individual's income is rising, the access to basic needs (food, shelter, clothing and urban services) is considerably improved.[33]

One contemporary scholar who studied the informal sector and illegality is the Peruvian economist De Soto Hernando. He defines informality as the popular response to the strict domination of the 'mercantilist' states, especially whose small elites are granted the privilege of legal participation in the economy.[34] He posits that the informal sector activities have the potential to generate income for the national economy and its workers, if only the state would stop regulating the economy. In other words, the informal sector demonstrates a crucial opportunity to generate wealth if the state shows interest in removing all the restrictions from the economy such as taxes.

The practice of defining the informal sector in terms of types of workers engaged in its activities is well established in the literature. In a study undertaken by Chen, Vanek and Carr, individual workers are categorized into three main groups: the visible, the less visible and the least visible workers. To begin with, the commonly visible workforce within the informal sector activities, in most developed and developing countries, relates to people who perform their activities as workers in the streets and in open-air areas.

33 Sethuraman, op. cit., 74.
34 De Soto, op. cit.

On the one hand, they provide a selection of economic activities, which are performed by the workforce in the shadow economy in urban areas, including 'barbers, cobblers, garbage collectors and vendors of vegetables, fruit, meat, fish, snack food or a myriad of non-perishable items from used clothing to locks and keys or soaps and cosmetics to electronic goods.'[35]

On the other hand, workers in rural areas may engage in activities related but not limited to: 'working on farms, raising livestock, making handicrafts or collecting and processing minor forest products' (Martha Chen , Joann Vanek, and Marilyn Carr, 2004:14).

The less visible category of workers is linked to individuals working in factories or small workshops. They include those who

> repair bicycles and motorcycles, recycle scrap metal, make furniture and metal parts, tan leather and stitch shoes, weave, dye and print cloth, polish diamonds and other gems, make and embroider garments, sort and sell cloth, paper and metal waste; and more. (Martha Chen, Joann Vanek, and Marilyn Carr, 2004: 14)

Additionally, the least visible category of workers in the informal sector is linked to women, who may perform their activities indoors and mostly invisible to others. Their activities range from

> selling or producing goods from their homes: stitching garments, weaving cloth, embroidering textile goods, making crafts, making shoes, processing food or assembling electronic and automobile parts. (Martha Chen, Joann Vanek, and Marilyn Carr, 2004: 14.)

It is crucial to mention here that the present paper focuses on the last category of workers in the informal sector.

The definition expands the focus to deal with the workforce[36] in terms of employment status. It includes two types of employment forms:

35 Martha, Chen, Joann Vanek, and Marilyn Carr. *Mainstreaming Informal Employment and Gender in Poverty Reduction: A Handbook for Policy-Makers and Other Stakeholders*. London: The Commonwealth Secretariat, 2004: 14.

36 In this paper, unless otherwise stipulated, I use the term 'workforce' in a broad sense to include both the self-employed and wage employed workers in the informal economy.

self-employed and wage employed. The informal economy is broadly recognized to include, on the one hand, persons who work as self-employed in informal enterprises (i.e. small and/or unregistered),[37] on the other hand, workers who are wage employed (i.e. without secure contracts, worker benefits, or social protection).[38] The most common criterion of informal workers, both self-employed and wage employed is the lack of secure work, workers' benefits, social protection and representation or voice.[39]

All these definitions and theoretical views about the concept of the informal sector show that it is characterized by its plurality. It differs from one context to another. This means that various definitions of the term may imply a multiplicity of conceptual understandings of informality. This is why scholars and researchers find it hard to provide a universal definition. In the present book, I refer to the informal sector as a variety of economic activities in which persons work to generate earnings. These jobs are not reported to the government. They are also absent from the official registration and taxation procedures. The shadow sector includes persons who work individually as self-employed or collectively in small scale businesses. Their operations take place mostly in invisible structures of some kind (homes) which are not licensed.

Characteristics of the Informal Sector

The understanding of the informal sector benefits from a diversity of forms that makes its definition a challenging task. One may shift to identify its main characteristics as a tentative way to define it. In what follows, the focus will be on four key characteristics that are widely accepted while referring to this type of economy. They include legality vs illegality of economic activities, way of payment, income and wages outside the records, and work conditions.

37 ILO. *Women and Men in the Informal Economy: a Statistical Picture*. Geneva: International Labor Office, (2002): 7.

38 ILO, 2002.

39 For a further discussion, see the section on the linkages between formal and informal sectors.

The growth of the invisible economy in different social and economic contexts may be either legal or illegal. Indeed, the distinction between formal and informal sectors does not focus on the character of the final product, rather it stresses the way it is produced or exchanged. For example, people producing or exchanging goods (e.g. food, clothes …) or services (domestic work, childcare …) provide legal commodities, yet they may originate in legally regulated or unregulated production processes.[40] Though economic activities are not illegal, but they rather violate some of the economic laws or rules such as evading taxes or abiding by the labor laws.[41] Furthermore, the distinction between economic activities may be made by the legal nature of the production and provision of products in addition to the legal status of goods and services themselves. Cross and Johnson criticize some researchers to confuse informality and illegality, especially while putting them in a single basket called 'underground economy' or 'black economy.' This amalgam confuses two activities that have very different etiologies. To illustrate their point of view, they give the example of a hot dog seller and a drug dealer and neither of them has work permission from the authorities.[42]

This example suggests that when a street vendor is selling hot dog, s/he is selling a legal product, which s/he purchased at a market, and it is offered after being prepared and served in a convenient location to a potential client. However, the health department may not authorize the product or the seller does not pay sales taxes. The hot dogs are still legal. Nevertheless, if the police stop the salesperson, they may fine him for evading the payment of taxes. On the contrary, if a person is a drug dealer and caught on the street, s/he may be ultimately fined for selling illegal products in public spaces. Both situations demonstrate that, technically speaking, both vendors have violated the law in a way or another. Nevertheless, the

40 See Rebecca Raijman. 'Mexican Immigrants and Informal Self-Employment: a Case study in the city of Chicago.' *Human Organization*. Vol. 60, No. 1 (2001): 47–45.

41 See Castells and Portes, op. cit.

42 John C. Cross, and Bruce. D Johnson. 'Expanding Dual Labour Market Theory: Crack Dealers and the Informal Sector.' *International Journal of Sociology and Social Policy*, Vol. 20, No. 1/2 (2000): 96–134.

situations in which both persons while stopped by the police are completely different. The former has transgressed the law by not conforming to the labor regulations while the latter has violated the law by the nature of the product s/he is vending.[43] Both examples of people who are working on the sidewalk on the same street, not paying taxes to the state, have the attention to a likely arrival of a police patrol. In another study, Tanzi noted that same activities are considered illegal in some countries and as perfectly legal and tolerated in other countries such as the case of prostitution.[44] To conclude, there is a broad difference between forms of legality and illegality of economic activities. There are some illegal activities, which evade taxation, and others, which gain income using criminal products such as through the use of drugs dealing, gambling, and trafficking in stolen or smuggled goods.

Another pertinent characteristic to identify the informal activities is the manner of payment. Most transactions between vendors and potential purchasers in the informal economy are performed using cash instead of other means (e.g. checks, credit cards, pay ball statements). Money becomes a particular type of asset in the informal economy that people use in their economic operations. The main purpose to use the currency method is to avoid the creation of exchange records of the activities.[45] In this regard, a person who receives a payment as a return for a good or a service in an informal economic activity is characterized by the untraceable nature of income. However, other transactions in the invisible economy are based on a bartering system. Indeed, some individuals prefer to exchange goods and services for other things rather than cash. In this respect, the currency looses so much of its value among workers in the informal economy. Instead, it is replaced by a barter transaction, which includes anything thought to be of worth value as currency. Having extra things beyond what a family will immediately need will have great value to the individual. In short,

43 Cross and Johnson, op. cit., 103.

44 Vito Tanzi. 'Uses and Abuses of Estimates of the Underground Economy.' *The Economic Journal*. Vol. 109, No. 456 (June, 1999): 338–347.

45 For more details, see McCrohan, Kevin, James D Smith, and Adams Terry K. 'Consumer Purchases in Informal Markets: Estimates for the 1980s, Prospects for the 1990s.' *Journal for the Retailing*, Vol. 67, No. 1 (1991): 22–23.

both money and barter are the generally accepted mediums of exchange in informal sector transactions.

As mentioned earlier, revenue exchanged between buyers and sellers in the informal sector is commonly outside official records. Indeed, transactions manifest in two forms. They are practiced either through cash or bartering systems. Moreover, these exchanges are characterized by the absence of proof of income or wage payment. Consequently, the income is not reported to government tax regulations. This means that both employees and employers in the shadow economy follow the unreported income or wage arrangement. In other words, those informal workers do not claim their incomes and employers hire informal workers and do not declare their employees' records state taxes.

Identifying the conditions of work under which labor is employed in the informal sector is another essential characteristic of this form of the economy. In their study, Castells and Portes point to health conditions, public hygiene, safety hazards, or the location of activities that ignore zoning laws as the most important work conditions.[46] Moreover, informal activities may seem to be oppositional to the ones in the formal sector as far as earning, social security, and protection from labor standards transgression are concerned. To illustrate, workers employed in the shadow sector may get an income lower than the minimum wage. In addition, revenues may disregard the legal labor benefits such as social security, compensation of workers or unemployment insurance. Informal work also ignores most of the formal employment standard requirement such as age, educational attainment level, the specific structure of the work as well as security and safety of work places.[47]

To conclude, the informal sector comprises an important part of the non-agricultural employment in different economies. Indeed, it is characterized by various key features. They encompass the nature of the informal activities, whether it is regulated or unregulated. The way workers receive

46 Castells and Portes, op. cit., 13.

47 Jan L. Losby, et al. *Informal Economy Literature Review.* Institute for Social and Economic Development (2002): 8. Available online: <http://www.kingslow-assoc.com/images/Informal_Economy_Lit_Review.pdf> (Retrieved: 8 September 2013)

their payment for the work they perform, the lack of records of the income gained via marketing informal products, the unsafe working conditions and the absence of social benefits such as pension and health insurance remain necessary to be addressed. The concern of the sub-sequent section is to examine the links between both sectors of the economy.

The Relationship between Formal and Informal Sectors

With interest in the informal economy, debates about the connection between the formal and the informal sectors have resurfaced. The precise determination of the linkages between the two sectors is a very complex task. This is because of the criteria for segmenting the productive system in both sectors do not always follow the same direction. For this reason, the discussion of the linkages between both sectors of the economy generally follows a common line. As mentioned previously in this chapter, the informal sector represents a mosaic of small businesses characterized by their heterogeneity and performance outside the regulations. On the contrary, the formal sector represents a platform for employment resources crystallized by their regulated aspect. Moreover, it is important to view the two sectors of the economy in relation to persons working in different activities. Along the same line of reasoning, Banerjee and Kolkata write:

> those in the formal sector are distinguished by being engaged in activities where they get an assurance of a secured living for themselves and their families, if not out of the activity itself, then, from the social security provided by the state. On the other hand, the rest, however large the numbers involved, would be in the informal sector since they lack this security and are subject to many uncertainties against which they have to devise their own defences. (Banerjee and Sachetana, 2004: 33)

This means that looking at the economy and its two sectors in relation to people who are working hard to secure a source of living is crucial to the discussion of the articulation between the formal and informal sectors. This perspective provides a prominent distinction between people who are structurally included in the formal economy, and the others who are either excluded or never found a work opportunity in it. On the contrary, drawing on the study of Loayza and Rigolini, a distinction between the informal and formal sectors concentrates on the types of production. The authors clearly said:

> The formal and informal sectors use different production technologies. In the formal sector, firms comply with regulation, incurring the corresponding costs, but benefiting from government provided services. In the informal sector, workers can avoid regulations but have restricted access to those services. (Loayza and Rigolini, 2011: 1505)

From this quotation, it is apparent that both sectors are broadly characterized by consisting of units engaged in the production of goods and services using formal and informal strategies. Enterprises in the first category abide by the legal organization and regulations. As a result, they are able to benefit from the governmental services. However, in the second category, the informal sector enterprises do not conform to the legal framework in any way. Thus, they face limitations in getting access to those services. In this respect, one may assume a natural relationship between non-regulation and informality.

Furthermore, the linkages between both sectors of the economy concentrate on the distinction between two segments of informal employment and their relation to the formal employment. These two homogenous subsectors include self-employment and wage employment. The first category is marked by the act of working and generating incomes without profiting from the workers' benefits. This is explained in the words of Loayza and Rigolini who refer to self-employment as being 'significantly correlated with popular measures of informal labor such as the share of the labor force not covered by a retirement pension plan, working without a job contract, or not having health insurance' (Loayza and Rigolini, 2011: 1508). Moreover, self-employed people generally operate their informal units instead of working for an employer that pays a salary or wage. According to Abzhad and Labchir, these informal units are described as the following:

> Ce sont des unités individuelles de production appartenant à des personnes travaillant pour leur propre compte et gérées par elles, seules ou en association avec les membres du ménage ou de ménages différents. Ces personnes peuvent employer des aides familiales et/ ou des apprentis. Les salariés sont parfois utilisés, de manière occasionnelle, pour répondre à des besoins spécifiques. Cette catégorie regroupe les

> personnes pourvues d'un travail indépendant (avec ou sans local commercial), les travailleurs à domicile, les aides familiales et les apprentis. (Abzhad and Labchir, 1998: 358)
>
> [They are individual production units belonging to persons working on their own account and managed by them, either alone or in combination with members of the household or individual households. These people can hire family supporters and/or apprentices. Employees are sometimes used occasionally to meet specific needs. This category includes persons who are self-employed (with or without a local), home workers, family workers and apprentices.]

Furthermore, self-employment encompasses different employment status. They are summarized by Chen into four categories. The first category includes employers who own enterprises and hire co-workers. The second one is about workers who own and operate their production units without hiring other people. The third one incorporates family members who contribute to family businesses without being paid. The fourth category involves members of cooperatives.[48] Overall, self-employment is characterized by the diversity of employment status of workers. Moreover, a strong intersection between workers in self-employment and informal activities is maintained. Loayza and Rigoloni testify this argument claiming that: 'most self-employed workers tend to be low-skilled and unregistered workers. Considering that self-employment may be a better proxy for the informal labor in developing than in developed countries' (Loayza and Rigolini, 2011: 1508). This means that self-employed workers include those in the urban labor force. They are neither concerned nor included in the wage employment. Both authors further added that the informal self-employment workers are not only responsible for taking care of themselves and other individuals, but also of employees in case they need to hire co-workers. This also holds true for unpaid contributing members in a situation when the enterprise is the family's ownership.[49]

48 Martha, Chen. 'Informality and Social Protection: Theories and Realities', *Institute of Development Studies*, Vol. 39, No. 2 (2008): 19.

49 Chen, Martha, Joann Vanek, and Marilyn Carr. *Mainstreaming Informal Employment and Gender in Poverty Reduction: A Handbook for Policy-Makers and Other Stakeholders*. London: The Commonwealth Secretariat, 2004: 25.

Informal wage employment is the second form of employment status in the informal sector. It consists of people who are employed without formal contracts or social protection. They are employed by formal or informal enterprises or by household units of production. This category of informal workers is defined by Abzhad and Labchir as: 'les unités de production qui appartiennent à des employeurs et gérées par eux, seuls ou en association avec les membres du même ménage ou de ménages différents, et qui emploient quelque travailleurs salariées de manière continue' (Abzhad, and Labchir, 1998 :358) [Production units belonging to employers and managed by them, either alone or in association with members of the same household or individual households, which employ some workers in a continuous manner]. There are various common categories of informal wage employment available in developing countries. They are divided into three types. First, informal employees who are unprotected and they have a known employer (s). Second, casual or day laborers as they are workers with no fix employer who sell their labor on a daily or seasonal basis. Third, industrial outworkers who are subcontracted workers producing for a piece-rate from small workshops or their homes.[50]

Furthermore, the classifications between the two forms of employment within the informal sector are crucially important both as concepts and as guides towards appropriate intervention. They break down the homogeneity of the idea of the informal sector, especially while recognizing the diversity and patterns of segmentation within the informal economy. In this scope, Chen (2008) said:

> … there is a significant range of average earnings and poverty risk across employment statuses within the informal economy with a small entrepreneurial class (comprised of most informal employers and a few own account operators) and a large working class (comprised of most informal employees, most own account operators, all casual day laborers, and all industrial outworks). There is also gender segmentation within informal labour markets resulting in a gender gap in average earnings with women over-represented in the lowest-paid segments and earning less on average than men in most segments.

50 See Chen, 2008, op. cit., 19–20.

From this quotation, one may understand that the informal segments of work provide opportunities of income, though they are low in comparison to their counterparts in the formal sector, to many individuals. The revenue differences are also recognizable on the basis of gender, as women earn less than men as a return for their work in informal activities. In the same standpoint, some people seek labor-force participation in informal markets due to the lack of income resources in the formal sector. This means that they either create new economic activities in the informal sector or join the already existing jobs.[51] Moreover, in times of unemployment or in situations of insufficient incomes in a low-wage market, the informal economic opportunities serve as a buffer of sources of employment.[52] For example, in her case study of ethnic entrepreneurship in Mexico, Raijman referred to the work of Portes and Sassen-Koob, who focused on the linkages between the two sub-sectors of the economy. According to her, both authors clearly indicate that formal firms appreciate the use of informal strategies as a means to operate their enterprises. These strategies help in reducing the costs. They allow the participation of marginal individuals as labor force. Furthermore, they grant the participation of sub-contractors who provide services to formal firms in different sectors. With regard to this, the informal sector represents a direct outgrowth of the restructuring of the economy. Accordingly, it flourishes in post-industrial economy. At this level, formal firms show more interest and demand for services provided informally.[53]

To conclude, the present sub-section attempted to provide a review of the links between formal and informal sectors. Indeed, the former represents economic activities that occur within the scope of legal framework and regulations. Moreover, formal employment is viewed as an employment originating from firms that are registered by authorities. In contrast, informal economic activities occur outside the regulations. Informal workers perform their activities in businesses that are not registered.

51 Raijman, op. cit.

52 See Hart, op. cit.

53 Raijman, op. cit., 49.

Briefly, the formal/informal sectors and the formal/informal employment represent a benefit for the overall economy.

Overall, the literature reviewed in this section testifies to the significance of the informal economy in Western countries. Many researchers have debated its existence from different perspectives. This segment of the economy has become an increasingly popular subject of study not just to economists, but also to sociologists and anthropologists. For instance, sociologists have analyzed its operation, structure and place in relation to the formal economy. Anthropologists, on their side, have discussed the experience of its participants. Together, both these disciplines documented the major aspects of the informal economy. The next section shifts the attention to the discussion of the existence of the informal sector in the Moroccan context. It focuses on the main factors of its development in the Moroccan history, its importance in creating work opportunities and labor absorption, with particular reference to women as constituting a crucial proportion of society. Finally, it highlights the relationship between the informal sector and the state.

Debating the Informal Sector in Morocco

The informal sector plays a major role in the Moroccan economy. Given the scale and interest it continues to generate, one cannot deny the importance of the shadow sector in terms of production, income generation, promotion of employment, the fight against unemployment, and ultimately the social integration of large proportions of society.[54] In 2003, estimates provided by the Moroccan Directorate of Statistics show that the contribution of the informal sector to the total GDP amounts to 17%.[55] Based on data provided in the 2007 report by the same institution, the number of the informal sector units in 2006–2007 is 1.550 million units, of which 69.8% are located in urban areas, and one out of 10 units is headed by a female. These informal units are highly concentrated in commercial activities 57.4%, followed by

54 See Direction de la Statistique, 2003, op. cit.
55 Direction de la Statistique, 2003, 19, op. cit.

industrial activities 17.2%, services 20%, and construction activities 5.4%. In effect, almost half of the Informal Production Units (IPU) are without any fixed address and 6.7% of the units are located in homes.[56] Furthermore, results from the 2006–2007 survey show that 9.9% of units are headed by females as compared to 12.4% of informal units in the 1999–2000 survey.[57] Therefore, the informal sector is crucial for creating job opportunities. Hence, these activities are not only essential for the generation of revenues, but they are also important for the social regulation of the country.

The present section provides an overview of the Moroccan informal sector since the independence era. The focus will be on its various factors of emergence. More particularly, this section attempts to give insight on the role of the informal sector as a labor absorber, with particular reference to the participation of the female workforce. The last issue addresses the role of the state in the informal sector. Statistical data to be used in this section are based on the national surveys on urban informal enterprises. They relate to the latest national surveys on the informal sector in Morocco, which were conducted by the Moroccan Directorate of Statistics in (1999–2000) and in (2006–2007).

Factors of Emergence

The present sub-section aims to grapple with basic questions relative to the understanding of the Moroccan informal sector. Special emphasis is on the urban informal activities as a crucial means of production, service provisions and promotion of employment. The importance of this segment of the Moroccan economy is related to four main factors of emergence. First, it is a consequence of movements of urbanization and migration. Second, it emanates from the industrialization process. Third, augmentation in poverty constitutes a pivotal indicator of the growth of the unorganized sector. Fourth, economic policies (SAP) implemented by the state present an important pressure process. These factors are essential to the development and consolidation of the urban informal activities.

56 Direction de la Statistique, 2007, op. cit.

57 Direction de la Statistique, 2003, op. cit.

Both urbanization and migration represent fundamental demographic trends, which accelerated the growth of the informal sector in Morocco. Indeed, urbanization in Morocco results in an explosive augmentation in the size of cities. The increase of the urban population is aggravated by the migration scale of large numbers of people from rural to urban areas. For instance, the rate of the countryside migration to cities has been unprecedented in the years of 1960, 1970 and 1980. For example, the growth rate is higher than that of the total population with an average about 4.3% in the 1960s-1970s, 4.4% in the 1970s-1980s and 4% in the 1980s-1990s. Consequently, the development of the informal sector is indivisible from the pattern of change in migration and urbanization.

Table 1. Increase of the Population of Morocco by Period and Place of Residence: 1960–2020[58]

Periods	Total Population	Urban Population	Rural Population
1960–1970	2.5	4.3	1.7
1970–1980	2.6	4.4	1.6
1980–1990	2.2	4.0	0.8
1990–2000	1.7	2.8	0.5
2000–2010	1.1	1.8	0.3
2010–2020	1.0	1.8	0.0

Source:[59] High Commission for Planning.

Rural migrants to urban areas present an essential category of the informal workforce in Morocco. Indeed, people who become the dwellers of the cities created their own sources of living. In this regard, the informal sector

58 The following data relating to the years 1960 to 2004 are estimated on the basis of actual rétroprojectes of the population by age, the results of general censuses of the population and habitat of 1960, 1971, 1982, 1994 and 2004. Data from 2004 onwards are based on the updating of population projections carried out taking into account the results of the census of 2004 and the national survey of the population to repeated passages of 2009–2010.

59 <http://www.hcp.ma/Taux-d-accroissement-de-la-population-du-Maroc-en-par-periode-et-milieu-de-residence-1960-2050_a683.html> (Consulted 10 November 2013).

becomes a substantial strategy to absorb these migrants who locate their economic activities in cities, shanty towns or in *medinas*.[60] In addition, rural migration is inextricably related to low strengths of the agriculture sector. The latter becomes unable to lessen the waves of the rural exodus who contributed to the rise of the urban population for many years. Thus, migration and urbanization symbolize chief factors determining the genesis and the expansion of the informal sector in the Moroccan society.

Sometimes, the reintegration effort of the rural migrants is likely to happen through the creation of informal employment opportunities in urban areas. The stay of this proportion of society in cities is particularly beneficial in terms of newly participation in modern structures and acquisition of urban norms that would help them to secure a job. In the same standpoint, in her description of rural migration to urban areas, Moser writes: 'with increased participation in the urban structure and increased assimilation of urban norms [migrants] would shift from their "marginal" position towards "integration", moving from peripheral occupations in the "exaggerated" tertiary sector to the industrial sector wage employment' (Moser, 1978: 1042). Consequently, this would demonstrate a process of integration of people coming from rural areas to cities. It also shows a visible consciousness of the substantial role of the unorganized sector in creating income generating opportunities. This means that this segment of the economy initially indicates the process of integration of the rural migrants into the cities. In the same vein, in his discussion of the efficient role of the informal activities as sources of integration in the city of Marrakech, Sebti said: 'Très lié à l'urbanisation et à l'exode rural, le phénomène atteint son apogée avec celui-ci et va de pair' (2009: 149) [Closely linked to urbanization and rural exodus, the phenomenon reached its peak with this one and goes]. Thus, the urbanization and migration processes grant people more

60 It is the singular of *medina*. The term refers to the old part found in many Moroccan cities. It often contains historical monuments such as palaces and schools. Moreover, they are characterized by little and narrow streets, which generally make them free from car traffic. This makes this part of the city unique among other places in urban areas. the city of Fez has two ancient *medinas*, the largest of which is *Fes El-Bali* [the old Fez].

opportunities to enter the workforce, to be part of the active population in the Moroccan society, and to actively participate in different economic sectors developed due to industrialization.

To conclude, both processes discussed above are viewed as two main demographic trends behind the emergence of the informal sector in Morocco. They allow people to find more opportunities to join the workforce. They also help many rural migrants who become city dwellers to be part of the active population. Therefore, to actively participate in different economic sectors among which those emerged through the industrialization process.

Morocco has experienced crucial socio-economic transformations. Distinctive modes of economic development were implemented during and after the French protectorate. During the colonization era, the colonial authorities developed different modes of economic activities based on the already existing examples in the native country. In this respect, Mechouat stated that:

> they brought new techniques of farming, created new services and introduced dams. Agriculture was geared to the French Economy … The colonial power resorted to force and state coercion so as to develop industry, with both government and private companies using forced labor, and confiscated the lands and estates of indigenous farmers, which had a remarkable impact on Morocco's economic, social and cultural structures. (2009, 59–60)

In fact, it is apparent from this quotation that in the context of this period, this mode of economic change has proved to be somewhat employing. The colonizer's intrusion had its impact on the socio-economic and cultural systems.

Since the independence era, the Moroccan economy was characterized by the development of the industrial sector. Indeed, industrialization is regarded as a strategy to accelerate the accumulation of the human capital in order to provide the national productive system with required human resources. For instance, many men and women worked in the textile and garment industries.[61] More precisely, the industrial field promoted effi-

61 See Cairoli, op. cit., 30–32.

ciently the access of women to the labor market. Concerning this point, Mechouat quoted Barkallil about the importance of the industrial sector as an encouraging factor to women's work:

> Le boom industriel des années cinquante allait croitre sensiblement l'emploi féminin et élargir son éventail. Au recensement de 1951/1952, la population féminine musulmane urbaine de la zone Sud représentait 18.4% de la population active musulmane et avait un taux d'activité de 11.8%. (Cairoli, 1999 : 30–32)
>
> [The industrial boom of the 1950s increased and enlarged the range of feminine employment. In 1951/1952 consensuses, the Muslim urban feminine population of the Southern zone represented 18.4% of the Muslim active population by 11.8% as a rate of activity.]

Moreover, the industrial process in Morocco was crystallized by its diversity. In fact, to optimize the promotion of the national system of the economy, it focused on the import system until the late 1960s.[62] Since 1973, after the exhaustion of the industrialization model based on import, Morocco focused on the promotion of the export mode of interactions. As a consequence, this resulted in the absence of the division between the modern and the traditional sectors of the economy already known in the 1960s and 1970s. Based on a dualist perspective of the economy, the former, which refers to the formal sector, should absorb the latter, which stands for the informal sector. In this respect, dualists view informal economic activities as transitional with absent links with their formal counterparts. However, in the case of the industrial process, whether through import or export systems, the modes of economic development implemented at that time proved insufficient and unable to massively promote the wage system. Thus, the method of export promotion, initiated in the late 1970s and its extension into the context of the structural adjustment demonstrated a decrease in the wage rate for the sake of remaining competitive in the markets outside. As a result, this situation allowed the development of the informal activities of small productions or services. In general, the

62 Alan Gilbert and Josef Gugler. *Cities, Poverty, and Development: Urbanization in the Third World*. New York: Oxford University Press, 1982: 65.

industrialization process corresponds to one of the factors responsible for the emergence of the informal sector in the Moroccan context.

Morocco witnessed a substantial rise in poverty between 1991 and 1999. Based on the national household survey, poverty is omnipresent among people living in rural areas as they constitute 66%. The poor living in urban areas accounts for 34% of the total population.[63] Both rural and urban dwellers who are commonly characterized by the lack of educational attainment and the residence in large families with few members in the labor market are more likely to be living in poverty than others. This is pertinent regardless of whether the economy is in an expansion of recession. Moreover, the sharing of the poor by the participation of the breadwinner in different economic activities shows that the agricultural sector attracts more than half of the population 57% of the working poor, followed by service sector 26% and construction sector 13%. In urban areas, among 58% of the poor heads of the household find their job opportunities in the service sector while in rural areas 75% of the poor create their own income generating activities in the agriculture sector.[64]

Affected by the dynamics of the urbanization process in Morocco, the structural causes of urban and rural poverty are closely intertwined. Indeed, most poor rural households having productive activities typically have access to agricultural lands. However, these lands are characterized by their small ownership and minute production. Consequently, due to the absence of the legal regulations of the lands, most holders are deprived from formal credits and proper property's investments. Most often they resort to conduct their productive work outside the agriculture sector, namely as workers in the informal sector. In this respect, they keep moving back and forth between rural and urban areas. In the same vein, the poor living in urban areas are faced up with difficulties that hinder their socio-economic development. They include lack of employment opportunities, inadequacy of access to land, insufficiency of access to basic services, among others as

63 Minot, Nicholas, et al. 'Agriculture, Trade, and Poverty in Morocco.' In Nicholas Minot, et al. *Trade Liberalization and Poverty*. Washington, DC: International Food Policy Research Institute, 2010: 171.

64 Minot, Nicholas, et al. (2010): 172.

they are crucial for the development of a human being. All these factors aggravate their chances to have access to employment opportunities in the informal sector.

Generally, it can clearly be stated that poverty in Morocco, in a way or another, has an important role in the development of the informal sector. This is due to the impact activities within this segment of the labor market has on the generation of incomes. As a consequence, households are more likely to opt for an alternative source of revenues via other forms of work. Thus, the increase in the overall poverty contributes to the significant change of the strategies followed by both the urban and the rural poor.

Morocco, as many other different countries, experienced troubles related to external debts and economic crisis, which forced it to launch a structural adjustment program. In the middle of the 1980s, the use of the wide-reaching program of changing the patterns of the economy had targeted the achievement of two main objectives. First, it aims to stabilize the national economy through better implementation of the macro-economic policies. Second, it aims to change the economic structures in the medium and long terms. With the support of the International Monetary and the World Bank, the SAP happened in order to achieve the aforementioned goals through the expansion of the private sector and stringent fiscal policies. Describing this national initiative, Minot pointed out that: 'The structural adjustment program aimed to reduce the budget deficit, establish a coherent pricing policy, move the real exchange rate closer to equilibrium, and correct the country's trade imbalance' (2010: 168). This means that the program has set as its main objective to support the state to overcome its different economic hindrances, achievement of accelerated growth, increase in employment opportunities and gain of sustainable economic development.

Most countries in the Maghreb region resorted to alternative economic development strategies as a way to react to the economic crisis. Almost invariably, Tunisia, Algeria and Morocco used SAP to achieve structural reforms. In his article about the discussion of the economic and political crises experienced by these North African countries, Layachi summarized the situation as follows:

> These programs helped reform the economies of Morocco and Tunisia with a relative success at the aggregate level, but at a relatively high social cost. As for Algeria, whose SAP started more recently, structural reforms have not had significant results. However, in all three countries, and as a result of stringent austerity measures, more people fell in the poverty trap; unemployment rose and state services were severely curtailed. (2001: 18)

This means that these programs were helpful to manage the crisis in the three countries. Their prominent contribution was obvious in avoiding a total breakdown. However, they had pitfalls on the social structures. In other words, the outcome of the use of the SAP allowed the restructuring of each country's economy, yet with relative success.

In conclusion, the experience of the use of the SAP denotes an important management style of the crisis that ensued from the economic exclusion. Indeed, Morocco succeeded in stabilizing and structuralizing its economy notably through different strategies. For example, the privatization process which primarily helped in securing a constant situation. However, a complete success did not uplift the status of large proportions of society. In this regard, many persons resorted to create their job opportunities in the informal sector after being excluded from the mainstream economy due to layoffs or inability to secure a first job. In other words, many individuals became subject to job recession, marginality, economic and social exclusion. They formed a new class in the Moroccan society. It is a group of marginal working class, who found their source of rescue in the informal sector as income opportunities.[65] However, this does not mean that the emergence of informal activities had primarily its origins in the SAP but it is certain that shifts from the state economy to the private economy plays a great role in their development.

As a result, the adoption of a structural adjustment program by Morocco was only the beginning of a change in the national economy. This initiative helped in consolidating the changes in the country that provided a path to the creation of a more flexible informal sector. The latter has a crucial role in absorbing different categories of the Moroccan workforce.

65 See Aksikas, op. cit., 256.

The statistics, available after the evaluation of the structural adjustment program, demonstrated that regardless of the development during the 80s, the informal sector has been a safety source of employment during the period of adjustment[66] and continued to develop over this period.

The present sub-section tackled in general the various factors of the emergence of the informal sector in Morocco. It focused on the discussion of the impact of the demographic trends mainly migration and urbanization, the industrialization process, poverty rise and the implementation of the structural adjustment program on this emergence. These represent initially the Moroccan society's main causes for the development of the informal economic activities outside the modern and agriculture sectors. They also represent sources of the integration of the informal enterprise sector, which is viewed as a substantial potential engine for economic growth and labor absorption. The subsequent section attempts to unveil the key issues addressed in the literature concerning the role of the informal sector in providing employment to many people with particular reference to the female workforce.

Informal Sector as a Labor Absorber

In Morocco, the informal sector emerges as an alternative to the mainstream economy. Indeed, the informal economic activities become a significant source in absorbing the workforce. Its dynamism is triggered by the important role it plays in the creation of employment opportunities.[67] For instance, it receives different categories of workers who are seeking revenues, especially in periods of crisis. Abzhad and Labchir provide the examples of the dismissed workers from the formal sector, the urban newcomers to the labor market who have not been able to obtain a formal employment, and the rural migrants in search of work in order to meet

66 Direction des Etudes et des Prévisions Financières. *Bilan du Programme D'Ajustement Structurel*. Rabat: Ministère de l'Economie et des Finances, 1995: 9.

67 Ali Fejjal. 'Le Secteur Informel: Concept et Mesure.' *Annales Marocaines d'Economie*, No. 4 (Spring 1993): 29.

their basic needs.[68] This means that this sector functions as a refuge for many active individuals who are unable to secure an employment in the formal sector. Its social vital role would enable it to substitute for the official employment crisis.[69]

The recognition of the essential role of the informal sector as a source of employment represents a proliferation if not a rapid evolution. However, I cannot ignore the fact that the informal employment cannot constitute, in almost all the cases, a persistent solution towards the formal employment crisis. Based on the estimation by Charmes, the Moroccan informal sector absorbs the highest rate of workers 56.9% of the population in the non-agriculture sectors.[70] Along the same line of reasoning, a recent study conducted by the Moroccan Directorate of Statistics in 2007 confirms that the informal sector contributes to the national economy by 37.3%.[71] The total of informal employment stood at 2,216,116 jobs in 2007 in contrast to 1,901,947 in 1999.[72] However, it should not be hastily deduced from these statistics that the importance of the informal sector as a labor absorber is a sign of poverty or a low economic development. It is rather a clear evidence for the manifestation of the underestimation of the GDP, especially taking into account the importance of the informal sector and the inability of the national accounts to correctly evaluate the contribution of the informal sector to the overall national economy.

Furthermore, the multi-criterion of workers in the informal sector is vital for the evaluation of the role of the informal sector in absorbing the workforce in Morocco. Indeed, most of these people share different interconnected issues while working informally. First, most of the informal

68 Abzahd and Labchir, op. cit., 359.

69 Rajaa Mejjati Alami. 'le Secteur Informel au Maroc: 1956–2004.' *50 ans de Développement Humains au Maroc et Perspèctives en 2025* (2006): 443.

70 Jacques Charmes. 'Emplois et Revenus dans l'Informel (non agricol) au Maghreb.' Bernard Chantal. *Nouvelles Logiques Marchandes au Maghreb: l'informel dans les Années 80*. Paris: Centre National de la Recherche Scientifique (1991): 50.

71 These data are based on a national survey on the informal sector conducted by the Moroccan Directorate of Statistics. It includes 10,259 informal production unit representatives of different categories of informal producers.

72 Direction de la Statistique, 2007, op. cit., 39.

workforce performs unorganized and marginalized activities because of their lack of the basic qualifications needed to enroll in the mainstream sector such as education and professional skills. Moreover, they also have in common various conditions of existence relative to place of origins, educational attainment, level of income, standards of living, among others.[73] Second, the informal sector mobilizes different workers who work in various sub-sectors outside the former sector. For instance, based on the statistics of the Directorate of Statistics, trade alone represents more than half of the jobs in the sector 53.2%.[74] The industrial sector comes second with 21.5% of the total labor in the informal sector followed by the service sector. The latter creates 19.1% of informal jobs. The construction industry and public work, meanwhile, have lower contribution to the supply of informal employment and this contribution rarely exceeds 6.4%.[75]

Third, the dynamics of the informal sector reveal that people choose different forms of working informally. Indeed, self-employment is the dominant component of job creation as it constitutes a source of survival. This idea is emphasized by Fejjal: 'En effet, en deça de 10, l'emploi dans le secteur informel est caractérisé par la prédominance des indépendants, des apprentis et des aides familiaux' (1993: 32) [Indeed, less than 10, employment in the informal sector is characterized by the predominance of own account workers, apprentices, and family helpers]. Based on the national survey by the Directorate of Statistics in 2003, 69% of the active population in the informal sector works as workers on their own account, with the help of family members and/or non-paid apprentices, and only 28.6% is rural workers.[76] The type of work may be exercised in a permanent or irregular manner and usually may have some effects on the household, which are exposed to irregular income. However, one cannot deny the fact that professional associations and cooperatives are also essential components of this sector. They constitute a strategy to minimize the risk of employment crisis. In a context of crisis in formal employment, individuals

73 See Aksikas, op. cit., 256–257.

74 Direction de la Statistique, 2007, op. cit., 117.

75 Direction de la Statistique, 2007, op. cit., 46.

76 Direction de la Statistique, 2003, op. cit., 130.

resort to different mechanisms to create small associations or cooperatives of two or more people to work together.[77] Considering the development of self-employment and the growth of small units of production, wage employment is less presented in the informal sector. Statistics reveal that wage-employment represents 15.8% of the entire informal sector employment in 2007, against 66.7% of global non-agricultural employment.[78]

Fourth, geographically speaking, the informal sector includes mostly workers who are generally active operators in urban areas and surrounding. In his study about the informal sector in the Moroccan context, Fejjal found that this sector includes workers from urban areas who are mostly locating their businesses in the old Medina, the new Medina and urban slums or *douars* [village].[79] This means that, in terms of the relation between sources of employment creation and the geographic placement of the economic units of production, urban areas constitute a crucial open door that attract many individuals to exercise their informal activities. This mostly includes both forms of job creation in this sector, urban self-employment and wage employment.

Another key characteristic of the informal sector in Morocco is the nature of the economic unit. Data revealed that most of the informal production units mobilized generally one person 70.5% of total units, in comparison with the units, including four workers 4.8% of enterprises in the sector.[80] Taking into account the development of self-employment and the growth of small units of production, wage employment is less presented in the informal sector. Statistics reveal that wage-employment represents 15.8% of the entire informal sector employment in 2007, against 66.7% of global non-agricultural employment.[81]

77 It is important to mention here that this form of work is based on trust between its members and collaborative work to produce a particular product without being sanctioned by any type of contracts. Most importantly, workers under the umbrella of associations or cooperatives have in common the willingness of sharing and minimizing the risks. In fact, women are a crucial proportion of the workforce who find their employment opportunities in different informal activities.

78 Direction de la Statistique, 2007, op. cit., 46.

79 Fejjal, op. cit., 33.

80 Direction de la Statistique, 2003, op. cit., 131.

81 Direction de la Statistique, 2007, op. cit., 46.

The informal sector presents a primary source of employment for many women worldwide and in higher shares. This basic fact is emphasized in the words of Chen, Vanek and Heintz who noted that: 'throughout the developing world, informal employment is generally a larger source of employment for women than formal employment and generally a larger source of employment for women than for men' (2006: 2133). In other words, this means that women are more economically active in the informal sector rather than in the formal sector. Moreover, the composition of the informal workforce trespasses the simple division of workers in self-employed or wage-employed activities. It focuses on the gender segmentation within both categories. Based on the findings of the UNIFEM publication, Chen, et al., found that with respect to the non-agricultural informal employment women likely work 'as own-account workers, domestic workers, and unpaid contributing workers in family enterprises' (2005: 9). In contrast, men are more likely to work as employers and wage workers.[82]

Using the results of the same publication, it is apparent that the male workforce is omnipresent in the informal agricultural activities, though sometimes exceptions are available. However, the female workforce constitutes a vital share of the total population of persons who are agricultural own-account workers or unpaid workers on family farms. In this regard, one may deduce that the gender-based differences in employment status are important. Compared to the male informal workers, a vast majority of women are more likely to be own-account workers and sub-contractors and they are less likely to be own operators or paid employees. As a result, these differentials in work may put workers at risks of gaining low and uncertain incomes as well as facing poverty.[83]

Furthermore, the proportion of women workers in the informal sector is larger than that of men. In her consideration of women's work outside the home, Hoyman argued that the occupational categories are 'so sex-segregated that we can assume that nearly all the workers in a specified occupation are female or that all are male, depending on the occupation' (1987: 67). This means that the share of the informal workforce by gender depends on the types

82 Chen, et al. (2005), 44.

83 For further details see Chen, et al. (2005).

of activities performed. In this regard, women's involvement in the informal economy mostly concentrates on occupations that are in the service industry.[84] These activities include 'babysitting, housecleaning, sewing, laundry, and beauty care as the top female occupations in terms of selling occupation' (Hoyman 1987: 69). Regardless of the fact that the literature that has been conducted on the gender dimension and informal sector employment is not definitive, and which deduces that men are more likely to be active participants in the informal sector than women, another line of research is developed and suggests that women may be as much engaged as men, if not more.[85]

In Morocco, available statistics about women working in the shadow economy show that they initially operate their activities in urban areas. Based on the national survey of 2007 by the Directorate of Statistics, women occupy one employment often in the informal sector, against 18.6% of global non-agricultural employment. Their presence is mainly in the industrial sector with a share of 24.3%, followed by service sector 11.8%, 6.3% in commerce activities, and 0.6% in building and public work activities.[86] Moreover, findings also show that 90.1% of the informal production units are headed by men, against 9.9% led by women. This proportion decreased by 2.5% points since 1999. Women headed informal production units are almost absent from the building sector and public works. However, they run 28.8% of units operating the industrial sector.[87] Furthermore, most of the informal activities concentrated in big cities, which take the form of self-employment are subjugated to gender discrimination. Indeed, Women's work in the shadow sector is invisibly performed at home and indoor, which makes it not subject to regulation and taxation procedures. In the same line of argument, Mejjati found that home-based work is almost exclusively feminine where women perform informal activities from home, especially those available in the artisanal sector such as broidery, sewing, weaving and others.[88]

84 See Hoyman (1987): 68 for a list of female-dominated occupations found in the U.S. General Accounting Office.
85 Hoyman, op. cit.
86 Direction de la Statistique, 2007, op. cit., 85.
87 Direction de la Statistique, 2007, op. cit., 31.
88 Mejjati, op. cit., 438.

To conclude, the informal sector has preponderance in terms of job creation. This segment of the economy has enormously diverse categories of workers. Indeed, the female informal workforce holds various employment status and shows a higher representation than its male counterpart. This is because the female workforce finds employment in the informal activities a refuge. Thus, the unorganized sector constitutes a pivotal source of job creation to an interesting proportion of workers. However, the question to be raised here is what role does the state play in dealing with the informal sector of the economy?

Informal Sector and the State

This section attempts to demonstrate that the relationship between the informal sector in Morocco and the state is a double-edge process. The first relationship tries to look at the debate on the link between informality and the state. It is made clear that informality is defined as opposed to the state regulations. It is illegally constituted. The second one is related to the state relationship to the informal sector. It is concerned with the nature of the policies towards the informal sector. Thus, what support can the state provide to the informal sector employees? To what extent can the state make this informal work integrated into the sphere of the formal economy? The following discussion tries to give reflections on these potential types of interventions to be brought to this sector.

Concerning the state actions towards the informal sector, it is obviously claimed that in the late 1960s and 1970s the informal sector was negatively perceived by the state. Most of the informal activities appeared to be more or less ignored by the modern sector. In this respect, work in the non-formalized economic sector was considered as a source to absorb employment, provide income opportunities, and supply migrants pending their integration into the formal sector. According to Aksikas 'the informal sector was thus seen as merely a temporary phenomenon, one that would disappear over time with the right kind of help from the state and its institutions' (2007: 258). As a consequence, the state put in place initiatives to develop the formal sector while its counterpart knew a timid evolutionary scheme. The focus was mainly related to the artisanal sector and workers in self-employment. In short, one may deduce that the informal sector activities during this period seemed to be excluded at the same time from the formal sector and the public authorities.

In 1980s and 1990s, the informal sector started to attract the attention of public authorities. This is in fact due to the benefit of external funding. For instance, this sector is supposed to play an important social role in creating job opportunities for many Moroccan individuals. As a result, the intervention of the state during this period focused on the development of the sector through various programs. They encompass programs about the promotion of *Petites et Moyennes Industrie*[89] (PMI), *Petites et Moyennes Entreprises*[90] (PME), *Programme de Priorités Social*[91] (BAJ),[92] the creation of micro-loans networks such as *Al Amana* and *Zakoura* for small businesses, and the organization of campaigns for poverty reduction.[93] Consequently, the negative opinions about the informal sector started to gradually diminish. Therefore, the provided assets would allow the sector to be an alternative in terms of employment provision.

Given these points, one may assume that the efforts of the state to boost the informal activities and recognize its contributors were limited. In fact, the focus has been mainly on some sectors with neglect to others. For example, state's interventions were mainly oriented towards craft, small businesses and survival activities. Generally speaking, the government interventions and financial support for them remain inadequate and insufficient.

Despite all that has been stated above, one cannot deny the fact that the micro credit strategy is a crucial tool used to fight against poverty and promote informal sector workers. Indeed, micro-entrepreneurs face difficulties to access credits to develop their activities. The emergence of micro-credits institutes are encouraged by development aid. They aim to fight against poverty. They are also supposed to financially assist people.

89 Small and medium industry (my translation).

90 Small and medium businesses (my translation).

91 *Barnamej Al Aoulaouiyat Al Ijtimaia*/Social Priority Program (my translation).

92 The aim of this program is to provide people in need with certain social services and employment.

93 See Mejjati, op. cit., 443–444.

Sometimes, they even replace the state actions as well as official banks in providing loans for many people. The main micro-credits institutes in Morocco are *Al Amana*,[94] *Zakoura*[95] and *Fondep*.[96] They work initially with commercials, small artisans and micro-entrepreneurs, both men and women, who face problems in getting access to credits via the traditional banking system.[97] In short, the provision of financial services is an omnipresent strategy by the state to contribute to the economic and social inclusion of micro-entrepreneurs excluded from traditional financial channels. However, one would venture to say that the state has to put various initiatives in place in order to invest more in human resources and give them access to resources outside informality.

Concerning informality and state regulations, one may assume that the informal sector is not characterized in most of the times by its deliberate willingness to transgress the legal regulations of the state. In fact, most micro-enterprises are semi-legal as stated by the Directorate of Statistics.[98] In other words, they respect certain regulations and neglect others. For instance, micro-enterprises comply with tax legislations rather than social and labor legislations. Furthermore, the registration of informal activities or enterprises is changeable on the basis of whether these activities are practiced at home or in any other setting. Based on the findings of the Directorate of Statistics, 18.6% of informal production units are registered, a sharply lower rate in 1999 as it reached 23.3%. This decline mainly affected the commercial sector where the share of patented informal units decreased from 29% to 20.6%. In contrast, the construction sector has increased from 3.5% to 6.2%. In terms of employment status of the head of the production units: only 15.5% managed by the independent units are recorded against 42.8% of those managed by employers.[99] Thus, one may estimate that if certain regulations are not met or if enterprises are not registered or correctly recorded, is that there are other

94 See <http://www.alamana.org.ma/> (Accessed 12 April 2014).
95 See <http://www.zakourafondation.org/> (Accessed 12 April 2014).
96 See <http://www.albaraka.ma/fr/> (Accessed 12 April 2014).
97 See Mejjati, op. cit., 444.
98 Direction de la Statistique, 2003, op. cit.
99 Direction de la Statistique, 2007, op. cit., 32.

factors responsible for the violation of state's regulations. For example, the complexity of procedures of regulation, the costs of recording and formalization process are of great importance.

To conclude, this section provides evidence about the important role that the informal sector plays in Morocco. It is demonstrated that it has an essential contribution in the regulation of the labor market. The forms of work exercised under the umbrella of this sector are very heterogeneous. They serve as a refuge for many individuals who are unable to secure a source of employment in the formal sector, and lack the adequate criteria to be part of the organized labor market.

More importantly, the development of the informal sector in Morocco is characterized by various historical factors. Firstly, the expansion of economic activities exercised by migrants from rural to urban areas resulted in the acceleration of the urbanization process. Secondly, the development in cities appears as a necessary outcome of the growth of the industrialization and privatization of some sectors of the economy, which may lead one to assume the availability of an intimate connection between the industrialization and urbanization processes.[100] Thirdly, Morocco experienced the implementation of the Structural Adjustment Program as a way to reform the economy and a means to maintain a standard of living. This is supported by the analysis of Charmes in his investigation of the different trends of employment available in the informal sector in countries of the Middle East:

> in countries where structural adjustment programs have been implemented, a means of maintaining standards of living has been found through the marketization of goods traditionally produced by women for self-consumption in their households. This process has thrown them into highly competitive world markets where labor costs are the main comparative advantage. This entry into the labor market from the bottom end has certainly been a consequence of globalization. (Charmes, 2004: 182)

Finally, it is worth pointing out that the available data on informal sector employment and more specifically in relation to gender are still limited. For this reason, the third chapter will provide a sound analysis about women workers as informal self-employed in the city of Fez on the basis of empirical data.

100 Gilbert and Gugler, op. cit., 65.

But before proceeding with this analysis, the subsequent section is dedicated to the examination of poverty in relation to gender and informal employment.

Perspectives on Poverty, Gender and Informal Employment

Poverty is a constant problem in different countries and its conceptualization remains a hard task as the concept is multidimensional. On this basis, this section is divided into two main sections. The first one will be devoted to a discussion of the interconnection between gender and poverty. The second one will concern itself with the relationship between informal employment and poverty.

Gender and Poverty in Focus

The interaction between gender and poverty is essential in the debate around poverty. Two important distinctions emerge to shape how this relationship between the two concepts is understood: the feminization of poverty and female household headship. This section starts with an overview of the ways social division of gender shapes and mediates the way poverty is experienced. Then, it focuses on the examination of the experience of females in household headship and its relation to poverty.

The 'Feminization of Poverty'

Discussions of the intersection of poverty with gender have revolved around the feminization of poverty for the last decades.[101] Medeiros and Costa reported that: 'data on the feminization of poverty is particularly important because it combines two issues: gender inequality and poverty. But the two

101 Chant (2010b), op. cit.

are not synonymous; gender inequality extends beyond poor and, by its turn, poverty is not exclusive to females' (2010: 95). On this level, to understand whether there is a feminization of poverty or not, it is important to define the key terms. In answer to this question, this sub-section provides the meaning of different concepts of the feminization, which can be applied to poverty.

The concept of feminization provides a description of a phenomenon in which the female proportion of society experiences the burden of poverty in a particular context. It refers to the assertion that women account for a disproportionately higher share of the poor of the world. Medeiros and Costa used the term as a description of 'both static and dynamic situations, to examine the gender composition of the poor, to compare the levels of poverty between and within gender groups, and to evaluate the conditions of women and of female headed-households' (2010: 97).[102] In this respect, analyzing the feminization of poverty may differ from one social group to another. Measures of poverty among the 'female-headed households' are not similar to the 'women group' even though both of them capture the gender dimension of poverty though in a quite different manner.[103]

Moreover, the thesis of the feminization of poverty highlights that women's experiences of poverty are not only restricted to their gender but also include other elements. This means that the female face of poverty is distinct and indeed women's experiences of poverty are different. This is emphasized in the words of Bradshaw, who said that: 'The feminization of poverty as approached by feminists is not only multidimensional but multi-sectoral as well. It is experienced in different ways, at different times and in different spaces' (2002: 12). Furthermore, the feminization of poverty is characterized by many non-economic and economic causes. In Moghadam's in-depth review of the 'feminization of poverty', she provides three main factors that put women at risk of poverty more than men. Firstly, she refers to women's disadvantage in respect of poverty-inducing capabilities and entitlements (such as education, skills, access to land and property). Secondly, women's heavier work burdens and lower earnings.

102 Female-headed households represent a focus of the feminization of poverty approach. More details are given in the section entitled 'Female Headed Households'.

103 Medeiros, Marcelo, and Joana Costa (2010), 98–99.

Thirdly, she refers to the constraints on women's socio-economic mobility due to cultural, legal, political and labor market barriers.[104] Thus, the conceptualization of the feminization of poverty relates to the way women experience different levels of poverty in a given time and context.

Feminization of poverty, originated in the United States in the late 1970s and coined by Diana Pearce, refers to its concentration among the female proportion of society, especially that the fastest growing type of family structure was relative to female heads of households.[105] Generally speaking, it refers to the phenomenon in which women experience poverty excessively and at far higher rates when compared with men. In the same line of argument, Medeiros and Costa defined the concept of the feminization of poverty[106] as: '(a) an increase in the difference in the levels of poverty among women and among men, and (b) an increase in the difference in the levels of poverty among female-headed households and among male – and cool – headed households' (2010: 99). Since the seventies, the fast rising of households headed by low-income women and their children represented a growing proportion, especially among the Afro-American community.[107]

Poverty in its females' aspect is used without any elucidation of its meaning. However, many researchers attempted to provide a set of common characteristics of the feminization of poverty. They include women's experience of higher incidence of poverty than men do. Women experience greater depth and severity of poverty than their male counterparts. Moreover, women are prone to suffer more persistent poverty than men are, women's disproportionate burden of poverty is rising relatively to men, and women

104 See Valentine Moghadam. 'The Feminization of Poverty: Notes on a Concept and Trend.' Occasional Paper. Vol. Normal IL, No. 2: Illinois State University, Women's Studies Program, 1997.

105 Diana Pearce, 'The Feminization of Poverty: Women, Work and Welfare.' *Urban and Social Change Review*, 1978.

106 In the empirical part of this book, I focus on the feminization of poverty based on the sex of individuals and not the sex of the head of household. In other words, I base my analysis on women and not on female-headed household for the simple reason that the informants in the unit of analysis live in households also headed by men. The analysis includes all households' types however headed by women or men.

107 Moghadam, op. cit., 6.

face more barriers to lifting themselves out of poverty. Leading from this, my concern in this book is to emphasize that poverty becomes more complexly gendered as both sexes are often subject to differently experience it for different reasons. Women have also divergent capacities to survive with and or escape poverty. These differences are manifested through gender inequalities and gender power within households. In the words of Cagatay: 'gender-based power relations mean that women experience poverty differently and more forcefully than men do' (2001: 14). Consequently, the feminization of poverty is linked to the feminization of household headship. Hence, women headed households are the 'poorest of the poor' who may transmit poverty to their children.[108]

In the Moroccan context, poverty increases and gets a multi-dimensional perspective. Despite of the classical poverty aspect characterized by particularly destitute material conditions, another more recent form of poverty linked to non-material aspects is developed. Skalli rightly observes in this regard that: 'poverty has many dimensions. Its dominant face in Morocco is becoming increasingly female, rural, illiterate and unskilled. Among the total population declared poor in the country, women are disproportionately over represented' (2001: 73). This new and modern type of poverty, which has emerged in different countries, is found essentially in rural areas and among the most vulnerable groups. In this regard, research on the Moroccan population revealed that women are the most vulnerable group who are affected by poverty. Based on the national study on poverty within the Moroccan society, it is shown that in 2007 9.1% of women are poor, including 4.8% living in urban areas and 14.5% living in rural areas.[109]

Poverty among Moroccan women is characterized by different mechanisms of exclusion. This exclusion is related to the working world, social solidarity, the possibility of integration, to name but a few. Additionally,

108 Chant (2007, 2008); Moghadam (1997); Cagatay (1998); Medeiros and Costa, Poverty among Women in Latin America: Feminization or Over representation? Working Paper 20, Brazil: International Poverty Center – UNDP, 2006.

109 Direction de la Statistique. *La Femme Marocaine en Chiffre: Tendances d'Evolution des Charactériqtiques Démographiques et Socioprofessionelles*. Rabat: Haut Commissariat au Plan, 2008: 107.

there are various factors behind the spread of exclusion as Skalli further explained: 'many economic, social and cultural factors converge and reinforce each other to produce conditions of social exclusion for a sizable number of women' (2001: 73). Hence, despite the repeated emphasis on the links between feminization of poverty and female headship, a growing body of literature also showed that the concept of poverty is not only limited to the economic aspect alone, but it also extends to include social, cultural and human considerations. This, however, encourages new dilemmas, especially given the increase in targeting the consideration of the plausible links between informal employment, gender and poverty to emerge.

Generally, women represent the most vulnerable group experiencing poverty due to their gender, as Cagatay further claimed: 'women are more vulnerable to chronic poverty because of gender inequalities in the distribution of income, access to productive inputs, such as credits, command over property or control over earned income, as well as gender biases in labor markets' (2001: 6). This means that the feminization of poverty, as a lived reality concentrated among women, represents something larger than simply concentrating on the economic domain. While the very definition of poverty relates to the inability to secure the basic needs such as food, clothing, or shelter, experiencing poverty also implies the denial of opportunity to achieve life goals, and ultimately to lose hope in development. At this stage, one may venture to say that the feminization of poverty is not only restricted to the financial aspects such as income but also extends to include non-material needs. In this respect, one may be tempted by the argument that the feminization of poverty is linked to the mounting incidence of female household headship as its primary tenet.[110]

Female-Headed Households

Female Household headship refers to the situation where an adult woman (usually with children) resides without a male partner, or in some cases, another adult male such as a father or brother.[111] The interconnection

110 See Chant (1997a); Moghadam (1997).

111 Chant (1997a), op. cit., 5.

between the household headship and the feminization of poverty is important since 'Female-headed households were the focus of the original feminization of poverty proposition. Given the economic disadvantages facing women, female-headed households were expected to have a higher poverty rate on average than male headed households' (Heintz, 2010: 438). Consequently, the relationship between the feminization of poverty and the headship in households originates from the notion that women headed households constitute a proportion of those affected by poverty, and that their experience of poverty is highly relative to the extremes in contrast to their male-headed units.[112] Therefore, both the feminization of poverty and the feminization of household headship seem to take the twinning aspect. However, I argue that it is impossible for investigations focusing on heterogeneous households headed by women to use simultaneously generalizations about poverty and present reality without taking into account its diversity.

Households headed by women consist of a high proportion of lone mother units with the hardships of raising children alone and securing the survival of the family. According to Chant, development literature widely assumes this group to be the poorest of the poor.[113] Consequently, poverty shifts from mothers to children, where female heads of households become responsible for 'inter-generational transmission of disadvantage' (Chant, 2007: 114). Mehra, et al., confirm that poverty becomes an inter-generational perpetuated phenomenon because of the inability of female heads of households to 'properly support their families or ensure their well being' (2000: 7).[114] Indeed, due to the intervening effect of the poverty transmission, a list of generalized assumptions appears. It includes the participation of children in the labor market to support the households instead of being in school. However, the number of child labor is noticeably not higher in the female-headed units.[115] Along the assumptions of Chant, the

112 See Moghadam, op. cit.

113 Chant (2007): 100.

114 Also see ILO. *All Women are Working Women: The Feminization of Poverty*. Geneva: International Labor Office, 1996.

115 Chant (1997a): 230; Chant (2007): 107.

present research tries to challenge the assumption that households could actually be a source of empowerment for lone mothers and to enhance their children's well-being.

In the light of the above discussion, it can be deduced that there is a close connection between feminization of poverty and female-headed households. Indeed, the popularization of the link between these two relationships could be supported through the variables of informal employment, socio-demographic and economic characteristics, which are taken into account with an eye to analyze and explain urban Moroccan women's experiences in this respect.

The Relationship between Informal Employment and Poverty

This section attempts to examine the relationship between informal employment and poverty and its intersection with gender. It is clear from the previous sections that a substantial proportion of females' participation in the labor market is found in the informal category. Women in informal employment, either as wage or self-employed, have a greater likelihood of being poor or/and affecting poverty. This section discusses the links between informal employment and poverty. It is followed by a distinction between household versus individual poverty level analysis. Then, it provides an examination of the role of informal employment in the contribution to the household income.

Informal Employment and Poverty

Discussions of the relationship between informal employment and poverty often focus exclusively on a process of twin feminization: labor and poverty. The former refers to the female workforce. The entrance of women into the labor market is characterized by their lower-cost provision of a source of labor that would substitute for men's labor.[116] Women's labor participation kept the traditional division of labor associated with women's work. For

116 Heintz, op. cit., 437.

instance, women are frequently concentrated in the types of employment with higher risks of being informal.[117] The latter refers to the assertion that women are at higher risks of being more affected by poverty than their male counterparts. This is justified by the fact that the female's proportion of society is in lower economic positions than males. For example, women face discriminatory practices based on their gender such as earning gaps, low work opportunities and assets. In this respect, given the economic disadvantage women may face, one would assume that they are more at risk to face poverty.[118] Female-headed households are the focus of the original feminization of poverty proportion. As mentioned previously in this chapter, female headed household are more at risk of being poorer than male headed household.

Empirical evidence demonstrates that the argument that female headed households are always at risk of facing poverty is not always true. Indeed, not all women face the same economic hindrances. They are not disadvantaged in the same degree or to the same extent. For example, in some cases, women may improve their financial situations by leaving a male-headed household through escaping domestic violence.[119] Moreover, the participation of women in various types of jobs and sectors matter for determining the risk of being poor. Women who rely on informal employment, as their primary source of income, face higher poverty rates in comparison with women who have access to formal jobs. This shows that there is a direct link between the nature of employment and women's risk of poverty. Thus, the female headship is not always necessary to be a factor determining the overall poverty risk.

However, contradictory views regarding the relationship between employment in the informal sector and poverty emerge to the surface. On the one hand, the feminist perspective considers the informal sector as a source of employment to trap its actors in poverty. The jobs available in this sector of the economy are characterized by various elements. They include lower quality jobs, poor working conditions, poor remuneration of

117 Chen, et al. (2005), op. cit.

118 For more details, see Heintz, op. cit.; Medeiros and Costa (2010), op. cit.

119 See Chant (2010a).

workers, absence of social protection, and exclusion of workers from social dialogue and decision-making.[120] Hence, its output to poverty reduction is minor. Therefore, this puts them at risk of injury and health harm on a daily basis. This means that poverty represents a crucial motive pushing people to end up performing informal work activities and working in the informal sector means experiencing poverty.

On the other hand, the economist view considers employment in the informal sector as a crucial means to contribute to the eradication of poverty. The size of this sector, particularly in terms of the creation of job opportunities, is relatively important in most countries and the Arab region is no exception. Generally, this serious problem is difficult to tackle without paying attention to the informal sector employment and poverty at both levels: the individual and the household level.

Individual Level vs Household Level Analysis

Individual level: The economist's perspective on welfare is essentially individualist. For instance, welfare pertains to individuals, and hence to poverty as the welfare shortfall is also a crucial characteristic of individuals. Poverty can be analyzed based on the economic autonomy through the income individuals have to satisfy their particular needs. The purpose of using this method is to get an idea about the poverty level of those who are unemployed, taking into account the gender differences, rather than using estimates of the total population.

Household Level: Economists consider that income and consumption data are normally collected from households, so that at the very least some adjustment and change are needed in translating a household resource in individual poverty. Such an adjustment has three aspects. First, it is to estimate the needs of different individuals. Second, it is to estimate the extent of economies of scale enjoyed. Third, it is to consider how household resources are allocated to different individuals within the household.

120 ILO, *Defining Strategies for Improving Working and Employment: Conditions in Micro and Small Enterprises and the Informal Economy: Overview of the ILO Learning and Research Agenda*. Geneva: International Labor Office, 2003.

In a study by Dubey, Shubhashis, and Wadhwa, the authors provide an analysis of the probability of the relationship between poverty and households based on their main source of income. Various classifications used focus on the regularity of salaries, form of employment as either self-employment or wage labor, as well as the size of the place in which they are located. The main findings of their analysis show that households with regular salaried employees have the lowest probability of being poor, unlike those households, which depend on casual day labor, have the highest probability. At the same time, those depending on self-employment fall roughly half way in between. They further maintain that all forms of employment have better experiences in larger cities.[121]

Income and Informal Employment

As noted above, the fastest growing source of employment for men and women in different countries and Morocco is no exception is the informal sector where both engage in a wide array of activities to secure an income. This has emerged as an important strategy, specifically for women to contribute to family income at a time when the formal labor market is stagnant. Moreover, it featured as another strategy to examine the link between informal employment and poverty. This is achieved via the examination of earnings in relation to different forms of informal employment. In other words, the focus is on a comparison of the differences in earnings based on various segments of informal employment. As mentioned previously in this chapter, the informal economy is segmented into wage employment and self-employment activities.

Although people have different reasons for their involvement in productive work, earning an income remains the most crucial one. Different earnings are associated with the type of activities performed. Hence, most households secure their livings through some form of employment. As such, employment income represents a substantial determinant while dealing

121 Amaresh, Dubey, Gangopadhyay Shubhashis, and Wilima Wadhwa. 'Occupational Structure and Incidence of Poverty in Indian Towns of Different Sizes.' *Review of Development Economics*, Vol. 5, No. 1 (2001).

with the income poverty status of the households. It is relative to the emphasis on the capabilities and individual freedoms instead of just focusing on income.[122] In this respect, employment earnings are crucial and significant to achieve the poverty reduction target.

Informal employment accounts for a larger share of total employment in many regions. More specifically, the informal employment income appears to be significantly important for a number of operators. Informal employment is not homogenous, but includes a variety of employment status, in particular self-employed workers and own-account operators who are omnipresent. However, earnings based on the non-waged forms of work are not statistically accounted, and they are not included in the official analysis of earnings. Furthermore, earnings from these forms of work are inferior and unstable comparatively with those earned through job opportunities in the wage employment form.[123]

Employment's earnings enormously vary in different situations. For instance, variation in work productivity provides an explanation of differences in employment earnings observed. These differentials have been well established in the literature. In this respect, Chen, Vanek and Carr provide a case in point while referring to the study by Charmes and Lakhel in different countries. The latter gave an insight on the differences in earnings within the informal sector.[124] They found that in most of the cases, except the Kenyan one, the average monthly incom of entrepreneurs is higher than the monthly average wages of the employees of micro-enterprises. Moreover, the earnings of the employees are around the minimum wage, which in most cases is not sufficient to secure the minimum needed for adequate survival.[125] Thus, one may deduce that there are significant gaps in earnings within the informal sector such as the employment segmentation,

122 Amartya, Sen. *Development as Freedom*. Oxford: Oxford University Press, 1999.

123 Chen, et al. (2005), op. cit.

124 See the results compiled by Charmes and Lakhel concerning the comparative data on the average monthly income of micro-entrepreneurs and the average monthly wage of employees of micro-enterprises in Martha Chen, Joann Vanek, and Marilyn Carr (2004), op. cit., 36.

125 Ibid., 36.

which has a crucial role to play in this regard. Same authors argued that on average, employers cherish the highest earnings while the earnings of home workers and wage workers are in between depending on the economic sector and the country.[126]

Employed women generally earn less than their male counterparts on average and within specific employment categories.[127] However, exceptions to this generalization occur on the surface, but they are specific to certain circumstances. Chen, et al., provide the example of women working in formal wage employment in the Egyptian case study who earn more on average than men do.[128] Nevertheless, this results from the low engagement of women in the labor force as well as the segmentation within the labor market in which large numbers of women perform unpaid work within family enterprises. Exceptions are relative to women who had access to education services, which gave them an opportunity to access the formal employment. Thus, the fact that those women's earnings in the wage employment are higher than those of men, which essentially indicate the gender inequalities, tend to increase inequalities among women as well as inequalities between men and women.

Conditions of employment are very important factors of employment income differentials. Indeed, the time to spend on an economic activity influences the rate of earnings. The increase of women's engagement in the labor force is relative to the increase of the time they allocate to paid work. However, evidence suggests that women are still less visible in remunerative activities comparatively to men, regardless of the increase in hours of paid work.[129] This means that the less time women spend on paid work, the lower earnings per hour or per day they may gain; therefore, their total income from employment falls below that of men on average. One justification for this relates to women's significant time spent in unpaid as

126 Ibid., 39.

127 ILO, *Global Employment Trends for Women*. Geneva: International Labor Office, 2004.

128 Chen, et al. (2005), op. cit.

129 Chen, et al. (2005), op. cit.

well as non-market work than men do.[130] Therefore, this has a limitation on the time workers can spend in paid employment. Moreover, the need to secure a balance in terms of reproductive and productive activities may provide explanations of the observed patterns of labor market segmentation. Chen, et al., found that in some countries, women working in informal employment, work longer hours in both market and non-market activities than women working in formal wage employment. One reason for these observed patterns of work is that own-account workers, for instance, may give women more flexibility to combine both paid and unpaid work, despite the evidence that it means long hours of work and lower average earnings.[131]

Conclusion

In line with the above discussions, these elements constitute a conceptual background and a theoretical framework. In fact, there are several studies on the informal sector and the relationship with poverty. However, to my knowledge, the kind of study, which focuses on the role of women's informal employment as a means of reducing household poverty in the city of Fez, seems to be scarce, if not almost absent. The present book focuses on women performing self-employed activities to convey the possibility of poverty reduction. It, therefore, adopts quantitative and qualitative approaches as techniques of collecting data to be the core on which my exploration will be hinged upon. This will be the main concern of the following chapter on methodology of data collection.

130 Lourdes Beneria. *Gender, Development and Globalization: Economics as if All People Mattered*. New York: Routledge, 2003.

131 Chen, et al. (2005) op. cit.

CHAPTER 2

Methodology

ABSTRACT
The use of a methodological framework is of great importance to investigate a phenomenon in social sciences. Indeed, the research design and the analytical process of any study should adopt a specific methodological direction based on the research objectives. To framework this process means that methodology is a set of procedures, whether quantitative or qualitative by which answers to research questions are found. In other words, the methodology is a process of discovery of how data are collected, organized, and interpreted. In this respect, selecting a particular methodology depends on the nature of the study and the choice of the suitable methodological steps is determined by the phenomenon under investigation. The focus of the present chapter is to provide justifications of the methodology used in this book. The first section is about a description of data collection and fieldwork. It starts with a discussion of the sample survey. It is followed by an overview of data collection techniques. Afterwards, I provide an explanation of the fieldwork. Ultimately, the second section is dedicated to the data analysis framework adopted in this study focusing on both the qualitative and the quantitative analyses. A discussion of the main limitations faced during the process of the investigation is addressed respectively.

Data Collection and Fieldwork

The present section attempts to provide an overview of the main data collection techniques and the process of the fieldwork. As mentioned earlier, this book uses both qualitative and quantitative research methods. They are important components of the survey[1] research by which a researcher collects information from a large group of people rather than a smaller number. This system also allows the researcher to find the link between various social, economic and psychological variables and behaviors.[2] However, the distinguishing features of surveys in social sciences research are the form of data and the method of analysis.[3]

There are two types of surveys, the census and the sample survey. The former 'includes information on the characteristics of the entire population in a territory. It is based on what people tell officials or what officials observe ' (Neuman, 2006: 237). The latter is used when the population is too large. The researcher uses either descriptive survey in order to describe a phenomenon or explanatory survey to explain something.[4] There are two types of data collection in the survey research: primary and secondary data. The primary sources refer to data collected by the researcher himself/herself using data collection instruments (questionnaires, interviews, focus groups, etc.). Secondary resources involve data offered by government agencies, local institutions, health and educational establishments to name but a few. My concern in this study is the sample survey and the primary data collection through the use of the mixed methods approach.

Sample Survey

To conduct a survey in the social sciences, a researcher needs to select a sample. It is a group of individuals who are selected from a larger population for investigation.[5] Therefore, the researcher has to use instruments not

1 For a summary of the main steps in conducting a social survey, see Lawrence, Neuman. *Social Research Methods: Qualitative and Quantitative Approaches* (6th edn). Boston, MA: University of Wisconsin at Whitewater, 2006: 276–277.

2 David, Gray. E. *Doing Research in the Real World* (2nd edn). London: Sage Publications, 2009: 218.

3 David, De Vaus. *Surveys in Social Research* (5th edn). London: Routledge, 2002: 3.

4 See De Vaus, op. cit., 31–32 for more details on descriptive and explanatory research.

5 See Alan, Bryman. *Social Science Methods (3rd Edition)*. Oxford: Oxford University Press, 2008: 168 for a further definition of the term sample. Also see De Vaus, op. cit., 70.

only to collect data but also to generalize the findings to the population from which the sample is selected. However, the critical factor determining the validity of these generalizations is the extent to which the sample is considered truly representative of the main population. This refers to the concept of 'sampling error' which makes the results of the fieldwork biased if they are not based on a good representative sample.[6] There are two types of sampling in the survey research: random and non-random samples.

Random sampling is a sampling technique to select a group of subjects (a sample) representative of a larger group (population). It is also known as probability sampling in the sense that it gives the sample element[7] the same chance of being selected.[8] Thus, the likelihood of being bias is reduced. There are various ways to select a random or probability sample. They are summarized as the following:

- *Simple random sample:* this is the most basic form of probability sampling.[9] It allows the possibility of inclusion of each single element in the population in the sample.[10] The selection of a specific unit does not affect the selection of another. This means that the process[11] of sample members' selection is done without informing them.[12]
- *Systematic sample:* similar to the simple random sample, the systematic sample gives the unit equal chance of being selected from the larger

6 For a further discussion on sampling error, see Bryman, op. cit., 170–171.

7 In the words of Babbie, the sample element refers to the unit of which a population is composed and which is selected in a sample. Distinguished from units of analysis that are used in data analysis (2013): 134. Similarly, Neuman refers to sample element as the 'unit of analysis or case in a population. It can be a person, a group, an organization, a written document or symbolic message, or even a social action (e.g. an arrest, a divorce, or a kiss) that is being measured' (2006: 224).

8 See Neuman, op. cit., 227; Bryman, op. cit., 117.

9 For a detailed definition of the concept, see Earl, Babbie. *The practice of Social Research* (13th edn). Austria: Wadsworth Cengage Learning, 2013: 147.

10 Bryman, op. cit., 171.

11 As an example of how to select a sample using random sampling technique, see Bryman, op. cit., 171–172.

12 Bryman, op. cit.,172.

population. As Bryman advances: 'with this kind of sampling, [the researcher] selects units directly from the sampling frame – that is, without resorting to a table of random numbers' (2008: 172). It is rather based on the selection of K*th* case in the sample frame using a sampling interval.[13]

- *Stratified random sampling:* it is based on the selection of the sample from a diversity of strata.[14] It refers to 'a random sample in which the researcher first identifies a set of mutually exclusive and exhaustive categories, divides the sampling frame by the categories, and then uses random selection to select cases from each category' (Neuman, 2006: 231). This technique of sampling is used when a researcher is interested in sub-groups.[15] This means that this technique divides the sampling frame into groups according to the variables the researcher requires for the study, such as gender, age, social class, marital status, etc. Then the sample is selected from each of these groups respecting the same proportional representation. Opposite to the simple random sample by which a homogeneous population is used to select the sample, the stratified sample demonstrates to be more representative of the population understudy since it gives the opportunity of representation of the sub-groups of the heterogeneous population and reduces sampling errors.[16]
- *Cluster sampling:* this is a 'type of random sample that uses multiple stages and is often used to cover wide geographic areas in which aggregated units are randomly selected and then the samples are drawn from the sampled aggregated units, or clusters' (Neuman, 2006: 233). It considers the units in a particular population as not only being members of the total population, but also as occurring members in cluster[17] population. Thus, this technique entails the multistage cluster sampling,

13 Neuman, op. cit., 230. For some examples on the systematic sampling, see 230–231.

14 Gray, op. cit., 152.

15 See Babbie, op. cit., 150.

16 For a further discussion, see Neuman, op. cit., 231; Babbie, op. cit., 150–151.

17 A cluster in the words of Neuman means 'a unit that contains final sampling elements, but can be treated temporarily as a sampling element itself.' Neuman, op. cit.,

which involves the repetition of two basic steps: listing and sampling.[18] A researcher who uses the cluster sampling is likely to reduce the costs of the research because this type of sample is 'less expensive than simple random sampling, but it is less accurate' (Neuman, 2006: 234).

- *Multi-stage sampling:* as the name denotes, is a technique based on the selection of the sample from another one. It follows many stages until the sample is identified. This form of sampling focuses on two main stages. The first one is about the selection of specific clusters and the second one is concerned with the choice of the population units in the selected clusters. Opposite to the cluster sampling, multistage sampling is based on random selection of sample units derived from each cluster rather than including all the units of clusters.

The non-random sampling is essentially an umbrella term to cover all types of sampling that are not conducted according to the canons of the random sampling outlined above.[19] In other words, it means that social research is taking place in situations that do not permit the use of the previously mentioned criteria of random sampling. It is also called non-probability sampling.[20] Unlike probability sampling used in the survey by which a list of units can be made, the non-random sample does neither allow the use of a list nor its creation. There are four main types: reliance on available subjects, purposive or judgmental sampling, snowball sampling, and quota sampling.

- *Reliance on available subjects:* this type of sampling is also called 'convenience' or 'haphazard' sample. The researcher relies on available subjects through stopping people on the street corner.[21] In this respect, he/she chooses the individual units without any random mechanism, as some individuals may fill out the survey, and others may ignore the researcher's inquiry. This form chooses the sample elements that are

---

234. It is used when there is the impossibility or the impracticality of compiling an exhaustive list of elements composing the target population.

18 Babbie, op. cit., 154.

19 Bryman, op. cit., 183.

20 For further discussion, see Babbie, op. cit., 128.

21 Babbie, op. cit., 128.

the most convenient for the investigation. It is mostly used among journalists as it does not permit any control among the representatives of a sample.[22]

- *Purposive or judgmental sampling:* this consists of tools that researchers use to 'deliberately select the subjects against one or more trait to give what is believed to be a representative sample' (Gray, 2009: 152). It is concerned with the selection of the unit of analysis[23] based on knowledge about a population, its elements, and the purpose of the study.[24] Accordingly, it is based on the judgment of an expert in the identification of cases, or it focuses on the selection with a particular aim in mind.[25] However, the purposive sampling puts the researcher in a disadvantageous position because he/she may inadvertently omit an important characteristic or may be subconsciously biased in selecting the sample.[26]
- *Snowball sampling:* as another crucial non-random strategy of sampling, the snowball sample is often used during data collection to ask each individual included in the sample to suggest additional people for fieldwork. This is emphasized in the words of Neuman, who said that it is a 'sample in which the researcher begins with one case, and then based on information about the interrelationships from that case, identifies other cases, and repeats the process again and again' (2006: 223). In other words, it encompasses personal contacts to build up a sample of the group to be studied. This technique is mostly used when the members of a particular population are not easy to locate. It allows the research to conduct a field research with the located subjects and ask them to suggest other subjects. The snowball sampling is good to use while investigating populations, which are neither delimited nor well-enumerated (e.g. homeless people). Snowball sampling, as a network

22 Babbie, op. cit., 128.
23 According to De Vaus 'A unit of analysis is the unit about which we obtain information: it is the unit whose characteristics we describe' (2002: 30).
24 Babbie, op. cit., 128.
25 See Neuman, op. cit., 222.
26 Gray, op. cit., 153.

of referral or reputational sampling is a method, which is based 'on an analogy to a snowball, which begins small but becomes larger as it is rolled on wet snow and picks up additional snow' (Neuaman, 2006: 223).
- *Quota sampling:* with the quota sampling, the researcher can non-randomly select the target population, which is stratified based on some variables until the planned number of subjects is reached. So, the researcher may choose to stratify the study based on some pre-specified characteristics 'so that the total sample will have the same distribution of characteristics assumed to exist in the population being studied' (Babbie, 2013: 130). To use the quota sampling, the individual needs to prepare a particular matrix or table describing the characteristics of the target population. These characteristics, depending on the research purposes, may include the gender of the proportion of the population, age categories of each proportion, educational level, marital status, social class, and so forth. Once the matrix is established and assigned, a relative proportion of each cell in the matrix, the researcher needs to move to the collection of data from people having the same features of a given cell.[27]

A survey research based on a non-random sample using a snowball sampling is therefore chosen as the research methodology best suited to the present mixed methods investigation. This is because it adequately addresses questions pertaining to attitudes and perceptions unlike the other options of social research (history – case study – experiment and archival analysis).[28] Moreover, it allows the accommodation of a larger population demanded by the study objective. Furthermore, it was decided to conduct survey research because it offers the ability to derive valuable results. However, before turning in details in the discussion of the data collection techniques used in the present study and the fieldwork, it is important to provide a general overview about the research methods in general. This would be of

27 Babbie, op. cit., 130. Also see Neuman, op. cit., 221.

28 For more details on other options of social research, see Bryman (2008); Neuman (2006); Babbie (2013) among others.

outstanding value when it comes to a description of the mixed methods approach adopted in this book.

The aim to use mixed methods approach is to generate credible findings via both quantitative and qualitative methods of research, which are used in a concurrent manner. The latter is also called the convergent parallel design.[29] According to Creswell and Clarck, this type of design allows the researcher to use different methods by directly focusing on the comparison and contrast of statistical quantitative findings with qualitative results. This process has as an objective to do corroboration and validation.[30] Thus, the convergence between quantitative and qualitative data[31] is essential to the provision of comprehensive analysis of the research question(s).

Qualitative approach is a process of exploration in social research whereby the researcher tries to understand how individuals make meaning of their social world.[32] Its main interest is to explore dimensions of the social world on the basis of everyday life experiences of the research participants,[33] the ways that social processes, institutions, discourses or relationships work, and the importance of the meanings they generate.[34] This means that qualitative research focuses on collecting impressions, words

29 Creswell, Vicki and Clark, *Designing and Conducting Mixed Methods Research* (2nd edn). California: Sage Publications, 2011: 77. The purpose in converging both quantitative and qualitative research methods is to provide a comprehensive analysis of the main research question(s) by converging both quantitative (statistical trends) and qualitative (detailed views) results for analysis. In this type of research design, the data are collected using both forms at the same time and then the results are interpreted on this basis (see John, Creswell. *Research Design: Qualitative, Quantitative, and Mixed Approaches* (2nd edn). Thouasands Oaks, CA: Sage Publications, 2003: 16.

30 Creswell, Vicki and Clark, op. cit., 77.

31 Neuman defines data as the 'empirical evidence or information that one gathers carefully according to rules or procedures. The data can be quantitative (i.e. expressed as numbers) or qualitative (i.e. expressed as words, pictures, or objects)' (2006): 8.

32 Sharlene Hesse-Biber. 'Qualitative Approaches to Mixed Methods Practice.' *Qualitative Inquiry*, Vol. 16, No. 6, (2010): 455. For further details see Bryman (2008): 366.

33 See Hesse-Biber, op. cit., 455.

34 Jennifer, Mason. *Qualitative Researching* (2nd edn). London: Sage Publications, 2002: 1.

and sentences, among other things to reflect on different views about a particular phenomenon. This is done through various steps: designing a study, collecting data, analyzing and interpreting them using qualitative techniques. In this respect, the researcher is able to build a new perspective as well as to draw on existing theories during these steps. Contrary to the quantitative research approach, which focuses on testing hypotheses in the interpreting data stage, the qualitative approach targets the creation of new concepts and emphasizes the construction of theoretical interpretations. Generally speaking, one may conclude that qualitative research is about collecting, analyzing and interpreting data using non-numerical data. In other words, it is based on gathering information using observations, interviews and analysis of documents.

Quantitative approach is a process of investigating a specific social phenomenon based on numerical data. Indeed, it is an ongoing procedure to develop and test hypotheses[35] pertaining to a phenomenon. This objective is achieved through the collection of data to be converted to statistics to answer the research question(s). In this respect, the quantitative research process follows different steps. It begins with the choice of a topic. It represents the main subject around which social research is conducted. The second step, afterwards, is to choose a theory by which 'a broadly deductive approach to the relationship between theory and research is taken' (Bryman, 2008: 141). It is common for summarizing the similar characteristics of the quantitative approach to suggest a focus question.[36] In contrast, other researchers prefer the use of inductive theory by which they choose to 'begin with observing the empirical world and then reflect on what is taking place, thinking in increasingly more abstract ways, moving toward theoretical concepts and propositions' (Neuman, 2006: 60).[37] The next

35 In the words of Neuman a hypothesis is 'an empirically testable version of a theoretical proposition that has not yet been tested or verified with empirical evidence. It is most used in deductive theorizing and can be restated as a prediction' (2006): 58.

36 The logic to connect the ideas in a theory to concrete evidence starting with abstract thinking and then testing these ideas against the evidence is known as the deductive direction of theorizing.

37 See also Gray, op. cit., 15.

step entails the selection of a research design. This latter 'requires making decisions about the type of case or sample to select, how to measure relevant factors, and what research techniques (questionnaire, experiment) to employ' (Neuman, 2006: 14). Step four entails collecting data using the research instruments.

A quantitative researcher has to choose between a set of techniques, which differ from one research to another.[38] Once the data are all collected, the researcher begins the fifth step related to the analysis of data. This typically entails coding the information. It means transforming it into numbers to facilitate the quantitative analysis of the data, especially if it is going to be processed with the use of a computer. This consideration leads into step six dealing with the interpretation of data. In this step, the researcher is concerned with the use of a number of techniques of quantitative data analysis to give meaning to data collected. Finally, the researcher informs the reader through a description and analysis of the results. Thus, an important part of the quantitative research process necessitates convincing the reader of the significance and validity of the research findings.

The mixed research approach is a multi-research methodology combining both quantitative and qualitative approaches. In the words of Creswell, it is defined as:

> [An approach] in which the researcher tends to base knowledge claims or pragmatic grounds [...]. It employs strategies of inquiry that involve collecting data either simultaneously or sequentially to best understand research problems. The data-collection also involves gathering both numeric information [...] as well as text information [...] so that the final database represents both quantitative and qualitative information. (2003: 18–20)

38 Bryman outlines three research types: *the experimental research*, which entails pre-testing subjects, manipulating the independent variable for the experimental group and post-testing respondents. The cross-sectional research uses social survey research instruments, which involves the use of structured interviews of the sample members or administering a self-completion questionnaire. Research using structured observation focuses on the task of the researcher as an observer to watch the setting and the behavior of people and then assign categories to each element of behavior (2008: 142).

In this scope, the mixed approach is distinguished in the sense that it combines the best of both fore-outlined approaches to collect, analyze, and interpret quantitative and qualitative data.[39] This means that the use of this approach allows the researcher to generalize from a particular sample to a larger population[40] and to provide an understanding of the phenomenon under investigation.[41] The strategy of the use of mixed methods approach is applied in order to marry the strengths of both methods in this research. The quantitative data are represented by the analysis of the questionnaires with women self-employed. The qualitative data focus on conducting interviews with females in professional associations to explain, validate and support the information obtained from the questionnaires. This stage focuses on semi-structured interviews to get the attitudes and life stories of these female workers. The discussion of the three types of research approaches is going to be maintained in the upcoming sections. Before turning in details to a discussion about the fieldwork of this study, it is important to provide a lens on the main data collection instruments used in this survey research.

Data Collection Techniques

Every fieldwork in the social sciences is about the use of specific techniques to collect data. These techniques are essential to get information about the population under investigation. In this respect, quantitative and qualitative methods are designed to count, compare, understand, interpret and

39 See Nancy L. Leech and Anthony J. Onwuegbuzie. 'A typology of mixed methods research designs.' *Springer Science*, Vol. 43 (2009): 265. See Creswell, Vicki and Clark, op. cit., 2–6; Bryman, op. cit., 603.

40 Babbie defines the term population as the group or collection that we are interested in generalizing about. More formally, a population is the theoretical specified aggregation of study elements (2013: 134). Equiventaly, Neuman stated: 'the large pool is the population, which has an important role in sampling […] to define the population, a researcher specifies the unit being sampled, the geographical location, and the temporal boundaries of populations' (2006: 224).

41 Hanson, et al., as cited in Gray (2009: 204).

give meaning of the findings based on the situation under investigation, taking into account various variables. It is for this reason that the present study includes two main research instruments. First, it is based on the use of interviews to get non-numerical data. Second, it focuses on the use of questionnaires to get statistical data. The following is a description of both data collection techniques.

Interviewing is a technique that the researcher uses to collect in depth and comprehensive information about a particular research subject. The collection of data, which rely on interviews, includes mostly people's attitudes, opinions, behaviors, motives, feelings and so forth. Typically, interviews deal with words and observations not numbers. This means that the interview is considered as a qualitative research method opposite to questionnaires by which information is quantifiable. Actually, the researcher has to pose questions in three different formats. First, the structured interview uses the same predetermined and standardized questions. That is, its aim is to give all interviewees exactly the same set of questions. This means that each respondent receives exactly the same fixed questions as any other. The questions are mostly very specific taking into consideration that the researcher has knowledge of the population or area under investigation. They are mainly in the form of closed, closed ended, pre-coded, or fixed choice questions.[42] This type of interviewing very often uses pre-determined answers and focuses the attention on a given issue by asking specific questions. Second, the semi-structured interview is a non standardized type of interviewing used in social research. Questions take frequently a more general form in their frame of reference from that typically found in structured interviews. Opposite to the structured interview, the semi-structured interview allows the researcher to ask further questions to what is seen as significant replies.[43] Third, the unstructured interview is based on a spontaneous conversation between the interviewer and the interviewee. It is also called the 'informal conversational interview'.[44] Unlike the structured interview, which is formal and has strict guidelines, the unstructured

42 Bryman, op. cit., 195.

43 Bryman, op. cit., 196; Gray, op. cit., 373.

44 Gray, op. cit., 374.

interview avoids the use of highly structured and pre-defined questions. The researcher has to ask questions by which the respondent freely reflects his/her viewpoint.[45]

In the present study, the interview technique will be used as a qualitative research method. The aim is to get women workers in professional associations as trainers and practitioners to express their ideas concerning the research's main themes. More importantly, the purpose is to employ women's knowledge, views, interpretations, experiences and interactions to give a meaning to the social reality which the research questions are designed to explore. Indeed, face to face interviews are employed to collect these data, as a follow-up to the information collected using quantitative methods, to further and strengthen the investigation of the responds' answers.

In addition, the study adopts a semi-structured interview technique to learn more about the central phenomenon of inquiry. This is done through the use of an interview guide.[46] It gives us the opportunity to ensure that the same information is gathered from each interviewee and to have the opportunity to ask further questions whenever needed. This type of interviewing remains more focused and restricted. This is because of openness and adaptability in comparison with the conversational or unstructured interview where the interviewer 'goes with the flow.' In this regard, it allows the research to be enriched by women's experiences, behaviors, opinions about their work in the informal sector and how they manage to reduce poverty and therefore, to move out of social exclusion.

Women informal workers are interviewed at their places of work. It is mainly performed either in the morning or the afternoon at a time chosen by the respondents. Each interview took around 30 minutes. Moreover, the use of a tape recorder is vital in this phase of the research since according to Gray it: 'not only does it record the essential data; it permits the interviewer to concentrate on the process of listening, interpreting and re-focusing the interview' (2009: 385). Moreover, confidentiality is ensured to the respondents in the beginning of each interview. To sum up, interviews

45 See Bryman, op. cit., 437–438 for an illustration of an unstructured interview style.

46 Translated versions of the interview guide into standarad Arabic and English are included in the appendices.

as a qualitative method help in the understanding of certain results of the data collected using questionnaires.

Questionnaires are data collection instruments widely used to gather information from a potentially large population at a short time. Gray defines them as: 'research tools through which people are asked to respond to the same set of questions in a predetermined order' (2009: 337). Inevitably, the aim of questionnaires is to obtain confirmatory information from each individual in the group in contrast to qualitative data, which are explanatory. Accordingly, questionnaires are the only way to secure statistical analysis of the findings of an inquiry.[47] Moreover, questionnaires are mostly not expensive. They are cheaper to administer in comparison to other forms of data collection.[48] They are frequently self-administered whereby respondents are given the opportunity to complete the questions themselves.

However, the main body of the questionnaire comprises either closed or open questions. Closed questions[49] are the most frequently used questions in the survey research. They usually take the form of multiple choice questions as they require a selection of the appropriate answer. Thus, the respondent has to choose between one or two alternatives whereby he/she has to choose and answer for the appropriate response. The researcher also has the chance to select from a set of answers either through two-way questions or liker-type scale.[50] Therefore, the closed questions do not allow the researcher to write down everything said by the respondent, to embellish what is said or even to misinterpret the answers.

Closed questions are easy to analyze in the context of survey research. Bryman stated: 'one advantage that is particularly significant [...] is that closed questions greatly facilitate the processing of data. When an open question is asked, the answers need to be sifted and coded in order for the data to be

47 They are tools employed to gather data to be converted into numerical forms. Therefore, statistical calculations can be made and conclusions drawn. The main aim is to test hypotheses and to find answers to the overriding research questions, hence, more objectivity is guaranteed about the research findings.

48 Gray, op. cit., 238.

49 See Creswell, Vicki and Clark, op. cit., 177.

50 For more details, see Bryman, op. cit., 207–222-223–349.

analyzed quantitatively' (2008: 195). This means that close questions provide respondents with a structure in their answers. Opposite to closed questions, open questions do not require the respondent to select from the alternatives. Instead, they allow the respondents to answer freely the questions and express their opinions without the intervention of the researcher.[51] Moreover, there is a kind of compromise between closed questions and open questions, which is relative to semi-opened questions. These latter refer to yes/no questions, which require the respondent to choose an answer and justify it in his/her own words. Both forms of questions are essential to design a questionnaire.

To investigate the role of women's participation in self-employed activities and poverty reduction, the present investigation focuses on the administration of a questionnaire, which represents the primary instrument of data collection. It is given to different women in the city of Fez. The informants, whose number is 300, work in an informal activity belonging to the self-employed type of work. It is important to mention here that the questionnaires are administered in person because many respondents are either illiterate or have lower educational levels. In this regard, most women have the feeling that they are participating in an interview rather than filling in a questionnaire as I write down their answers on their behalf.

After the introduction to the questionnaire, by which I explain to the respondents the purpose of the study and thank them for their willingness to devote some of their time to answer the questions, the questionnaire includes 55 questions classified under four axes. The first one aims to gather information about the informants' personal information, demographic characteristics of women employed in self-employed activities, which are considered influential in understanding women's profile. In the second part, informants are asked about the characteristics of their economic activities within the informal sector, the nature of work, their motives to end up in this type of work, and obstacles they confronted. The section afterwards deals with women's contribution to poverty reduction of the household. Finally, the last set of questions addresses the contribution of women's work to their empowerment.

51 Bryman, op. cit., 231.

The questionnaires include different types of questions. Apart from the background questions, there are different closed (limited response format) and open ended questions (text response format). They are designed in the Arabic language because only few women are supposed to be literate enough to answer by themselves. Where appropriate, some of the questions included in the questionnaires based on the general overview of the literature were modified to suit the context of the survey. Then in order to make sure that the reliability, which is important to retrieve valid measures of a concept, and to be sure that the statements are comprehensive for the respondents, the questionnaires were reviewed by my supervisor. Furthermore, confidentiality is ensured to the respondents because they are informed beforehand about the aim of the study. This means that the information, which is provided by the respondents, will be held in confidence except in the general analysis.

All in all, the data collected from the questionnaires provide the study with a framework of quantitative data on which I will be able to build up hypotheses. Besides, more credibility, reliability and objectivity will be given to the research. Quantitative data gathered using questionnaires will be presented in this research as tables and graphics accompanied by deep quantified analysis through significant intersections. Qualitative data collected using interviews will also provide desirable information to support the analysis of the quantitative data.

Fieldwork of the Study

To facilitate the fieldwork of the study and to guarantee the effectiveness of its results, I follow various exploratory steps. To begin with, I devise the questionnaire and the interview guide, as the main instruments to be used in the book to collect data, in order to ensure that the survey questions operate well and to avoid any difficult expressions to the informants. In this regard, I used piloting as a process of pre-testing elements of the survey tools, questionnaires and interviews, prior to implementation.[52] As a result,

52 According to Bryman, piloting the research instruments is very important for many reasons. First, it allows a researcher to achieve the reliability of the study. Second, it

some modifications are vital to the investigation, new questions are added while some are deleted, and others are rephrased. Due to the nature of the target population, questions are written in Arabic and a translated version into English is made available for non-native readers.[53] I have submitted a version to two editors who are fluent in Arabic to be sure that there are no significant language problems as well as style, and that the wording is correct. During the period December 2012–February 2013, I administered the questionnaires and the interview guide to a piloting population of 50 women who are comparable to members of the population from which the sample for the full study is taken. They are women working in the informal sector as self-employed in the city of Fez.

The aim of the pilot test survey is to check the validity of the questions and to identify any problem. I basically asked the respondents to answer the questions, and afterwards give their opinions about the appropriateness or inappropriateness of the questions. I also requested them to give me their point of views concerning the technique's ease of usage, its clarity, its ambiguity, its length and the wording of the questions and if there are some important questions, which are lacking. The next step is the evaluation of the results, which allowed me to make some adjustments to prevent any kind of misunderstanding. Finally, with the help of the supervisor, a final printed version of both tools is available after they were carefully tested.

In any fieldwork, it is important for the researcher to select a unit of analysis, which is going to be representative of the total population under research. Indeed, this unit necessarily needs to meet the same criteria and characteristics of the population. The researcher has to depend on the objective of the study to define the target group. In the present investigation, the focus is on the city of Fez as a case study. Moreover, informants are the main source of useful information in any ethnographic research, and this book is no exception here. I work with two kinds of informants:

---

helps him/her to reduce the incidence of non-response to the questionnaire. Third, it allows the researcher to identify the type of questions that are more likely to make respondents uncomfortable. Finally, it is a way to detect any tendency for respondents' interest to be lost at certain junctures (2008: 247).

53 See appendices.

those working within professional associations who teach women basic skills as well as the informants who respond to the questionnaires. The first group refers to the teachers and transmitters of the basic professional skills in various sectors of informal activities. It is noteworthy to mention that members of these associations participate in recommending women who are the informants of the second group. For this reason, I have contacted many professional associations in the city of Fez known to have a good membership of women beneficiaries of their services. I contacted 50 women whose main role in the associations is to transfer their knowledge to other women. These informants are interviewed in order to reveal their knowledge concerning their employment as well as their attitudes about women's self-employment in the informal sector and poverty reduction by answering the same questionnaire.

Moreover, the second group of informants includes many informal operators working invisibly. Some workers, however, are visible as they operate from public spaces like workshops or cooperatives. They are sampled via networks and relatives. The respondents are selected on a snowball basis as it represents a suitable means to use in this type of hidden populations of workers. A target sample of 300 total respondents is set encompassing mainly seamstresses, embroiderers, hairdressers, cosmeticians, vendors and so forth. It is noteworthy to mention here that the survey is limited to urban self-employed activities practiced by women and excludes those wages employed activities as well as units in the agricultural sector. Moreover, the population under investigation does not include domestics employed by managers.[54]

To conclude, the goal of this section is to situate and direct the reader towards the research design and various techniques used in the investigation. In this respect, two data collection instruments are used to probe general results. The subsequent section attempts to provide insight on the way the findings of the data collected in the city of Fez will be analyzed, the process of quantitative and qualitative data analyses as well as the constraints faced during the research process.

54 See Chapter 3.

Data Analysis, Processing and Limitations

Data analysis is a very important step in the social research process. As an empirical style of research on human and cultures, ethnography represents a good method of analysis in the present book. Mason defines ethnography as: 'an approach (some say strategy) which is grounded in a particular ontology. It is generally about the study of culture (or similar concepts), and is based on an epistemology which says that culture can be known through cultural and social settings' (2002: 55). Its aim is to observe a social phenomenon on the basis of the viewpoints of the subject of the study. In other words, it is a means to reflect the meanings in the lives of a cultural group. In the words of Gray, the main task of ethnographers is 'to pay attention to language and the ways in which terms are used in certain cultures' (2009: 23).

Ethnographers use a wide range of methods to explore a particular social or cultural setting. For instance, some researchers use observational techniques while others prefer to employ other instruments.[55] There are mainly three approaches to ethnography: conventional, phenomenological and critical. The conventional approach to ethnography does not locate much attention to the meanings. Opposite to the phenomenologist who has an interest in discovering and interpreting meanings, the conventionalist suggests hypotheses about meanings and tries hard to test them. Its overriding characteristic is related to the provision of detailed empirical knowledge about a subject to reveal a social process rather than providing generalizations. The phenomenological approach to ethnography, afterwards, deals with the exploration of what people think they are doing and why they are doing it. It is not concerned with the description of a social process, but rather deals with the process of interpretation of people's behaviors from their points of view. However, the critical approach to ethnography explores the meaning of a subject in relation to all aspects of the society

55 For further discussion on the main features of ethnographic approaches and the techniques a researcher may use to explore a social phenomenon, see Mason, op. cit., 55.

in which the subjects operate. As it is the main method of data analysis in this book, critical ethnography focuses on giving a deep insight into the meanings and locate them within a 'broader setting.'

To sum up, the present book adopts the critical ethnography approach to analyze the data collected using a mixed methods approach. It is employed in the practical part of the research to either confirm or refute the hypothesis that women's participation in self-employed activities in the informal sector contributes to the household poverty reduction in the city of Fez. This sub-section provides a description of data processing followed in the present book, namely focusing on ways of quantitative and qualitative data analysis. Finally, it focuses on a description of the main limitations faced during the research process.

Qualitative Data Analysis

Analysis of qualitative data takes mostly the form of written words. This type of analysis rarely uses numerical or statistical analysis. In this respect, the present investigation uses words and opinions expressed by women in the survey to provide texts to convince the reader along side with the statistics derived from the questionnaires. Through analysis, the data are broken down into new concepts, which allow the basis for a description using ethnography.

The qualitative data follow a coding process. First, I transcribe the data derived from the interviews and make them in a text format that can be easily read and interpreted. Second, the coding stage helps me to be more familiar with the data collected and allow me to identify different themes emerging from the analysis. Afterwards, I focus on the reading stage by which I become able to identify any duplicated phenomenon and remove the additional codes. Finally, the creation of codes allows me to connect and combine them to the emerging findings from the quantitative data to see if they can confirm or refute the hypotheses developed in the beginning of the research process. Thus, some of the respondents' quotes are presented in the practical part of the research whenever I find it relevant. This process helps me to go beyond description. It provides a path to interpret, to understand and to explain certain features revealed in the empirical study. These analyses, therefore, will allow for the achievement of new insights into my data.

Quantitative Data Analysis

To achieve the purpose of the present study, the data collected using the questionnaires are coded using the SPSS.[56] For instance, a number is assigned to the responses each respondent provided. They are entered into a data record that includes all the answers from the respondents. More specifically, the SPSS software helps me in providing a set of different statistical techniques to do the analysis. In this respect, before analyzing the data, I went through the following steps:

- A data entry file is created in SPSS package coding the questionnaires administered to women workers as self-employed.
- Data are coded in a format that is easy to analyze using a computer.
- Data are entered and these entries are checked before the final version of tables and graphs is used in the analysis.

Furthermore, different statistical techniques are used to retrieve data from the survey research as well as to achieve the objective of the study. Indeed, statistics included in the present study encompass descriptive statistics, as they are summaries based on the initial description of the data. They are based on univariate and bivariate analysis.

The univariate analysis is used to describe the distribution of variables.[57] It is defined by Bryman as: 'the analysis of one variable at a time' (2008: 322). It concentrates on the distribution of a single variable using frequency tables, which are used to indicate the number and the percentage of each variable.[58] Another way of displaying quantitative data is through

56 It refers to Statistical Package for the Social Sciences.

57 De Vaus, op. cit., 212.

58 See Bryman, op. cit., 322–323 for more guidance about how to identify variables of each type.

the use of diagrams. They are concerned with the demonstration of the findings in a readable manner. Bryman claimed that: 'their chief advantage is that they are relatively easy to interpret and understand' (2008: 324). The study utilizes three main types of diagrams: bar charts, pie charts and histograms.[59] In addition, measures of central tendency are among the most frequently used methods of exhibiting quantitative data. For example, the arithmetic mean as it represents '[the sum of] all the values in a distribution and then [their division] by the number of values' (Bryman, 2006: 325).

The bivariate analysis is used whenever descriptive statistics are needed to describe the relationship between pairs of variables. Bryman said: 'bivariate analysis is concerned with the analysis of two variables at a time in order to uncover whether the two variables are related' (2006: 325). In this respect, a variety of techniques are used to examine the relationships between two variables being analyzed. However, their use changes with the type of the variables involved. A variety of bivariate analysis methods are employed in the present book. Cross-tabulations are one of the simplest and most frequently used techniques of showing the relationship between variables. De Vaus said: 'cross-tabulations are the main tabular method for displaying data for detecting an association between two variables' (2002: 242). For this study, these tables allow two variables, which are set side by side in one table, to be simultaneously analyzed in order to check the relationship between them. Moreover, the analysis of quantitative data focused on the correlation analysis. This latter is concerned with 'associations between variables [...] correlation is concerned with describing relationships (e.g. between X and Y)' (Gray: 2009: 485).

Problems and Limitations

Any research project inevitably faces problems and constraints. Indeed, I encountered many difficulties along the way of carrying out this investigation. First, because the present research faced different time and financial

59 See De Vaus, op. cit., 214–220 for more details on the use of graphical analysis.

resource constraints, it was only designed to study the role of women's self-employment in the informal sector in reducing household poverty in the city of Fez. Therefore, the results and conclusions may not be generalized to other work categories or regions in Morocco.

Regarding the practical part of the research, the realization of this study confronted some difficulties in order to collect the data. These difficulties are summarized as the following: Firstly, I had to rely on a sample to conduct the empirical study. The latter represents a practical constraint on the nature of the informal sector and the characteristics of the target group with whom the practical part is concerned. For this reason, the preliminary informal interviews conducted with some women critically revealed the invisibility of this type of employment, the lack of data on their work, and the difficulty to find this category of women except in cases when it is via family networks or connections.

Secondly, collecting data using questionnaires represents another major constraint. Indeed, the majority of the respondents have less than primary education, which could not allow them to fill in the questionnaires themselves. So, I was obliged to do the task of reading, explaining the questions, and writing personally, which was time consuming. Moreover, some women refused to do the questionnaires or to be interviewed by providing certain excuses.

Another problem that I faced during the data collection process was related to the reluctance of respondents to talk in the presence of a member of their families, especially the husband or a male relative. Indeed, both questionnaires and interviews included some questions about income spending or household responsibilities division, among other sensitive issues. Therefore, I deliberately planned my meetings with these women in the absence of their husbands or their male relatives to escape any kind of misunderstanding.

The last limitation is related to the translation process. Both quantitative and qualitative data collection are done in Arabic considering the linguistic nature of the sample. In this respect, because surveys are conducted in the Arabic language and the book is written in the English language, then this took much more time for the researcher as it was planned. Moreover, some words are used by women relative to their work activities in Arabic, and they should be translated into a language other than their own. Thus, while translating into another language, which is not the original one such as English, the translation is evidently a hard task as there are some words, which are culturally bound.

Conclusion

In general, during the process of this research, I succeeded to overcome all the constraints and limitations I encountered in the different stages of the research project. This is due to the great patience and willingness to investigate the phenomenon and thanks to the help of many respondents who contributed to face all the challenges. Thus, the goal of this chapter was to situate and direct the reader towards the methodological framework adopted in this research as well as the points of views used in the construction of the research enterprise. The empirical study in the city of Fez is crowned with four chapters devoted to data analysis and interpretations. The third chapter deals with informal self-employed women in the research area. The fourth chapter concentrates on examining the role of self-employment in poverty reduction. The fifth chapter, afterward, discusses the work of women and its role in their emancipation. The sixth chapter focuses on the limitations and perspectives of women in their self-employment.

CHAPTER 3

Women and Self-employment in the City of Fez

ABSTRACT

In the previous chapters, it has been assumed that women's opportunities to enroll in an informal economic activity are caused by their lower socio-demographic and socioeconomic characteristics. It is further assumed that the informal sector is an important source of job creation for women whose motivations are diversified. The current chapter explores the socio-demographic and professional characteristics of self-employed women. It also examines women's interests in their shadow work. This would allow the understanding of the type of women working in this form of employment in Morocco in general and in the city of Fez in particular.

Women's Profiles in Self-employment

This section is divided into two main sub-sections. The first one has an objective to determine the profile of the workers through the examination of their socio-demographic and professional characteristics that promote or hinder the development of the informal self-employment. The second sub-section examines the main reasons and motivational aspects that pushed these women to end up working informally.

Socio-demographic Characteristics

Based on the findings of the quantitative data, the age variable of my informants ranges from 20 to 70 years old. Women informants whose age is between 30 and 45 years old come in the first place with a percentage of

37.3%. Informants whose age is less than 30 years old come in the second place with a percentage of 26.3%. In the third position comes women whose age is between 45–60 years old. They make the percentage of 23.3%. The last category is that of women whose age is 60 and above. They represent 13% of the total population.

Table 2. Age Categorization

	Frequency	Percentage
20–30	79	26.3%
30–45	112	37.3%
45–60	70	23.3%
+ 60	39	13%
Total	300	100%

Source: Fieldwork Results

Data retrieved from the questionnaires reveal the predominance of the adult active population. The remarkable presence of adult women whose age is less than 45 years represents 63.6% of the workforce. This shows that the younger age classes remain the most highly represented. This finding is enhanced by the results of the qualitative data, which show that younger women may be active participants than the older ones due to certain factors. For instance, they have strong physical conditions, enjoy tolerance of family members and have the intention to secure economic stability and independence, to name but a few. Moreover, among women who are relatively advanced in age, a low proportion continues to work. They are those who take charge of transmitting work knowledge and ensuring the well-functioning of the work based at home.

Most respondents consider the creation of job opportunities within the informal sector as a viable solution regardless of their ages. For instance, the interviewees' choice of the informal sector is justified by the following reasons: for the respondents whose age is between 20 and 30 years old, the main motives are the lack of education or the financial resources. As to the second age group category (30–60 years old), they saw that in addition to a steady source of income comes the dependence on their men and family members as sources of financial support, which encourage them for self-autonomy and financial independence. The last category of respondents whose age is 60 years old or above remain the least represented. The main motive for their choice of the informal sector lies in the fact that they do not have an alternative to find a job somewhere else. This is explained by Fatma, a woman whose primary job is carpet making, she said: 'I become old and it is impossible for me to find a job opportunity in another sector.' Furthermore, these women are the transmitters of work knowledge from one generation to another, especially in craftsmanship. In this respect, one may deduce that priorities differ among young and older women. Thus, age remains an important variable. It determines the major differences between women's age groups and their participation in informal segments of work.

With regard to the marital status, data from the city of Fez reveal that 21.6% are single, and the big majority has family responsibilities with a share of 34.3% for married women; 14.3% for divorcees; 13.6% for widows; 9% for abandoned women; and 5.3% is the percentage dedicated to the group of one of the wives[1] while single mothers are the least represented in the sample with a share of 1.6%.

Table 3. Women's Marital Status

	Percentage
Single	21.60%
Married	34.30%
one of the wives	5.30%
Divorced	14.30%
widow	13.60%
single mother	1.60%
Abandenned Women	9%

1 I used this term to refer to women who live in polygamy.

Examining the distribution of women based on their marital status, it can be noticed that the issue of marriage is a significant factor. It determines women's participation in the informal work. For instance, questionnaires' responses reveal that the highest rate is allocated to married women. They accessed the self-employed activities because they cannot rely only on a source of income provided by their partners or other male family members. Additionally, married individuals, specifically the household heads, are in fact the initiators of the family ties. They mobilize the energies of the family facing the challenges of daily life problems as well as the demands of survival in the research area. This denotes that in most situations, the economic activity, even though precarious, supports many families even though with the availability of a male figure as the main breadwinner. Women are also financial providers of the family who seek multiple sources of income. Likewise, women who belong to the category of one of the wives share the same idea of the category of married women. Their participation in informal activities is mainly for financial sources to support the husband in the daily expenses of the household.

Furthermore, questionnaires' responses show that divorced, widowed, abandoned women and single mothers consider the issue of 'no husband' as a major cause for their involvement in such a type of work. Indeed, women who experienced divorce or separation from their spouses, generally, create their own units of living either with their family members or with their children and sometimes both. Added to this, based on their unsuccessful experiences with marriage and cohabitation, the majority of divorced informants, regardless of their cultural backgrounds, declared that they would rely on their own resources to support themselves and their families.

In the same line of argument, despite of the fact that cultural belief about the importance of making a family may diverge from divorcees' positions, most interviewees declared that they would not seek a new husband anymore. Most of them have similar ideas about living without a partner and being self-supporters. It is crucial at this stage to mention that the data about the profile of husbands reveal that they have a low educational level. They are either unemployed or do not have a stable job. Their incomes are in most cases lower. This shows that their marriages are with lower class citizens and who have marginalized positions in the labor market. Thus, this type of marriage affects the living standards of the family. For this reason, many divorced women prefer to stay alone in order to stand up by themselves and become independent. Therefore, the rejection of some women to cohabit with men and get married again show their need for independence and gender equality in an expression of their agency. In this regard, Safia, a young traditional clothes maker who was divorced for four years confirms: 'I do not want to marry for a second time. All that I need is to work for myself because I want to be my own boss. No one to interfere with my work because I want to have flexibility in time and place of work.' From this statement, one might deduce that this category of women struggles to secure a living and survive on the margins of marriage and male domination.

Furthermore, widows and abandoned women are mostly illiterate. They do not have work experiences. They are unprepared to confront the hardships of daily life because of the loss of the main breadwinner. For this reason, self-employment activities are a source of living in most cases. Additionally, it is worth noting that they are also responsible to ensure different basic needs of the family members (food, shelter, clothes ...) This denotes that informal work has two interrelated outcomes for women. For some, it is a means of social emancipation while for others it is a source of survival for them and their families. In other words, informal work has purely social and economic outcomes.

Single mothers in this research present a key group to understand the enrollment of women in the informal work. Qualitative data demonstrate that this category of women faces several discriminatory practices because of their gender and their marital status. Against the dominant norm in the Moroccan culture of the nuclear family,[2] single mothers are considered as incomplete and castrated from the norm of society due to their sexual experiences and pregnancies outside the wedlock. Almost the 1.6% share of the single mothers in the case study declared their stunning experiences

2 This type of the family is considered to be normal in the Moroccan society. It includes both the parents and their children who are born within a marriage institution. This is in contrast to a single-parent family and to the extended family. For further details on the Moroccan family types, see Sadiqi (2014: 101–102).

of discrimination, and stigmatization. Indeed, most of them complained about their financial difficulties, social humiliation and stress. All these things are tangible reasons that pushed them to seek an employment in the informal sector to secure a source of living.

The willingness of single mothers to work and sustain themselves and their children is an essential way to challenge their victimization. Indeed, instead of perceiving themselves as victims, they do their utmost to deal with their vulnerable situation. A case in point is the declaration of Meriam who became pregnant at the age of 24 years in spite of her use of contraceptives. In fact, she found herself in a bad situation, especially when her boyfriend refused to recognize the pregnancy and take care of her. Because she wanted to keep the baby, her family rejected her and considered her situation as her own fault. As she did not receive any family support, she decided to be responsible for her doings and solved her problems by herself. She said:

> I was first rejected by my family because of my pregnancy. However, I could not stay with hands crossed. I started to prepare bread and sell it in open areas. When people knew about my activity, they started to demand it more and more. The material and emotional support I received from my network allowed me a certain financial assistance.

The case of Meriam shows that considering single mothers as an exception and a deviation from the norms do not affect women's readiness to support themselves and seek independence. Still, this help and support do not go without both implicit and explicit blames for women's violation of the norms. That said, despite being financially supported by social networks, they are socially stigmatized and pointed out as 'social outlaws'.

The analysis of the situation of women also shows the participation of single women in the informal workforce. They represent 21.6% of the total population in the city of Fez and exercise different activities. These young females often face a difficult daily reality. The everyday problems are also affected by the residence of these women with their parents. This situation pushes most of them to exercise any activity to support them and help their families. For this reason, the parental home remains a productive place of work for these young ladies. Unfortunately, their informal activities are usually characterized by their fragility, uncertainty, scarcity of benefit, and absence of a guarantee of permanence. Apart from the uncertainty of economic activities, fear of the future, the situation expresses obviously a certain inability to realize their own home and secure their own life outside their family circle.

Another reason behind women's access to the job market before marriage, which contradicts the case of the married women, is their perceptions of equality with men. In other words, single respondents want to secure a source of income before getting in the responsibilities of marriage. Some of them articulated that they prefer to work before marriage to challenge the tradition that women are forbidden to work by their husbands. However, they seek employment as a basis for independence. Others want to secure a financial source before getting married and having children. They prefer to remain single so as not to face the constraints of the institution of marriage. Houria, a single and 30-year-old interviewee said: 'women are not allowed to do what they want when they are married. I prefer to stay single in order to work and do as much exposition of my products as possible.'

Given the above information concerning the marital status of the respondents in the city of Fez, one may deduce that marriage is a variable associated with positive and negative impacts on self-employment of women. The findings are partly confirmed by the conclusion reached by Wellington, who reveals that women with family responsibilities are more likely to seek employment in the self-employment form.[3] In this regard, married women showed much preference to informal activities as a solution to balance productive and reproductive tasks. Thus far, the data analysis shows that the respondents to the survey who are categorized as single mothers, divorcees and widows would seek chances to make money more than others, especially those living with a husband in the same household. This means that there is more impetus for securing an income than there is for women who share the responsibility of supporting their families with their partners.

In what concerns the places of origins, Table 4 provides the place of birth of the operators. Statistics show that 57% of the participants originate

3 Alison J. Wellington. 'Self-Employment: the New Solution for Balancing Family and Career?' *Labour Economics*, Vol. 13, 2006.

from the city of Fez, as it represents the largest rate in the survey. In contrast, 43% of respondents originate from other places in Morocco such as the region of Fez Boulman. They come, especially, from some rural areas. In this regard, one may notice the role of the informal sector in the process of absorbing migration flows. Migrants's reasons are linked to marriage, education, family reunification, and employment, to name but a few. From the figure below, almost one-third of the respondents originate from other urban cities such as Beni Mellal, Zerhoun, Meknes, El Jedida, among others.

Table 4. Women's Places of Birth

	Percentage
Fez	57%
Region of fez Boulmane	13.67%
Outside Fez	29.33%

Despite the fact that the area of research is the city of Fez, it can be noticed from the statistics that 43% do not originate from Fez. As it has been discussed in the literature, urbanization in Morocco is higher and it remains one of the key factors behind the increase of the informal economy and also where this kind of economy is localized. However, what is clear from the Table 4 is that there are significant differences in the origins of the respondents within the research area. For instance, this figure is linked with the urbanization figures being especially pronounced for those coming from the region of Fez, particularly rural areas surrounding the city.

Another critical factor in increasing the numbers of the female migrant workforce in the informal sector, in Fez in particular and in Morocco in general, is the cocktail of privatization, restriction of the public sector, and the opening up of the Moroccan economy to foreign goods. All led to a dramatic shrinking of formal job opportunities in the Moroccan context. This resulted in its turn in a substantial increase in the numbers of those who opted for the informal sector as an alternative of employment creation outside their places of origins within the city of Fez as well as other regions of Morocco.

The findings of the present empirical research cannot be complete without a discussion of the educational level of women informal workers. Indeed, the data demonstrate different educational attainment levels among women self-employed in this region of Morocco. Most respondents have low education. It is inferior and inappropriate for the demands of the formal sector employment. According to the data of the quantitative research, Table 5 indicates that 27.7% of respondents did not trespass the primary educational level; over 25% of the respondents are completely illiterate; 11.3% who benefit from illiteracy courses. Moreover, almost a similar percentage is allocated to women who reached the secondary level 14% or high school level 15%. Among the rest of the sample, few women graduated from university 5.7% or other private schools 1%.

Table 5. Women's Educational Level

	Frequency	Percentage
Illiterate	76	25.3%
Illiteracy courses	34	11.3%
None finished primary level	53	17.7%
Finished primary level	30	10%
Secondary level	42	14%
High school level	45	15%
University level	17	5.7%
Others	3	1%
Total	300	100%

Source: Fieldwork Results

The educational level of women in this study is generally miserable. Over half of the respondents did not complete formal schooling. The average education level for those involved in the informal sector is not higher than primary school level or they are illiterate 64.3%. These statistics indicate that the informal sector by so far is the largest employment absorber of illiterate and poorly educated women. This finding correlates with the results of Sedjari who emphasized the important role of the informal sector as a labor absorber of many disadvantaged, marginalized and excluded people. This sector provides them with an opportunity to work and earn money.[4]

Similarly, qualitative data about the educational level of interviewees show that the informal sector represents the only source of employment for disadvantaged women with less educational attainment. A similar argument is pinpointed by Fatima who works as a cookie maker. She said: 'in the absence of schooling and diplomas, the only outlet for me and for many others is to prepare cookies at home and sell them.' Generally, most of them demonstrate their willingness to remain in their jobs despite of the availability of opportunities to develop their skills or to change their jobs. Khadija, a 30-years-old married woman, complained that quite often, being a female child, education and skills development are not considered an important thing for the family and a priority for their daughters. Little girls have to assist in the home with household chores, to get married at an early age or to be sent into other houses to work as little maids to contribute to the income of the family.

However, other informants consider their low level of educational attainment as a negative point. It influences their performance of work, management and development of their units of production. In other words, women who do not have an adequate educational attainment cannot find opportunities to get access to credible benefit from mechanisms to integrate the formal marketplace. Thus, education plays a crucial role in the participation of women in the labor market, both in its informal and formal forms.

Almost all the non-literate women workers in the sample in Fez have either never been to school or have not benefited from illiteracy classes. Moreover, there are some women who may be considered as semi-illiterate because they take illiteracy classes. They know some basics in calculations, reading and writing. As a vivid example, Fatiha, a traditional button maker in the city of Fez benefits from the classes of literacy provided by an association in her neighborhood, claimed that these courses enable her to learn how to read and write. She further mentioned that she faced some obstacles in the very beginning because she has to do domestic work as well as

4 Sedjari, Ali D. 'Quelle Intégration du Secteur Informel Urbain au Maroc.' *Le Devenir de la Ville*. Paris: L'Harmattan, 1999: 231.

her economic activity. However, this did not stop her to make efforts to discover her hidden talents and develop her skills. Consequently, she successfully passed her primary sixth grade. Learning how to read and write was regarded as an effort to lift her self-esteem and her image within her community. This means that some self-employed workers demonstrate that they want to free themselves from a situation of dependency caused by the power of culture and the patriarchal system.

Nevertheless, both non-literate and semi literate women consider their level of education as a factor behind their involvement in the informal activities. For example, Karima who had never been to school commented on her personal situation by saying: 'my parents did not value education, and they did not send me to school. I had to look for a job in the informal sector to survive because I am not qualified to other forms of employment since I do not have any formal schooling.' Similarly, another seamstress of traditional clothes decided to study again regardless of her old age and family responsibilities. She took illiteracy courses to change her situation and to know how to deal with her clients when selling her products. She sews traditional dresses and she is not aiming to stop for a variety of reasons, among which is her lack of educational attainment. She described her situation as follows:

> I have practiced sewing for many years because I lack the basic education to be in the formal market. I wanted to be in school, but my parents were poor and could not afford the expenses of schooling. I had no job to support myself, but I had the skill of sewing. When I got married, I had to look for a source of employment and help my husband. I decided then to look for a source of income by working with other tailors and sew some traditional dresses. At the same time, I came back to studies and joined the illiteracy courses.

From these statements, one may suggest that women's access to education would help in the development of their income and productivity in the labor market. This idea may be confirmed by the explanation provided by Khadija who successfully started up her own business and became her own boss. She pinpointed that: 'in the past, my parents did not value the educational attainment of girls, but now since I have a source of income, and I can go for literacy courses.'

Moreover, the presence of women workers with secondary or high school education level in the self-employed activities in the city of Fez reveals an important fact. The number of years spent in attaining higher education does not automatically secure a job opportunity in the public or private sectors of the economy. In this respect, Salma said: 'after graduation I did not find a job and I found myself unemployed, so I decided to join the informal sector for an employment opportunity till I secure an adequate job in the public sector.' This means, therefore, that they seek income generation in the informal sector, which in turn enables them to earn a decent living. It is clear that there is a close link between low educational attainment and employment in the informal sector.

However, women who finished their schooling and obtained diplomas are those who are vulnerable because they do not find work opportunities in the formal labor market. Fatima, a young and single lady pinpointed an observation shared by almost all highly educated respondents in the survey: 'it is difficult if not impossible in the Moroccan society to find young and educated females' decent jobs corresponding to their levels of educational attainment or meeting their professional trainings.' It follows from the above statement that this category of women feels both economically and socially excluded because they do not find work opportunities that fit with their real career aspirations. Therefore, they seek salvation in the informal sector.

As shown in Table 5, women with university level of education are less concerned with the informal work in comparison with the female illiterate category. The former represents 5.7% while the latter rises up to 25.3%. Two opposite explanations can be given to this trend. Firstly, members of the first group seek informal employment to fight against unemployment.[5] At the same time, their work in self-employed activities is in parallel with their search for other job opportunities in their field of study and in the

5 Unemployment is conceived as a major problem that looms large for educated members as well as disadvantaged groups in the major cities of Morocco and Fez is no exception. As a consequence, it intensifies the pressure on them to obtain a livelihood outside the economic mainstream. Thus, under this condition, the informal sector becomes a refuge for those who desperately are looking for relief from unemployment.

formal sector.[6] In addition, many young graduates want to invest their human capital acquired by the educational system and the improvement of their productivity in the labor market. However, it is worth emphasizing that the slower the economic growth and the working conditions in the formal sector are, the higher the pressure they put on diploma holders who tend to accept low paid jobs and informal careers occupied by their non-educated counterparts.[7]

Secondly, as what concerns members belonging to the second group, they seek employment in the informal sector because of their lack of educational attainment and formal skills required for entry to the formal job opportunities. In other words, working in another sector of the economy apart from the informal one requires relatively high-quality job qualifications, which these proportions of workers really lack. Therefore, the informal sector represents their sole source of work and income. The overall data of this study reveal that the share of self-employment becomes increasingly important as an alternative of job creation since both the public and the private sectors suffer from limited absorptive capacities.

Generally speaking, in urban informal employment settings, results show that most of the self-employed operators have very low levels of education or no education at all. There appears to be a relationship between the levels of education and work in the self-employment. Indeed, findings reveal the availability of an association between less-educated respondents and occupation in which higher percentage of jobs are in the informal sector. Therefore, occupations in the informal sector jobs are more likely to be held by persons with less educational attainment. These findings are enhanced by the results found by Gallaway and Bernasek. They concluded

6 According to the statistics provided by la Direction de la Statistique, the rate of the unemployed females in Morocco for the year 2012, which equals 29.1% of the total population (2013: 96). Consequently, one may deduce that the high rates of unemployed educated people may be attributed to a large extent to the weaknesses of the Moroccan educational system and its inability to meet the requirements and needs of the job market, which can be considered as good predictors for choosing a career in the informal sector.

7 See Strangleman and Warren for more details on the impacts of unemployment on the unemployed person, the family and the community (2008: 254–258).

that people with the highest levels of education are more likely to be found in the formal sector, whereas those with the lowest levels have the highest probabilities of working in the informal sector.[8]

In what concerns the presence of children, quantitative data retrieved from the sample demonstrate that 53.7% respondents have children. However, nearly a third of the sample does not have children 24.7%. The presence of children, especially as babies or at a young age in the household appears to have a significant negative impact on women's overall work participation. One would think that this is perhaps related to the absence of someone to help women with children.[9] Consequently, the presence of children in the household contributes to the employment disparities among women more than men since it lowers their commitment to employment.[10] Moreover, one may suggest that women who have more children might have less time for work and earnings than do those who have fewer children. A possible explanation for this can be related to the fact that they have to spend more time taking care of their children than do those who have fewer.

Table 6. Presence of Children[11]

	Frequency	Percentage
No	74	24.7%
Yes	161	53.7%
Total	235	78.3%

Source: Fieldwork Results

As concerned the day-care centers, self-employed workers rarely benefit from their services. In other words, the informally employed woman faces

8 Julia Gallaway and Alexendra Bernasek. 'Gender and Informal Sector Employment in Indonesia.' *Journal of Economic Issues*, Vol. 36, No. 2 (2002).
9 Further details will be provided in Chapter 5.
10 More details will be presented in Chapter 6.
11 As the issue of presence of children concerns women who are married, divorced, widowed, abandoned wives, and single mothers, these statistics exclude 65 females who are single 21.6%.

obstacles in getting access to these facilities due to the high costs. The nature, the place, and the timing of women's working periods in the informal sector vary. So, the utilization of child care facilities becomes difficult and impracticable for most informal workers. Thus, a self-employed worker is assumed to take advantage of combining the domestic and the economic tasks. Along the same line of argument, Meagher claimed: 'informal employment is seen as an ideal solution to the 'double burden' of economic and domestic responsibilities, providing women with more flexible forms of employment that can be adapted to household and childcare demands.'[12] Therefore, women who have more children may not perform their productive work very well and with the same level as those who have less children because they have to focus more on their children's rearing.

Similarly, poverty increases with additional household members. The more members are available in a family the more needs are required as well as resources are needed. Data reveal that larger households are in need of more resources than small households. This is primarily due to the fact that additional household members may be either children or elderly people (parents or grandparents).

In sum, the presence of children can be seen as a strong negative effect on women's self-employment. Perhaps this is because childcare reduces women's time to work. In other words, despite being a means of survival, the self-employed activities chosen by women can only be exerted when those women are free of family obligations, viz., childcare.[13]

Statistical data indicate that most respondents are trained outside the formal system. This happens either at professional associations or via traditional ways with the help of a teacher[14] who is mostly available in the

12 Kate, Meagher. 'The empowerment Trap: Gender, Poverty and the Informal Economy in Sub-Saharan Africa.' In Chant, Sylvia. *The international handbook for gender and poverty*. Cheltenham: Edward Elgar Publishing, 2010: 473.

13 A range of tasks defined as childcare can be, and are, socially and culturally delegated to women. Such delegated tasks include feeding, washing, dressing, as well as playing with children, see more details in Strangleman and Warren, op. cit., 238–239.

14 In the Moroccan culture and Arabic variety, this instructor is called '*Mâalma*'. Througout the process of the book, the word *mâalma* refers to a woman who is known by her mastery of craftsman skills. She manages workshops, instructs and

craft's sector.[15] These women transmit their expertise from one generation to another. Only 23% of female self-employed have benefited from trainings in a professional institution. However, 77% of the workers do not benefit from a professional or a vocational training.

Table 7. Women with Vocational Training

	Frequency	Percentage
No	231	77%
Yes	69	23%
Total	300	100%

Source: Fieldwork Results

Self-employment focuses on the use of the human resources. They represent the skeleton and the main pillar for its development in the Moroccan context. In this respect, many individuals have the flexibility of being both workers and apprentices who benefit from the transfer of skills from one generation to another, especially in the craftsmen sector. Consequently, every self-employed worker who becomes a skilled person should, after a certain period of service, hand on its knowhow to the next younger generation, which is either marveled by the job or forced by unemployment. In this regard, data reveal that my respondents have acquired their occupational knowledge through traditional apprenticeship and self-training. Along the same line of argument, Rassam refers to learning through the traditional apprenticeship as the following:

> The choice is one of learning a *san'a*, a trade or craft which allows one to generate some income without loss of status or respect. These crafts consist of embroidery, sewing

trains apprentices in a particular production activity. She mostly occupies an important place in the craft industries in different regions of Morocco. Her position as the traditional instructor who transmits her knowledge and skills of a particular activity to other young people remains one of the characteristics of the Moroccan heritage.

15 The term craft refers to all craft activities performed by craftswomen as well as to all other different activities and services known in the Moroccan traditional milieu. For example, some crafts that exist in the city of Fez include belt makers, bags makers, *hanbal* weavers, caftan makers, crochet items makers, among others.

> and carpet weaving, all of which are considered 'respectable skills' as they permit the women to work at home and under the supervision of the family.[16]

The majority of women in the survey acquired different skills necessary to exercise their jobs through the traditional apprenticeship. This method is mainly found in the craft's sector. For example, the apprentice watches the actions and conducts of the master crafts woman (*Mâalma*), assimilates them into her behavior, and then the apprentices start to learn the technical tasks and perform their own production. The meetings I had during the fieldwork with *mâalmat* and interviews with heads of professional associations confirmed that the traditional apprenticeships are crucial to enable women gain work skills and transmit work knowledge from one generation to another.

The second prevailing and available method for workers in trades, especially in commerce is self-training. This means that learning by doing, (i.e. by repetition or imitation) is the pertinent way to acquire skills in the Moroccan informal sector. For instance, the development of those trainees in commerce is not only limited to get the technical skills,[17] but it is also to develop the workers' skills and abilities to deal with potential clients. That is to say, training shows different initiatives to indulge in different effective forms to acquire skills and to make it possible to prepare young girls and women for a better performance of activities. In sum, the analysis of the present ways to acquire skills and to be trained in the self-employed activities demonstrates that these methods present crucial mediums to develop women's skills.

However, the share of respondents who have access to vocational training is quite recognizable in the research area. It relates mainly to those who benefited from the trainings in sewing and embroidery.[18] Their main purpose is to improve their skills as reported by most workers as well as to improve their productions. This means that access to training may be

16 Amal, Rassam. 'The Silent Workers: Women and Craft Production in Morocco.' Patricia L. Fiske, W. R. Pickering and Ralph S. Yohe, eds. *From the Far West: Carpets and Textiles of Morocco*. Washington, DC: The Textile Museum, 1980: 66.

17 This refers to the way an individual may acquire how to reproduce and improve a particular object.

18 See Table 8.

effective at raising women's chances of work because women may be trained for the suitable kinds of jobs. Therefore, it can help secure better incomes. In the same line of argument, Kantor argues:

> training can also improve pay levels and access to more and regular work as higher skills can help workers be more competitive in the labor market. Workers perceived a clear payoff to skill training as many connected better skills to more work, more regular work and better pay. The challenge is in ensuring the quality and demand responsiveness of the training offered and its accessibility to all.[19]

This quotation suggests that the irregular economy functions as a school for most female workers. Presumably, employment in the informal sector promotes self-employment among female workers by providing them with opportunities for skills acquisition and importing knowledge about how it takes to develop their economic activities. This view is consolidated by the findings of the research. In this respect, data reveal that trainings in sewing and knitting as well as embroidery represent the same highest rates 6.7% among respondents in the research area. Moreover, sewing and cutting off clothes 4.3% and hairdressing 4% stand in the second and third position respectively. They are followed by decorating which is represented by 1% and secretariat skills represented by 3.3%.

Table 8. Types of Vocational Training[20]

	Percentage
Sewing and knitting	6.70%
Hairdressing	1%
Sewing and cut off clothes	0.30%
Embroidery	6.70%
Secretary	0.30%
Decoration	1%

19 Paula Kantor. 'A Gendered Analysis of Decent Work Deficits in India's Urban Informal Economy: Case Study Perspectives from Surat.' in Chant, Sylvia. *The International Handbook for Gender and Poverty*. Cheltenham: Edward Elgar Publishing, 2010: 483.

20 These data are concerned with women who have done training in public institutions and/or professional associations.

Many women in the field survey have never had access to schooling because of their low socio-economic factors. Some of them lost the few educational achievements they gained at school either because they were obliged to drop out of school or because they started working at a very early age. Many of them simply found a source of employment in a family or neighborhood activity and have no opportunity to develop their skills to be in another field of work. Because of these factors, many respondents in the city of Fez had the chance to have vocational training in order to strengthen their capacity and maintain their knowledge; and therefore, they are allowed to perform an occupation in the informal sector. Hence, this enables them to avoid the social discrimination and have access to an integrating place in the social and economic tissue.

In general, the Moroccan informal economy is characterized by the low training system that distinguishes the nature of workers. Indeed, trainings represent mechanisms by which the labor market is developed, workers are trained and skills are obtained. In the context of self-employed women workers in the informal sector, vocational trainings represent a key source to obtain technical knowledge. It prepares them to enroll in specific careers at various levels of craft, trade, services or a higher professional position such as the secretariat. From Table 8, one may notice that most vocational trainings are based on manual as well as practical actions that are related to traditional specific activities mainly crafts and services. In this respect, through these trainings, self-employed women are able to learn and practice the skills they need to enter their specific field of production.

Concerning the type and the nature of residence, the findings of the quantitative data show that 50.7% live independently and they own the locations where they reside. However, Table 9 shows that about 49.3% of the places of residence are owned by other family members and where women in the research area share the residence. These statistics have two major explanations. Women in the first choice living independently are living in nuclear[21] families consisting mostly of a couple and their children,

21 It typically refers to a married couple and their children whose number differs from one family to another. For example, a nuclear family may include the parents and two children.

or sometimes a mother with her children in cases where she is a widow, a divorcee, or an abandoned wife. In contrast, the extended[22] family is likely to be the core component of the second choice of the type of residence found in this research area. In this regard, most women living with others represent cases of a family that extends beyond the nuclear one. Most of the times, it encompasses grandparents, parents, aunts, uncles and others all living in the same household and sharing the same residence place.

Table 9. Type of Residence

	Frequency	Percentage
Independent	148	49.3%
Living with others	152	50.7%
Total	300	100%

Source: Fieldwork Results

The majority of respondents revealed that they live in middle to poor areas. They claimed that they suffer from various barriers. Such as substandard housing, overcrowded households and adverse environmental conditions. Moreover, owning a house is a farfetched dream that a family in the area of research could achieve. Having the shelter owned is by having it mostly through heritage or an ownership via credits and collaboration between spouses in the case of married category. Most of the female respondents said that their houses are either rented or a mortgage and even the conditions of their houses are not good for safe living.[23]

The investigation of the living conditions of women in the city of Fez shows that out of 300 women informal workers, 146 (48.7%) own their houses. This means that their place of residence in which either the respondent or any other family member of the respondent has legal ownership, 101 (33.7%) reside in rented houses and 49 (16.3%) live in houses

22 It is a larger family extending the nuclear one. It may consist of various nuclear families such as the grandparents and their siblings. It also includes grandchildren and other members. For example, an extended family in Morocco may include 10 or more members.

23 See Table 10.

which are mortgage, as well as only four women 1.3% who keep changing their places of residence, especially the ones living in slums. These women, whose place of residence is in slum areas face poor housing conditions, exposure to excessive heat, cold, and diseases, among others.

Table 10. Nature of Residence

	Frequency	Percentage
Ownership	146	48.7%
Rent	101	33.7%
Mortgage	49	16.3%
Others	4	1.3%
Total	300	100%

Source: Fieldwork Results

Generally, the aforementioned socio-demographic characteristics of women revealed the profile of participants working in the informal segments of work in the research area. It allows identifying the level of the existing workforce in the self-employed form. Indeed, the distinction to make between women based on their age should not make an individual believe optimistically. Based on their age levels, the younger age classes remain least represented in the research area. With regard to women workers in the informal sector, there is a presence of those belonging to the adult age classes. Their presence in small-scale activities is high as they require mostly qualifications acquired via '*maalmin*' or through self-training. Moreover, data from the survey showed that younger women may be active participants than older women for many factors. The first category is characterized by the absence of childcare responsibilities, physical strength and husbands' tolerance. The second category is equally free of childcare responsibilities, which allow to fully devote their time to their work.

Data analysis related to women's marital status is also crucial. The respondents in the survey were categorized in different status. Married women or those living in separation with the presence of children represent the highest percentages. They have double responsibilities, which are both productive and reproductive. In this respect, most women with children in the sample claimed the availability of tension between domestic and work responsibilities.

Additionally, findings indicated that the low educational attainment in the area under study is not only a crucial factor of the access of women to the labor market, but also serves as a decisive determinant of initial entry into the informal sector at least in self-employment activities. To put it differently, it could even be argued that as a consequence, low educational attainment is of major importance for a woman to decide to become a self-employed worker. Furthermore, most respondents based their training on the acquisition of professional skills via traditional means and apprenticeship, which in a way or another can influence the production. Consequently, in a competitive context, the product's quality presents a crucial handicap on the development of the production unit of self-employed workers.

In the following section, the understanding of women's situation in the informal sector as it relates to the socio-demographic characteristics discussed above will be further substantiated with a discussion about the main professional characteristics to the extent that empirical evidence makes possible.

Professional Characteristics

The present sub-section complements the previous one by delineating the salient professional features of women's work in the informal sector as self-employed. It is based on an extensive analysis of the data collected using quantitative and qualitative methods. In this section, employment of women is broken out by the nature of activities, types of work, employment status, place of work, the size of the unit of production, age and sources of capital, as well as registration of economic activities. In this perspective, the issues brought to light here – together with those that emerged from the previous section – will form the basis of the discussion of the reasons and motivations in the next section.

The first cluster of results in this section is relative to the nature of activities. As it was discussed in the literature, the informal sector plays a crucial and controversial role in the provision of job opportunities. It also reduces unemployment and underemployment among many portions of society. However, in many cases, the jobs are diversified. Indeed, the informal sector covers a wide range of labor market activities that combine three groups of different nature. Data revealed that women perform activities, which are stable 57%, primary 28% and periodical 15% of the total population.

Table 11. Nature of Activities

	Frequency	Percentage
Stable	171	57%
Primary	84	28%
Periodical	45	15%
Total	300	100%

Source: Fieldwork Results

These findings indicate that self-employed work is not transient or necessarily temporary, but to some extent, provides a sustainable living for many women. None of the respondents in this study are contract workers or have a formal employer. In addition, they do not have any supplementary or secondary employment. In other words, self-employment is their only source of income, except in some cases where women tend to perform multiple self-employed activities to add other sources of income to supplement their families' expenditures.

Findings in the research area indicate that women's ownership of economic activities can be classified into two main categories: individual or collective ownerships. The former refers to the complete belonging of the economic activities to the individuals. This means that the worker is the owner. Based on data of the present research, the individual ownership is more common and covers 69% of the total population in the research area.[24] The latter is concerned with businesses belonging to a group of people. It takes a variety of forms. It comes in the second position 30% of the total population of the present survey in the city of Fez.

24 See Figure 1 as an illustration of individual ownership.

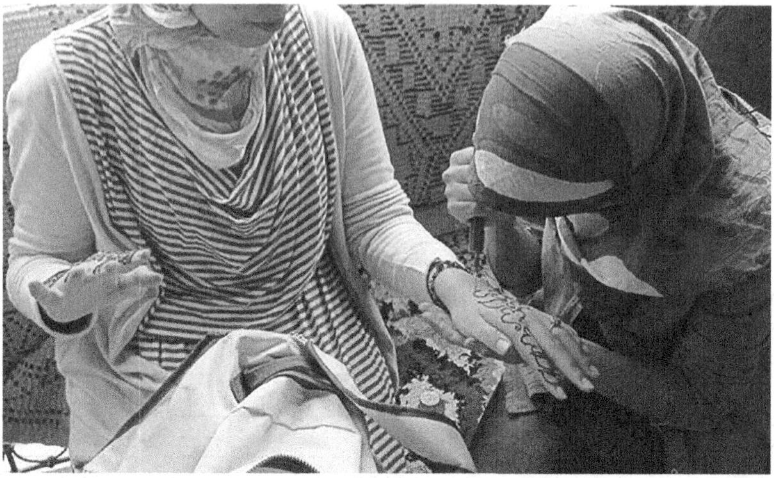

Figure 1. An own-account *Henna* Maker.

The status of workers within the collective ownership includes mainly partnerships 11%, cooperatives 10% as well as family-owned businesses 9%. This type of ownership is not governed by special rules, but rather it is based on kinship and family relationships, except in the cooperatives case. The family businesses are crucial in this study, as the extended family plays a role of great importance in ensuring business continuity and daily family survival. These businesses are mostly managed by the oldest person in the family. Most of the times, he is the father. Moreover, the ownership is allocated among women who are part of the group's members.

Table 12. Nature of Activity Ownership

	Frequency	Percentage
Personal ownership	207	69%
Family ownership	27	9%
Partnership	33	11%
Cooperative	30	10%
Others	3	1%
Total	300	100%

Source: Fieldwork Results

Additionally, women both produce and sell as a group in collective ownerships. For example, 'The Arts of Fez' is a cooperative producing and selling crafts products in the city of Fez. The board of directors is responsible for buying the raw materials. About half of the cooperative members make different artistic products and the board of directors finds distributors to whom they may market their production. Some of the collective workers produce the goods in their homes, but join together with other members to buy the needed raw materials and market the final finished product.

Furthermore, the collective ownership of a business has a double edge effect. First, respondents refer mostly to the absence of the individual's right to deal with the business resources and benefits. Moreover, because women have supporting roles in these types of partnerships, they mostly lack the stability of work and cannot develop their investment efforts. Second, the size of tasks of work allocated to female members is reported to be higher than their male counterparts. Furthermore, their benefits are becoming smaller and smaller as they are assumed to help a family project and since they are ignoring their working identity. The question to be answered in this perspective is what activities women perform in the informal sector in the city of Fez?

As far as the type of activities is concerned, an individualistic perspective would assume that the types of economic activities performed by self-employed women in the informal sector are a result of random individual decisions. It can help show what certain kinds of jobs women choose at certain times, but not why women as a group tend to enter the informal labor instead of the formal one. In this regard, to illustrate the occupation and employment categories used in the analysis, this section presents the leading occupations women perform in the study area. In this perspective, a detailed breakdown of the self-employment activities showed that sewing activities are also dominated as near the embroidery activities. They present 32% of the total self-employment. In this respect, women are more likely to be in the needle activities if self-employed, which indicates being handicraft operators.

Women working as bakers, carpet makers, tattoo makers, and crochet makers are represented by 6.7%, 6%, 5.7%, and 5% respectively. They are followed by hairdressers and cosmetologists, *makerami*[25] and *takerir*[26] makers, shoes as well as *mjadel*[27] makers who represent 4.7%, 4.7%, and 4% of the total population. Moreover, other women whose rate does not exceed 4% gain their incomes working as traditional button makers, ceramic makers, shoes and bag vendors, cook, decorators of tissue, drawers on glass, and finally cosmetic vendors. The final category least presented in the city of Fez with a percentage that does not go beyond 2.3% is representative of the following activities: bath attendants, pastry makers, wool items' makers, as well as clothes vendors.

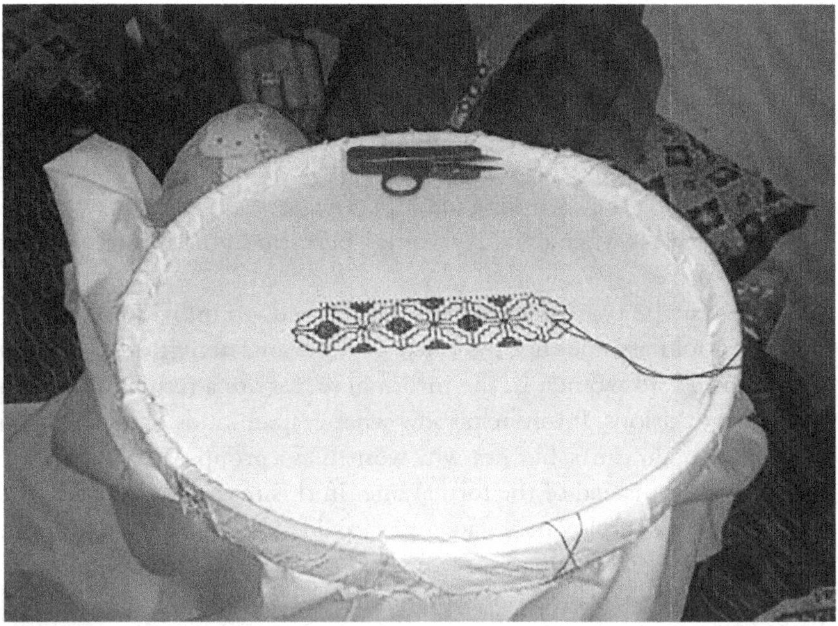

Figure 2. A woman doing *Terz Al Gherza*.

25 A type of handmade fabrication used to decorate pieces of tissue.
26 A type of handmade fabrication used to decorate pieces of tissue.
27 See Figure 5 for an example of a woman making a majdoul (singular of *mjadel*).

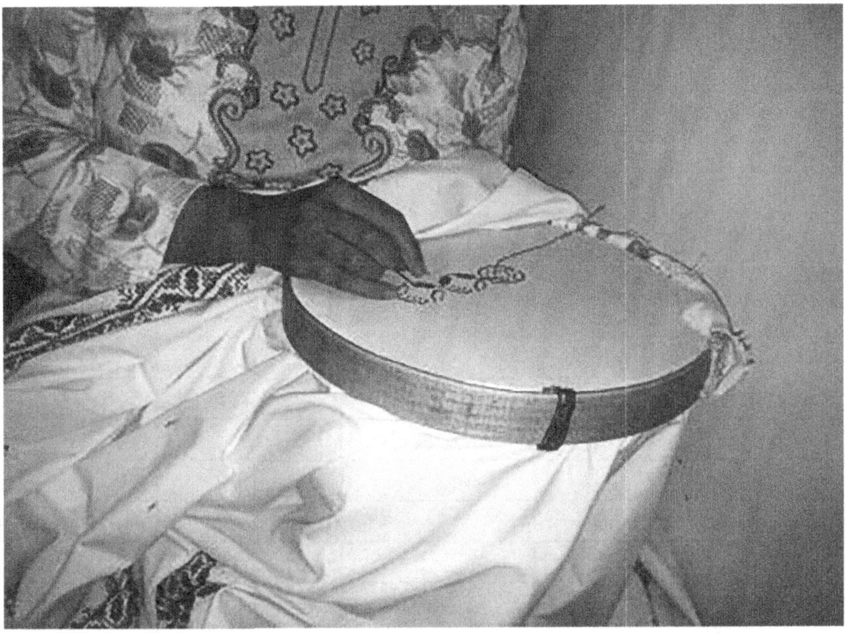

Figure 3. A woman doing *Terz Al-Rebatti*.

The breakdown is also done by broad industry categories in which a largely female workforce is employed.[28] For example, dressmaking industry (seamstresses, traditional dressmakers and those who fabricate items necessary for dressmaking), embroidery industry (embroiderers in all its types), gastronomy (cooks, bakers, pastry makers), personal services (bath attendants, shopkeepers ...), beauty industry (hairdressers and cosmologists). Needless to say that industry categories are by definition and automatically broad enough to include different categories of economic activities where females may work to gain their revenues.[29]

28 See Table 14.
29 See Table 13.

Table 13. Types of Women's Activities

	Frequency	Percentage
Seamstress	47	15.7%
Cook	10	3.3%
Embroiderer	49	16.3%
Hairdresser and cosmetologist	14	4.7%
Baker	20	6.7%
Traditional button maker	11	3.7%
Makerami and *Takerir* maker	14	4.7%
Clothes vendor	4	1.3%
Cosmetic vendor	9	3%
Carpet maker	18	6%
Henna maker (tattoo maker)	17	5.7%
Pastry maker	6	2%
Crochet maker	15	5%
Wool items maker	5	1.7%
Decorator of tissue (*Tenbat /aa'kik)*	10	3.3%
Drawing on glass	10	3.3%
Ceramic maker	11	3.7%
Shoes and bags vendor	11	3.7%
Mejadel maker	12	4%
Bath attendant	7	2.3%
Total	300	100%

Source: Fieldwork Results

The informal sector in its self-employed form is not limited to a one type of economic activity. It encompasses various activities such as those cited in Table 13. The sole commonality among these diverse activities is that, in the informal sector context, they are not officially recognized as well as not legally established and, hence they are not subject to state regulations. This means that these activities are characterized by their invisibility and difficulty to be localized, especially when exercised in unreported places to authorities.

The statistics in the table above show that most of the unorganized activities in the city of Fez are mainly concentrated on commerce and artisanal production. Indeed, although women are highly present in the variety of income-generating activities, high concentration is apparent in those activities which require a large amount of input and very little capital. Other women in the sample participate in the traditional jobs such as cooking and providing services. These are conventionally known as 'women's work.' It is part of their traditional gender-based roles to be performed in the private sphere.

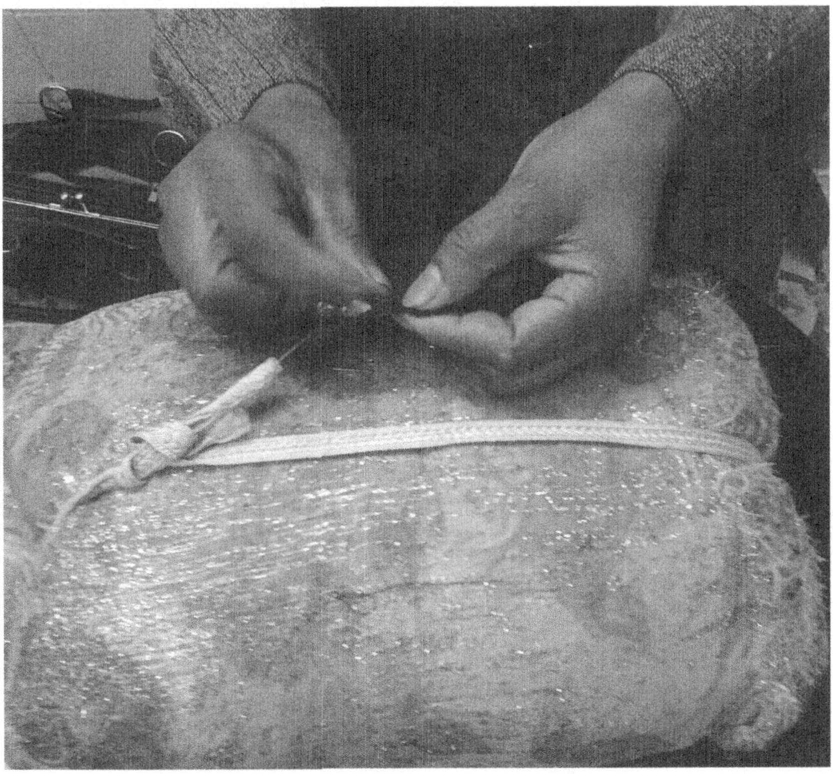

Figure 4. A woman sewing a traditional *Jellaba*.

More importantly, the findings of the qualitative data reveal that the duplication and diversification in activities performed in informal ways are almost common in the economic behavior of women workers in the city of Fez. It is not common to find an individual or family dependent on one resource for income. This might be justified by the fear of uncertainty of income generation. Another feature is related to the insecurity of employment for workers, which is not the amount of income attained, but the certainty of continuity of work and reliability. Thus, the informal activities play a crucial role in providing opportunities of work multiplicity and income generation.

The distribution of activities by informal sectors is characterized by the range of economic units as well as by the bulk of workers operating in various sectors. Indeed, out of the 300 self-employed women in the survey exercising informal activities in the research area, more than 52.3% of them work in the sewing and embroidery activities (craft sector), the service sector as the second absorber of self-employed workforce occupy the second place with 34.3% of the total number of participants. The least represented sector of activity is the textile sector with 7.3% and the informal trade sector is positioned last with only 6% of the total number of informal self-employed.

Table 14. Types of Sectors of Work

	Percentage
Sewing and Embroidery	52.30%
Trade	6%
Services	34.30%
Textile	7.30%

The preponderance of evidence suggests that women's participation in the informal employment is highly heterogeneous in terms of work activities. The relative distribution of these activities shows wide variation in the city of Fez, but by large, crafts (sewing and embroidery) as well as service sectors tend to dominate. They are followed by textile and trade sectors as they are less prevalent in the research area.

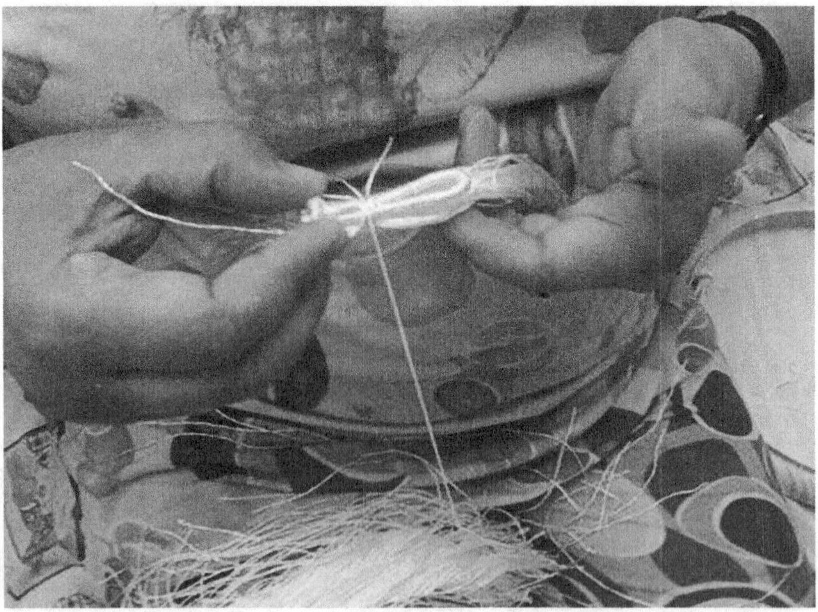

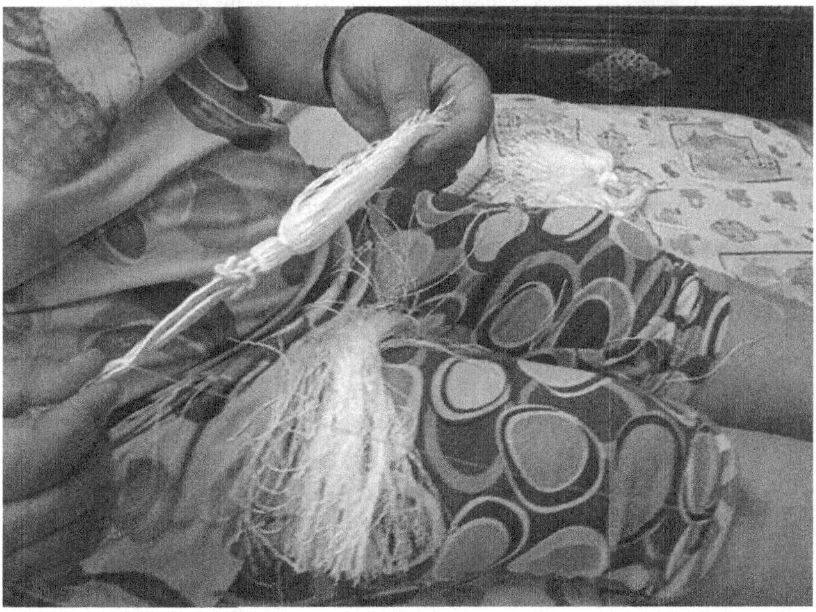

Figure 5. A *mâalma* showing the process of making a *Majdoul*.
Source: Fieldwork pictures.

Informal workers fall into a number of group categories. Among women who are working more or less in full time in crafts are women artisans. The craftsmanship represents a vital sector of work. It accounts for a rapidly increasing female labor force from one generation to another. The common thing shared by women in this sector is their reliance basically on the efforts they produce, their manual skills and their artistic as well as creative capacities. Moreover, the richness of the sector is relative to two main features. Firstly, its principle is that crafts are handed down for ages and from one generation to another.[30] Secondly, the new generations of craft workers benefit from the modern acquired skills and develop the craft products.

Women working in the trade sector are owners of a clothing shop, bags and shoes shops, and cosmetic shop. Their workplace is outside

30 See Figure 6.

their homes. Almost all women in this sector employed co-workers. They also hire workers under informal employment relationships. In most such cases, it is the employer not the informal worker who chooses to work informally and enjoys its benefits. These things also apply to the family members who are hired to manage the business and support their relatives.

Figure 6. A woman showing a young lady the techniques of embroidery.

Employment in the service sector is part of the shadow economy. In almost all the times, the activities of informal service workers are particularly small-scale operations. In this regard, data collected on self-employment in such economically marginal endeavors reveal that there is relatively a large share of the labor force. Accordingly, women in the informal service sector are mostly present in activities offering their knowledge, productivity and performance of their skills.[31] A sector as such succeeded in absorbing many women workers in the city of Fez against various economic structures. It is indeed an immune field and of which productive units and producers are able to create a source of livelihood. They are able to adopt themselves to the different economic changes. Thus, one may assume that the service sector stands as a pivotal sector. It plays an essential role in the local as well as the national economic tissue. Therefore, it is a sector that contributes to the development of the economy as well as the social development of its workers. Moreover, one may assume that self-employment in the informal service sector helped a meaningful number of women in the city of Fez to avoid unemployment. It also allowed them to secure a source of income to help them sustain the financial requirements of their households.

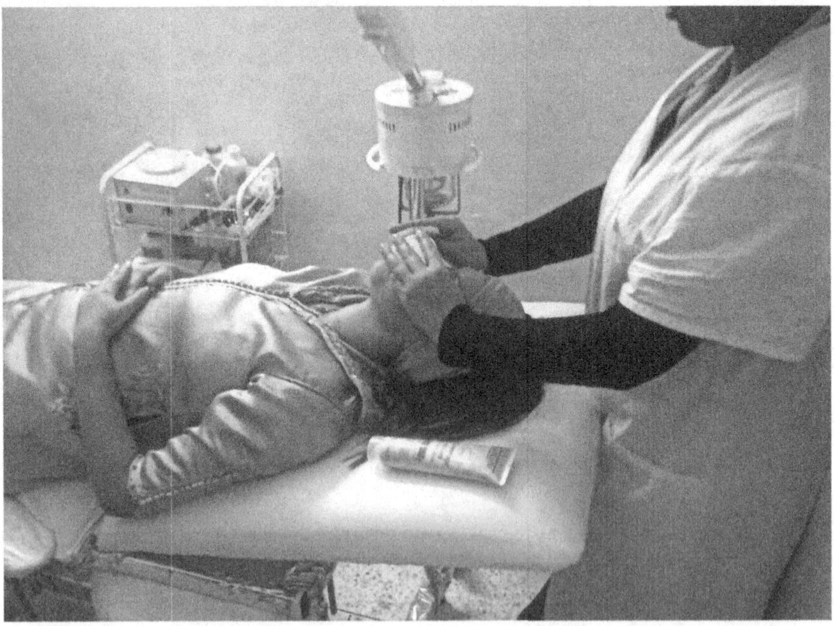

31 See for example, Figure 7.

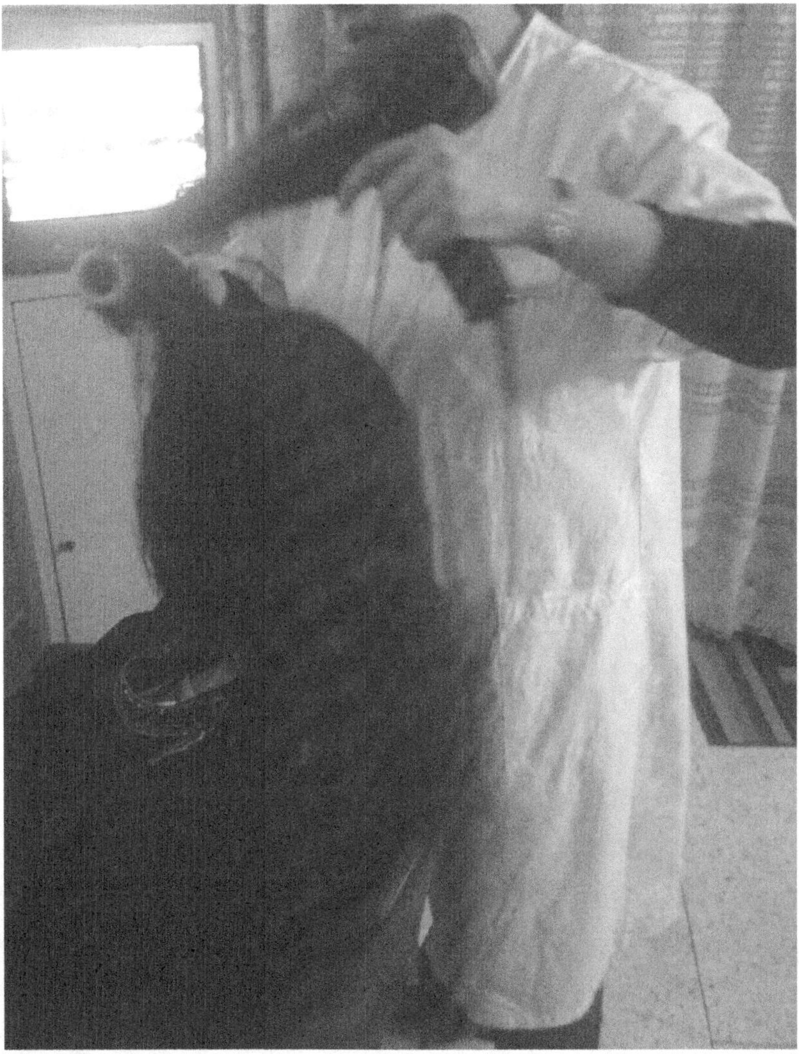

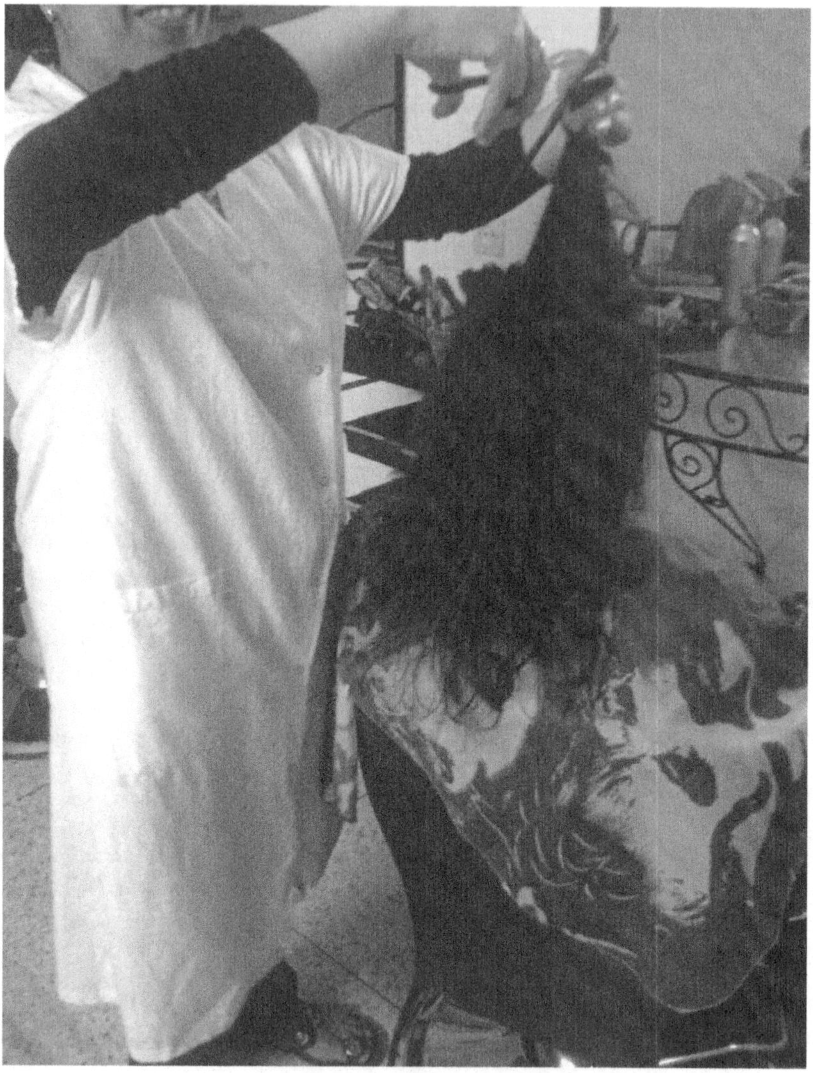

Figure 7. A hairdresser and cosmetologist.

Finally, women in the textile sector include those working as weavers as well as carpet makers.[32] This sector plays a key role in the provision of work opportunities. This is due to its different productive, artistic and service branches. This means that these informal sectors play a vital role for members of disadvantaged groups in the city of Fez. Their capacity to absorb the female workforce is frequently maintained by the scarcity of other alternatives in other sectors. Consequently, job seekers at the low end of the employment queue, especially women must often look for ways of sustenance through working as self-employed in the economy's textile sector in particular and various informal sectors in general.

In sum, the absorption of self-employed workers into activities of the informal sector represents an outstanding feature of the city of Fez. The informal sector's activities contain a plethora of income-generating opportunities as it was discussed in Chapter 1. Indeed, one may venture to say that such absorption helps ameliorate the inconvenient problem of unemployment among the female portion in the Moroccan society and the city of Fez in particular. Self-employment activities, as an effective form of individual and collective entrepreneurship, have a double edge impact. They are both risky and appealing since they are generally perceived as prominent sources of independence and satisfaction for the majority of business owners.[33] Many workers do not only evade the burden of being unemployed by starting up their own economic activities for themselves, but also create more job opportunities for others. They also increase labor demand for their goods and services. Thus, self-employment activities are important for growth, especially when they are associated with the creation of job opportunities.

32 See Figure 8.

33 See Chapter 6.

Figure 8. A carpet maker.

Generally, one may deduce that the revealed sectors of work in the city of Fez are rich and strong sectors with their distinguished contributions. They reflect the originality of Morocco and the genius of its producers. For instance, people in the craftsmanship as well as textile sectors use their fingers and creativity while those in the services and trade sector use their cleverness and skills to produce various products. Accordingly, women in these sectors rely on their skills and expertise to set up their own sources of income generation, with modest or no capital and secure an employment opportunity, which stand as a source of living for them and their families as it will be explained in details in Chapter 4. Acting so, women in the research area consciously or unconsciously contribute to the training of other young informal practitioners. Therefore, they maintain the role of the self-employed activities as crucial channels for various employment status.

Another way of classifying self-employed women in the informal sector, which provides us with a great deal about their working conditions, is by employment status. In the words of Chen and Doane, employment status refers to:

> The relative share of labor and capital inputs of workers. Historically, labor statisticians have classified all economically active persons into five employment statuses, as follows: employers, employees, own account workers, unpaid contributing family workers, and members of cooperatives.[34]

On the basis of this quotation, it is obvious that the informal sector is characterized by diversity in status of employment. Indeed, the examination of the informal units in the city of Fez immediately shows the indisputable predominance of the sole proprietorship. For instance, 64% of women are working for their own account. As regards to the informal units held by informal employers and which involve employees, they constitute 21% of the total population. They are followed by 10% of members of cooperatives while unpaid family members accounted only for 5% as the least proportion.

Table 15. Women's Employment Status

	Frequency	Percentage
Employer of informal enterprise	63	21%
Own-account worker	192	64%
Unpaid family worker	15	5%
Member of a cooperative	30	10%
Total	300	100%

Source: Fieldwork Results

Own account workers, as the sole owners of their businesses;[35] take up informal occupations than other employment status due to the lack of entrance into the formal activities. For instance, the formal occupation is usually associated with control and gender inequalities as compared

34 Martha, Chen and Donna Doane. *Informality in South Asia: A Review*, Working Paper 4. Cambridge: WEIGO (September 2008): 8.

35 See Figure 9.

to other forms of work, factors that high caste vulnerable groups such as women. This is maintained by the results in Table 15, which are perhaps a reflection of women's preference for own-account positions. In fact, such preferences among self-employed workers are often revealed during my field interviews where women in Fez repeatedly expressed aspirations for own-account jobs rather than formal activities. The following are some respondents' explanations:

Houria, who is a carpet weaver, stated:

> I know that I wanted to be in another job since I was a little girl. I had a dream like other girls of my age, but I always was fascinated by the work of my grandmother and mother. I think it is probably because I was reared in an environment where most female family members do not have salaried jobs and they have to contribute to the fabrication of carpets.

Meriam reported similar issues:

> I have never thought of doing any other work except needle work. All my female family members are their own boss and they have always had practiced the craft of embroidery in its different types. We do not know how to do another thing like others do.

Fatima, who is a traditional cloth maker, expressed:

> my father brought me into this job. I like it and I will stay here unless I die ... (Laughs) ... being your own account worker does not allow anyone to shout at you. It gives you security. It is less risky than going outside to work in companies.

Salma has a more enthusiastic vision about her employment status as own-account worker. She said:

> having my own business and being the sole responsible about it gives me the opportunity to have a place in the market, possibility for professional development, and I can implement my own ideas to develop my skills and therefore my activity. Moreover, no one intervenes regarding my own business decisions. I have the freedom to set my own goals as well as manipulate my working time.

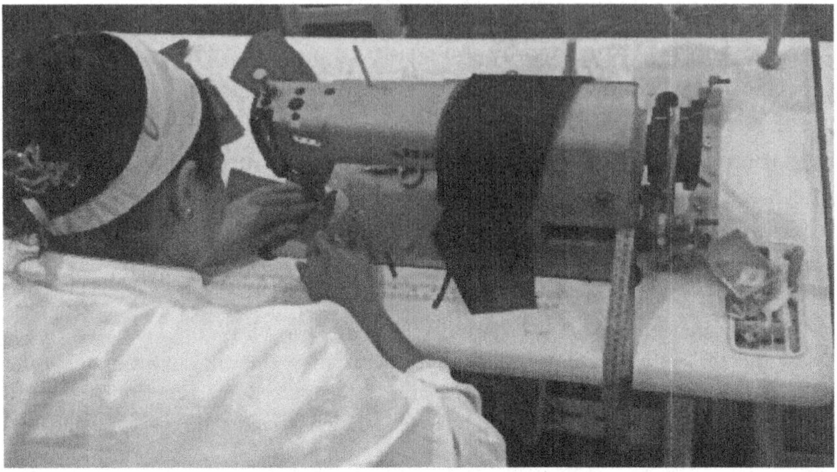

Figure 9. An own-account seamstress.

From respondents' experiences, it is obvious that the employment status of women as own-account workers appears to be relevant in the study area. In addition to the absence of work opportunities in the formal sector, most of them have similarities in their preferences of being their own-account workers because of the freedom they have in determining their employment status decisions. All of them show satisfaction from their work status as it helps them to be financially independent, support themselves and achieve self-esteem in family and society at large.

Other women informal workers in the city of Fez are members of cooperatives 10%. They choose to get involved in cooperatives to improve their productivity and income as a group through their collective organized efforts and group solidarity. They engage in this type of work to promote and protect their personal interests. As cited in Tesfay and Tadele, Majurin summarizes the roles of cooperatives as follows:

> Cooperatives generate considerable socio-economic benefits to their members. From the economic standpoint, cooperatives improve the income and the bargaining power of their members. While the social purposes of cooperation are more diverse than economic purposes. They provide a unique opportunity to members to education and training; encourage active participation in meetings, committee membership and leadership position. (2013: 2)

As a matter of fact, many cooperative members in the city of Fez reveal that their memberships in these organizations allow them to develop their businesses and their self-help capacities. This all happens in an atmosphere of cooperation and solidarity among its individuals. Consequently, this strengthens women's ability to be responsible for reproductive work[36] and be active entrepreneurs recording rapid growth in their economic activities.[37]

Data also suggest that women have preference to be employers of informal enterprises. For instance, most respondents demonstrate their interest in setting up their own enterprise as a source of employment. They do not often consider them a risk as they may be allowed a stable work opportunity regardless of their familial status and condition. Moreover, women may escape experiences of discrimination in the work environment and the probability of work leave due to age increase. For this reason, women may seek out a job in their own enterprise that allows for self-employment. This way, the individual is better able to be an employer.

Another pertinent employment status found in the research area is the unpaid family workers. In fact, their preference to become self-employed may be their willingness to help generate the family income. For example, Kaoutar, a wife of a traditional tailor contributes to the provision of help to her husband without being paid back for her services. She narrated her story as follows:

> The sole factor that affected my work in the informal sector is the business of my husband. Both of us are aware that making traditional clothes might be more lucrative than performing other activities because clients in Morocco consider traditional clothing as necessary as it is part of our culture. So, during certain seasons, my husband spends sleepless nights to prepare the dresses for the native clients or foreign tourists. At this moment, I decided to join a professional association and learn the skills of sewing. After a one year training, I am now able to help my husband in his work though I do not have an official payment.

36 Reproductive work is referred to in this paper as all those activities, which are classified as non-income generating work needed to sustain a family. This type of work includes unpaid activities such as caring for children, preparing food and doing household chores. Productive work, in contrast, is about all activities generating revenue whether performed inside or outside home.

37 Tesfay and Tadele, op. cit.

In all four types, it can be observed that the informal sector makes up a high percentage of self-employed women who occupy diverse status. Indeed, women are often thought to choose to perform their income opportunities either as own-account workers or employers for the freedom of operation and flexibility schedules it offers. For those who choose to work in cooperatives, I might infer to their choice of being in collective work and benefit from the skills of others. However, those who prefer to be unpaid family workers are solely interested in developing the outputs of the family's work and financial outcomes.

Data concerning the place of work show that the informal economic activities in the research area are located in two types of workplaces. According to Chen and Doane they are labeled as conventional or non-conventional workplaces. The former refers to registered shops, office spaces, hospitals. The latter is linked to places such as private homes, open spaces, unregistered shops or workshops.[38] In this regard, the characteristics of self-employed women workers on the basis of their place of work show the predominance of the non-localized informal activities. Indeed, more than half of the respondents practice their economic activities from home 54.3% against 25.3% of workers who have a fixed business local. Furthermore, 13% of self-employed women exercise their productive activities without having a proper local and 7.3% perform their activities in the locals of cooperatives.

Table 16. Place of Work

	Frequency	Percentage
Home	163	54.3%
With local	76	25.3%
Without local	39	13%
Cooperative	22	7.3%
Total	300	100%

Source: Fieldwork Results

38 Chen and Doan, op. cit., 17.

Most of the respondents in this study work and sell their productions from home. This relatively coincides with the argument of Rassam: 'in common with other traditional societies, most goods and services in Morocco were produced and consumed at the level of the household' (1980: 65). In other words, women's houses become their workplace where they perform their informal activities and market their productions. This means that the home serves both as a place of residence and a workplace.

From the data collected, most noticeable are the problems of overcrowded and large households. Many women complain about their small working space. They strongly feel that it is not conducive to run a successful business from home. There is no separate room to use it as a workplace. Therefore, they habitually sit down in one of the rooms, salon or kitchen to perform their economic activities.[39] This makes their work invisible, unknown to others and not accessible to the public. Along the same line of reasoning, in his prominent investigation on the informal activities in Morocco, Sebti pointed out that: 'Les activités exercées à domicile représentent un cas extrême dans la mesure où il n'y a rien à déclarer de la part des ouvriers. Ce sont des indépendants exerçant hors de l'espace de l'entreprise, donc invisible' (2009: 155) [Activities carried out from home represent an extreme case insofar as there is nothing to report on the part of the workers. They are independent working outside the enterprise space, so invisible]. However, the findings of the current investigation demonstrated that there are some advantages about working at home that were highlighted during the interviews.

39 See Figure 10.

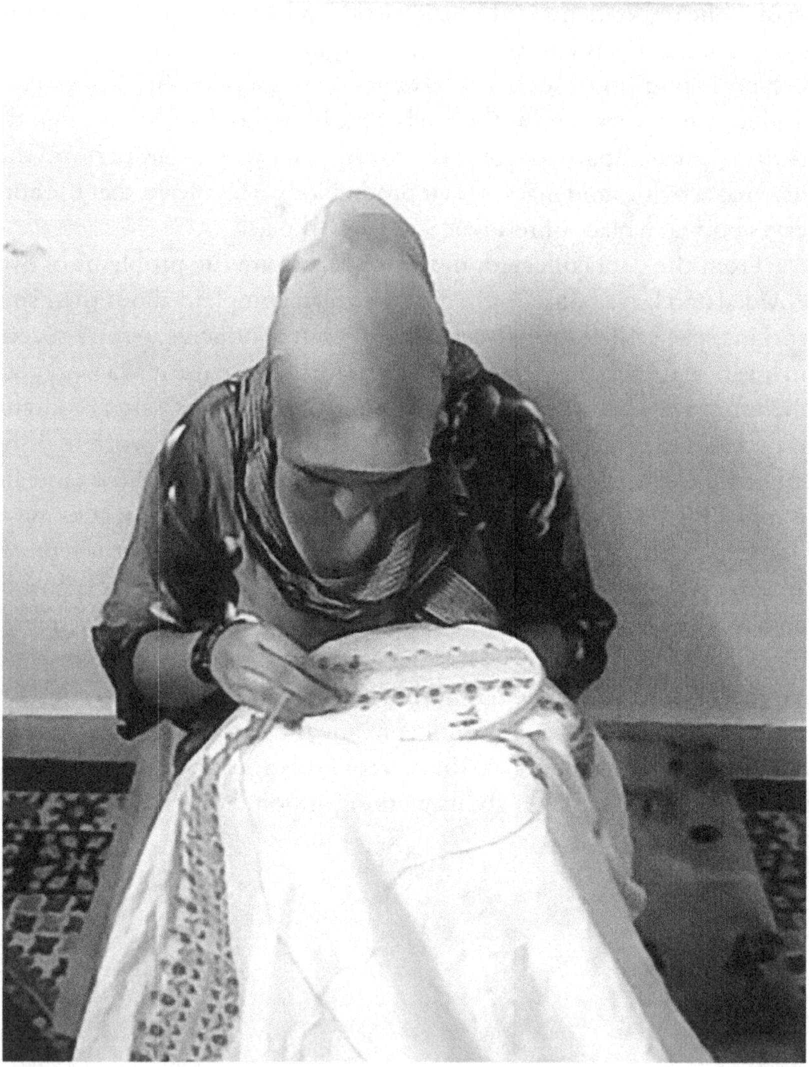

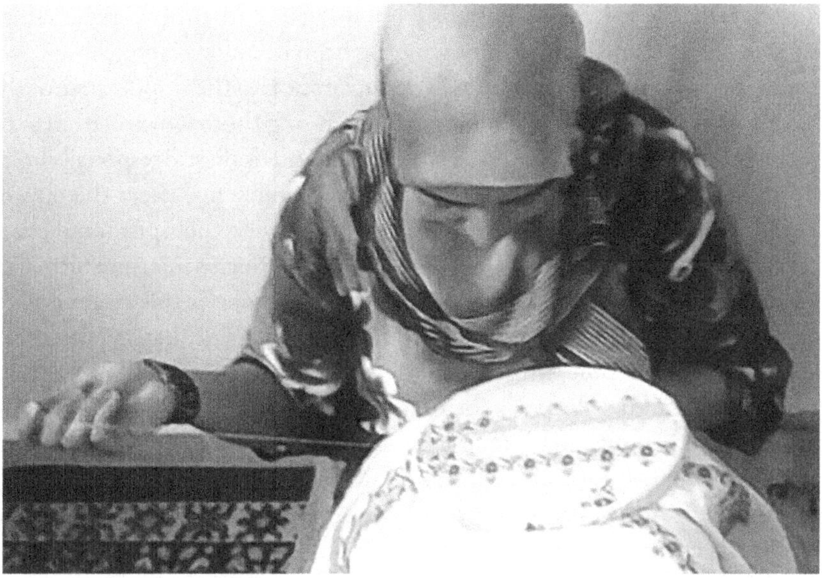

Figure 10. A young lady doing embroidery in a corner of the salon.

Firstly, most of the interviewees claim that their choice to perform their work at the household is due to their possibility to reduce the rental component of costs, which other activities in its formal enterprises counterpart strongly demand. Secondly, many women agreed that home-based work[40] is not only a source of generating income, but also provides them with opportunities to do their domestic work and private sphere responsibilities. For instance, they confirm that their domestic duties are exercised first before their self-employed activities. As a result, the number of hours they spend in their productive activities varies. Data show that there are many women who start their economic activities when their children are out for school and after they finish their housework (cleaning, cooking ...). This is relevant mainly to married women who are in craft work and embroidery.

Thirdly, most respondents referred to flexibility of hours of work. Baxter alluded to the distinction made by Wolcott and Glezer concerning flexibility

40 In this paper, it is used to refer to an arrangement where women do all their paid work at home.

in work hours, which 'may mean different things – part-time work, job sharing, varying start and finish hours, working from home, averaging hours over weeks, months or a year' (200: 17). The declaration of the importance of the flexible working time is particularly strong among those workers in marital situations or those with heavy family demands and domestic responsibilities. Most respondents claim that flexible working hours give them the opportunity to some extent to have reconciliation between their productive and reproductive work.[41] This is enhanced by the belief that women are primarily responsible for the domestic chores and the ones who are associated with the private sphere responsibilities. To justify this point, Latifa, a married and 34-year-old respondent stressed the idea that the informal employment is flexible and allows the workers to do both responsibilities. She said: 'I do my household chores such as cleaning the house and preparing food for my family in the morning and sewing and knitting in the afternoon.'

Women in the city of Fez tend not only to work shorter hours and receive lower incomes but they are also more likely, because of the nature of their economic activities, to work early mornings, late evenings as well as weekends. Consequently, following these kinds of patterns, they further stress the gender division of labor at home. Similarly, Rassam provided others to justify why women prefer to set up their business at home: 'the women say that they can set their own place at home, attend the needs of family members, receive visits from relatives and friends and feel relaxed away from the supervision and anonymity of the factory' (1980: 66). However, this situation mostly might become a crucial constraint. For instance, I can deduce that it hinders their productivity, isolates them from other workers in the same or other domains, and undermine their knowledge and access to the market. Moreover, it may weaken their bargaining power and limit their chances to expand the clientele network. Therefore, the impediments faced by some workers are often quite similar in the research area – notably, but not exclusively, seamstresses, embroiderers, bakers, pastry makers, button makers, and others.

25.3% of respondents choose to practice their economic activities outside home. They choose to have their own workplace, either on a rent or an

41 See Chapter 5 for more details.

ownership basis.[42] However, many respondents in this category reveal that the conditions under which they operate their activities are precarious and unstable. They are threatened by the inability to afford a regular income to pay the rent and the basic services of the shops. In addition, their shops are located in poor areas, which are in most cases unsafe working environment. Therefore, for many informal sector operators, their home and workplace represent another predictor of their vulnerability. This is justified by the conditions under which they operate their informal economic activities.

Figure 11. A seamstress working in a rented workplace.

42 See Figure 11.

Most of the respondents claim that their activities are performed in areas which lack the necessary facilities. This can be explained by the concentration of most economic production units in the old Medina and the most precarious open places. Self-employed women face difficulties in finding a permanent and stable place of work where they are able to exercise their activities. Nearly most of the respondents in the research area practice their activities in the open air and they do not have locals 13%.[43]

Figure 12. An old woman selling clothes in an open air area in Fez.

Additionally, data demonstrate that 7.3% of the total population sampled in the city of Fez performs their activities in cooperatives. Indeed, women working in

43 See Figure 12.

cooperative enterprise exercise their activities on the same place in a harmonious environment. The main characteristic of these workers is that the majority of them share the responsibility of the local expenses and needs, as well as concerning the majority of benefits' shares are owned by the workforce.[44]

In sum, data reveal that women's places of work in the informal sector are diverse. The most prevalent type is of those indoor working women. They are more numerous in comparison to those practicing their activities outside their houses. This category of workers is more or less visible. While participation of women in the shadow economy can be characterized by their place of work, the size of the economic activity is undoubtedly a recognizable feature of informal ventures.

The examination of Table 17 gives the distribution of units of production by size.[45] It shows the predominance of economic activities headed by one person as they represent 61.3% of the entire sample in the research area. Those employing two people come second with a rate of 13.3%, followed by those units encompassing three workers with a rate of 6.3%. The larger units, including a higher number of employees, are poorly represented 5% and nearly 4.7% for seven co-workers.

Table 17. Size of the Unit of Production

	Frequency	Percentage
0 Co-worker	184	61.3%
1 Co-worker	12	4%
2 Co-workers	40	13.3%
3 Co-workers	19	6.3%
4 Co-workers	11	3.7%
5 Co-workers	2	0.7%
6 Co-workers	3	1%
7 Co-workers	14	4.7%
10 Co-workers	15	5%
Total	300	100%

Source: Fieldwork Result

44 More details are provided in Chapter 5, sub-section on cooperative involvement.
45 It is based on the employment of co-workers.

From these statistics, it is noticeable that many economic activities are structured and organized without recourse to other employees. The presence of co-workers is low in informal employment in the research area. On average, operators employ no more than 1.5% co-worker as a mean of the total population. Most of those employed by the informal operators are members of the family operating in the enterprise. Other respondents declare that they employ workers from outside the immediate family. This is mostly among tailors and embroiderers. Consequently, the respondents in the research area maintained the general norm of the size of the enterprise in the informal sector as described by Abzahd and Labchir: 'L'emploi informel regroupe les employeurs informels et leurs associés, ainsi que les salariés travaillant dans les petits établissements employant moins de dix salariés' (1998: 358) [Informal employment includes informal employers and their associates. It also includes employers working in small enterprises employing less than 10 employees].

In this respect, one may notice that many informal units of production and operators start out as individuals or family scale operators. And while it is true that some of them are successful entrepreneurs, they tend to enlarge their businesses. However, even when they might otherwise profit from enterprise size, it does not seem to be an appropriate means of determining formality. In other words, one may assume that this type of informal work is harder to formalize than the own account informal employment since the process should start first by formalizing the firm, registering it and having it pay taxes, and then formalize its workers by registering them.

The informal self-employed female workers are also distinguished by the age and sources to start up their own businesses. Indeed, the fieldwork conducted in the city of Fez has revealed that self-employment activities are largely undertaken by women plagued by socio-economic and personal factors, which pushed them to perform informal activities for years. Table 18 below shows that 54% of women in the informal sector have entered relatively these activities in different periods of their lives. Those who started working before the age of 20 years old represent 41.7%

of the total population of the sample while those who work since their early ages represent 4.3% of the whole sample examined.

Table 18. Age of Start-up Business

	Frequency	Percentage
Before the age of 15	13	4.3%
Before the age of 20	125	41.7%
Other	162	54%
Total	300	100%

Source: Fieldwork Results

The justifications provided by respondents regarding their work history are diverse. For example, among the married respondents, almost all of them reported that they started working after they got married. Most of them are initially engaged in self-employment to supplement their husbands financially. For example, Samira pointed out that: 'my husband is a jobless person and I have to work so as my family members could survive.' Similarly, Khadija stressed the fact that her work in the informal sector stems from her willingness to support her husband financially speaking. She said: 'the income of my husband is not sufficient and I have to work to help him.' Moreover, the work history of most married respondents, especially the family workers reveal that the majority did not work before marriage except for two women who are members of the same cooperative where their husbands are working as piece rate carpet weavers. Thus, upon marriage, these women had no alternative but to engage in an informal economic activity. As for the other categories of women, there are no significant differences between the type of activity they used to do before and after marriage.

Single women reveal that their work is not essentially designed for the survival of the household. They rather take up different craft and service oriented activities to earn pocket money. After moving to the husband's house; however, their work turns to be a source of the household survival. As for many women without a partner, such as divorced, widowed, single mothers and abandoned wives, they are expected to actively start their businesses since they are mainly obliged to rely on their own sources of finance for the survival of their families. In the same line of argument, Safae, an embroiderer pointed out that: 'I do not have another source of income. Broidery is one of my hobbies since childhood. It is the only thing I know to do. My needlework is my only source of living and my family's survival means.'

Findings also show that there are some respondents who began their activities before the age of 20. They work in self-employment activities either because of personal reasons or because of their occupations, which are traditionally handed over from one generation to another. These situations are clearly indicative of women's pressures to find a means of livelihood. In addition, it reflects the high possibilities of entry and exit across employment status within the informal sector. For example, Siham explained that she learned the skills of *Terz Al-Fassi* (a type of embroidery known in the city of Fez) since she was in secondary school. Her mother is an embroiderer (*terraza*) who taught her the techniques of embroidery. Siham used to study during the school year and work during summer holidays. When she became skillful, she started to help her mother and do some embroider tissue for her. Later on, Siham said that she left school and decided to work as an embroiderer of *Terz Al-Fassi*.

As for the third category of workers who started their work at an early age, their reasons are linked to their family's cultural beliefs. Indeed, many respondents claim that their families obliged them to drop out of school to enter the labor market. Parents are not interested in investing in their daughters' education. They taught them the skills of the job to perform it at an early age. However, for these women who are now *mâalmat* (i.e. who teach other young females the skills of a particular craft), their entry into the low skilled occupations was a significant stage in their lives, which was physically demanding and from which they did not gain higher incomes.

The data derived from the sample in the city of Fez are most useful to clarify the main sources of finance and start-up of women's economic activities. In fact, respondents in this study area reveal that the initial capital of their businesses results from various sources. For example, the data show that 34% of the economic activities are financed by the workers themselves from their personal savings without recourse to others. Similarly, 33.3% declared that their activities do not require a capital. However, a share of 19.7% of respondents resorted to family members and relatives to help them create their own businesses. In case of the absence of the family support, some informants revealed their recourse to other sources. 5.3% said that they benefited from micro-credits while 4% said they benefited from bank loans. 2.3% of the respondents confirmed their engagement in another form of financial support and cooperation known as *daret*.[46] The last category represented by 2% of the total number of workers sold their ownerships to finance the creation of their businesses. These are clearly summarized in the following table:

Table 19. Financial Sources to Start-up Economic Activity

	Frequency	Percentage
Personal saving	102	34%
Bank loan	12	4%
Micro-credit	16	5.3%
Family/relative loan	59	19.7%
Selling of ownership	4	1.3%
No need	100	33.3%
Others	7	2.3%
Total	300	100%

Source: Fieldwork Results

46 *Daret*, as it is known in the Moroccan variety, is a process of collecting money from a group of people (the number of members differs from one group to another) each period of time (generally, it may be per week, per 15 days, or per month), which is most of the time agreed upon by the members of the group. The purpose is to collect the amount of money from each individual to hand the total to one member of the group on a rotating basis. The same process is repeated many times till all the members get the same amount of money. Usually, a member of the group takes in charge the collection of the money and give it to the person who is in turn.

The results in the table above indicate the dependence of most informal self-employed workers on informal sources to start up their businesses. They also show the limited access of women to formal types of funding. Therefore, given its relative scarcity, financial resources to start up business in the informal sector tend to be low if not to say absent. A logical consequence of the results is the small size of the informal enterprises in the city of Fez as it was previously indicated. More particularly, this idea is emphasized by the following statement by Rajae:

> My budget prevented me from starting my own business, with my own savings and funds, which I aimed to use in launching my activity. Because this budget was low, and the aid from the society was also absent, loans from banks and micro-credits were missing, which further prevented me to set up my business. Hence, I had no choice, but ask my relatives for a loan, and I still pay it each month.

However, there is a significant difference in the use of the capital in terms of the type and scale of the economic activity. For example, most self-employed in the research area rely on their own savings as a capital or raise the necessary financing at their own risk to start up their businesses. Moreover, personal saving represents a form of individual funding. It is a dominant source of starting up the activity or the creation of the enterprise. One may deduce from the results of the survey that women's purpose is to rely on oneself and be independent. Indeed, this is the general observation prevalent among workers of the informal segments. The findings corroborate this observation since the highest rate is for independent workers who preferred to create their business without relying on other resources. Moreover, taking into account the nature of some activities, other respondents declared that they do not require a capital to practice their activities. This is mainly found in the craft's sector with particular reference to seamstresses and embroiderers who take the raw materials in most cases from their clients. Najat, a cookie maker said: 'there is no need for financial resources to start up the business of the cookie maker. It depends on clients' needs and each one brings me his/her materials according to the chosen type of cookies requested for preparation.' The same thing happens with women working as cookie makers as well as *henna* makers.

Because the banks are reluctant to make loans to small businesses, most women are forced to find other sources to start up their own activities. For instance, they borrow the bulk of their funds from family members and friends. These people are also considered as informal lenders. Unlike the banks and the formal financial institutes, women most often lend money without official guarantees. Moreover, it is done at daily, weekly or monthly rates. The reason for this is the collateral requirement, which poor participants in the informal sector usually lack, and with the lengthy procedures banks require before providing any loan to people. In this respect, women are discouraged to get loans from banks because of their high costs. However, for the case of micro-credits as well as cooperative members, women focus mainly on sharing the capital between either the members of the cooperative or the participants benefiting from the micro-loans. These micro-credit opportunities provide women in this study with the small loans. These are mostly needed not only to purchase the raw materials or basic resources to start up or to expand their own businesses (i.e. to buy embroidery and sewing machines) but also to facilitate women coming together in groups.

As mentioned in the literature on the legalist school of thought, the informal segments of work implicitly refer to the economic activities that escape in part or in full from the control of the state.[47] Indeed, legality of work is important to the development of the unit of production despite the additional costs it requires. It allows the workers to enjoy certain tax and financial benefits such as access to loans and exemption from certain taxes. Hence, concerning the registration of economic activities in the administrative records, the vast majority of women's activities/units of productions in this study remain unknown to the public authorities with a rate of 69.7%.

Interestingly enough, although the Moroccan informal sector is characterized by being invisible, illegal, and even unregistered, 30.3% of the informal activities' operators, contrary to my expectations, affirmed that they pay some forms of taxes. The latter can take the form of the patent

47 See De Soto, op. cit.

tax paid to local authorities to license and legalize the workplace and the activities performed. As for informal activities performed at home, they are all neither registered nor listed on the license. This can justify the situation of informal activities, which lay further away from the public scrutiny. Accordingly, one may assume that the local of the informal economic activity has a significant role in the record of the activity in the public authorities. For instance, if a woman practices her economic activity in a shop, she is automatically obliged to register her activity, unlike a woman who works from her home. This means that the choice of the workplace identifies the process of registration of activities/units. It follows from the above arguments that what is informal is not necessarily invisible. Let's consider the following table:

Table 20. Registration of Economic Activity

	Frequency	Percentage
No	209	69.7%
Yes	91	30.3%
Total	300	100%

Source: Fieldwork Results

The registration of economic activities takes two forms: recording the license and registration in the trade register. The former as defined in the national survey on informal sector by the Directorate of Statistics is:

> L'enregistrement à la patente concerne toute personne ou société qui exerce une activité industrielle, commerciale, de service ou une profession libérale. Son paiement conditionne l'exercice de l'activité et permet de jouir de la reconnaissance des autorités. D'autre part, l'enregistrement à la patente est une condition nécessaire pour s'inscrire au registre de commerce, ce qui permet à l'établissement de se faire valoir tous les droits que lui accorde la législation en vigueur. (Direction de la Statistique, 2003 : 199–200)

> [Recording in the license applies to any person or company carrying on an industrial, commercial, trade or professional services. Its payment determines the exercise of the business and allows the recognition of authorities. On the other hand, recording the license is necessary for registration in the trade register, which allows the institution to enforce all the rights under the statutory provisions.]

One may estimate that the correlation between women's declaration of economic activities to the public authorities and informality is positive. In other words, the non-registration in the commercial register and the patent reveals what legalists argued in their approach to the informal sector. This means that the above information stresses the idea that informal activities performed by self-employed women are not registered, not because the workers want to evade taxation or the regulation, on the contrary, informal workers are not obliged to do the registration or they lack the information as it was reported by most of the respondents in the research area.

Generally, women in the informal sector are both economically and legally marginalized as they are neither recognized in the labor code not covered by the social security. As a consequence, this informal work is actually carried out in isolation from other economic activities in other sectors. The questions that might be asked in this regard are: despite the low-income and the job insecurity as well as the lack of worker rights, why do women join the informal sector particularly the self-employed form in large numbers? Do women work informally because they choose to, or because they have no alternative? The subsequent section attempts to discuss the main reasons and motives that pushed women in the city of Fez to end up working informally.

Women's Interests in Informal Work

An important lesson revealed in the literature is that informal employment is not homogenous.[48] It is not appropriate to deal with the informal employment as a whole when thinking about the situation of women workers. A self-employed woman like a seamstress, an embroiderer, a

48 William Maloney. 'Informality Revisited.' *World Development*, Vol. 32, No. 7 (2004): 1159–1178. Also see Guillermo, Perry, et al., 2007.

street vendor or a shop-keeper who may own a store and employ others, is not in the informal employment for the same reasons and probably does not have the same motivations to end up working informally. Nevertheless, the present study represents a source of information about self-employed workers in the sense that it aims to answer the question why women are interested in performing informal activities. It primarily concentrates on how women explain their own reasons and motives for choosing self-employment. Whether voluntarily or involuntarily, the data of the research provided in this section reveal both reasons and motives.

Reasons for the Choice of the Economic Activity

As clearly demonstrated in Table 21, women's reasons to perform an informal economic activity may be classified into different categories. Indeed, 78.3% of respondents in the survey stated that their social and economic needs are the main reasons for choosing to work informally. Moreover, 64.6% of them considered that the main reason simply lies in their personal choice in the search for a better life while those who prefer to follow the family professional tradition represent 25% of the total number of informal self-employed workers. However, 92.3% women saw that the husband's job does not represent a reason behind their choice to select a job in the informal sector. While 76.3% of respondents did not choose a habit as a main reason to practice their productive work informally, only 3.3% of women provided other reasons, which pushed them to end up working in such activities. Out of those respondents, some referred to the absence of the work opportunities in other sectors and lack of an educational level and trainings. Other respondents, in contrast, confirmed that their old age hinders them to seek employment in the formal sector. Only some married women pinpointed the need to support their partners financially as a main factor to work as a self-employed.

Table 21. Women's Reasons to Work in the Informal Sector[49]

	Yes		No		
	Frequency	Percentage	Frequency	Percentage	Total
Family tradition	75	25%	225	75%	100%
Personal choice	193	64.3%	107	35.7%	100%
Habit	71	23.7%	229	76.3%	100%
Husband's job	23	7.7%	277	92.3%	100%
Social and economic reasons	235	78.3%	65	21.7%	100%
Others	10	3.3%	290	96.7%	100%

Source: Fieldwork Results

Most participants selected various factors as their main reasons to work informally. Firstly, the social and economic reasons are the omnipresent in the research area. For instance, money represents a factor of prominent importance affecting women's choice of self-employment activities. Fatiha, a single seamstress who is 28 years old shared her experience saying: 'I joined the sewing and knitting activity because I needed a source of income. I was fed up with asking money from my parents. I had to secure a source of income to meet my personal needs.' From this quotation, we may understand that unemployment and the need to earn money represent the most recognizable key factors with which women justify their choices of self-employment in the research area.

Secondly, women's personal choice, as a reason of work in the informal sector activities, is also shown to be quite significant. For instance, prior knowledge about the business is the justification advanced by most interviewees as being the main reason that led them to personally choose to pursue their economic activities in the informal sector. Moreover, the findings of the survey in Table 21 corroborate the argument that the participation of women in the informal economic activities generally does not require an educational level. This is also confirmed by the findings relative to

49 Fraction of answers (multiple answers allowed).

women's educational attainment in the analysis provided previously in this chapter. In other words, working informally necessitates neither the high qualification nor the training. The findings of this study are emphasized by the argument developed by the Directorate of Statistics in the national survey about the informal sector:

> En un temps où l'accès à un emploi salarié exige, entre autres, de longs délais de recherche, un certain niveau d'études, une formation et/ou une expérience professionnelle, l'alternative d'exercer un emploi pour propre compte (auto-emploi), au moins au secteur informel, est relativement forte. (Direction de la Statistique, 2003 : 98)
>
> [At a time when access to employment requires, among other things, long search time, a certain level of education, training and/or professional experience, the alternative is to exercise own account employment (self-employment), at least at the informal sector, which is relatively high.]

Thirdly, one of the most available predictors for women's employment in the informal sector is following the family tradition of being workers in this sector. It is possible that some women in the sample might be pushed to work informally because of their families' need for a continuation of the tradition. Indeed, this was precisely the view of Maria, who said when I interviewed her that one of her major triggers to be successful in the informal economy was her determination to preserve her family's tradition of sewing traditional clothes and doing embroidery in all its types. One explanation for the interest of women to keep attached to their family tradition is the willingness to develop their economic situation and safeguard the cultural heritage of the Moroccan society.

These interviewees can be classified into two categories. The first one self-selects in the informal sector because of the barriers of their entrance to the formal sector. The second category includes women who have no possibility of joining the formal sector and find themselves obliged to join the informal sector despite their awareness of the socio-cultural barriers that may face them in this sector of work. Firstly, women's self-choice of participating in the informal economic activities is important. 54.3% of women operate their businesses in their homes. Working in their places of residence is their preferred option because it allows them flexibility in work.[50] This line of argument is emphasized by Hoyman who stated: 'The informal sector does provide more flexibility, greater probability of being household-based and greater potential for part time or occasional work, and it requires less stringent credentials to gain entry' (1987: 75). Nevertheless, it should not be assumed that the total validity of the participation of women in the shadow activities is out of choice.

Secondly, women are forced to work in the informal sector because of the barriers to participate in the formal economy. In fact, many women face difficulties to join the formal labor market because of discriminatory practices, job segregation, and wage differences. Moreover, women's work in low position jobs puts them at risk to leave the job market and come back to their traditional gender roles in the household. These findings are similarly found in the article by Hoyman who referred to Agassi Judith as follows:

> The informal economy may be thrust upon women as an economy of last resort rather than of choice. Barriers to participation in the formal economy, such as discrimination, rigid schedules, and low wages all push women to work informally. Another possibility is that the limited access to only the lower status, service oriented jobs in the formal economy in combination with the low self-esteem and acceptance of conventional gender roles by many women causes them to revert back often to a traditional maternal role. It is this combination of factors that drives them back to the informal economy. (1987: 75)

Thirdly, the availability of preschool children within the household has a crucial role in orienting women to select a job in the informal sector. This line of argument is also developed by Vinary in her study of the Italian women. Her theory of the life cycle suggests a distinction in the patterns of family household participation based on the number of preschool children availability in the household. She suggests that when children are present in the household, women automatically prefer to engage in informal sector activities rather than formal ones.[51] Similarly, in the present study, many female interviewees argued that the availability of children, especially babies or little kids, impeded them to join the formal market. For example, Khadija

50 See Table 22.

51 Paola Vinary, 'Family Life Cycle and the Informal Economy in Central Italy.' *International Journal of Urban and Regional Research*, Vol. 9, No. 1 (1985): 92–93.

commented on her situation as a mother of two school age children and said: 'I have kids at home who need my presence, and it is not of my interest to be in a formal work or a daily activity. I only need to fill in my leisure time and do my needlework. So, I prefer to practice my activity from home and take care of my children.' In fact, the maternal obligations are strikingly high in the early years of the children. As a result, this necessitates the presence of mothers in the household. Thus, many respondents show more preference for informal rather than formal activities: 'a woman should preferably stay at her household to take care of her children and make sure they progress in their education. She may work and develop from home' as maintained by Fatima, a crochet maker who preferred to work indoors.

Finally, women often lack the training and skills needed for employment in the formal sector, which push them to end up working informally. For educated women, entering the informal economy for a job achievement represents a way of supplementing declining sources of employment and income in the formal sector of the economy. In other words, according to the interviews' findings, the respondents' participation in the informal sector's activities is triggered by various factors, which are mostly relative to the rising of unemployment rates and lower wages in the formal economy. For example, a graduate student complained about the lack of adequate work opportunities in her field of studies. Faiza said: 'I graduated a few months ago, but I didn't find suitable work which could go hand in hand with my professional skills, so I had to work as a baker in order to gain some money to help my husband.' There are many other factors that force women to work in the informal sector employment in other marginal activities. Among these, we can point out sex-based discrimination in the labor market and/or cultural factors in Morocco, which restrict women's mobility. As a consequence, they result in a preference for home-based employment.

In sum, the main conclusions reached so far demonstrate many reasons behind women's informal work. On the one hand, the financial necessity pushes them to choose to work informally. That is to say, this is driven by women's own resort or their best option to gain a source of revenue. In other words, the materialistic reasons behind their work demonstrate the strong desire to satisfy their fundamental human needs.[52] This finding is validated by the same argument in Benjelloun: 'la motivation économique constitue la motivation general retenue par la grande majorité des femmes quelque soit leur catégorie socioprofessionnelle' (Benjelloune, 1993: 96) [The economic motivation constitutes the general motivation maintained by the vast majority of women, regardless of their socio-professional category]. Thus, women's economic necessity is a crucial element behind the women's search for a refuge in the informal sector.

On the other hand, many women work in the informal sector because of their social obligations. Indeed, women work as self-employed, either because of their voluntary or by constraining choices. For instance, some respondents are in the informal employment by personal choice. This relates to their choice of the work flexibility, the absence of the requirement of an education level and training, or a professional experience, to name but a few. However, others join the informal labor market because of their traditional gender-based roles, especially child rearing, which restricts their access to the formal sector and encourages many women to work informally. Generally, it is crucial to note that not all respondents in the self-employment are there due to financial reasons, but it is also because they are socially disadvantaged. The subsequent section develops the main motivations behind women's choice to be self-employed.

Motivations for the Choice of the Economic Activity

As noted in the previous discussion, informal self-employment workers reflected various reasons to opt for this type of work. Indeed, both the sociological and economic clusters offer important reasons why many Moroccan women in the city of Fez may actually prefer the self-employment form over other types of employment. In addition to the already discussed reasons, the

52 In the qualitative research, interviewees, for the most part, declared that the primary reason to practice an informal economic activity is to converge with the highly daily expenses and to provide financial support to their male figures at the household, their husbands or fathers for the sake of securing a comfortable livelihood to the children and other family members.

empirical evidence also gives another set of motives for distinguishing between the deliberate and involuntary desires that drive women's occupational choices. In what follows, this section reports the findings based on quantitative research simultaneously backed up with stories from qualitative data.

As shown in Table 22, many motives push women to opt for self-employed activities. 73.7% engage in this form of work to meet the family basic needs. Women seeking financial independence and women looking for a source of living come in the second and third position with a rate of 73% and 71% respectively. Equally important, almost 57% opt for this type of work because of its flexible nature and the use of homes as a workplace. Finally, more than 70% would not take an informal job in response to the challenges of the society, modern aspiration, or even as a response to traditions.

Table 22. Women's Motivations to Work in Informal Sector in the City of Fez[53]

	Yes		No		
	Frequency	Percentage	Frequency	Percentage	Total
In response to the challenges of society	81	27%	219	73%	100%
In response to modern aspirations	69	23%	231	77%	100%
Responding to traditions	77	25.7%	223	74.3%	100%
In response to family needs	221	73.7%	79	26.3%	100%
Search for financial independence	219	73%	81	27%	100%
Living source	213	71%	87	29%	100%
Flexibility in work	172	57.3%	128	42.7%	100%
Possibility of home-based work	171	57%	129	43%	100%
Others	71	23.7%	229	76.3%	100%

Source: Fieldwork Results

53 Fraction of answers (multiple answers were allowed).

Data from the case study in the city of Fez demonstrate that family financial needs are the main motives behind women's participation in informal segments of work. Many women say that they spend most of the money they earn to contribute to family expenses, as they referred to it as 'family.' From the same perspective, Amal, a married woman, with four children said: 'I have to work as a baker because family expenses are too much and life is expensive. Add to this, my husband's income is insufficient to cover all the family's needs. So, to procure our necessities, I have to work and support him and contribute to the house budget.' The second main women's motive is economic par excellence. For instance, almost all respondents seek financial independence while working informally. The informal sector represents a source of independence for the urban people, particularly, women as it provides them with informal subsistence activities for their livelihoods. The majority of Moroccan women working informally in the city of Fez maintains that despite the fact that their earnings are mostly low and not stable in comparison to their counterparts in the formal sector, without the informal sector as a source of income generation, their earnings would be negligible.

The third motivational aspect is linked to finding a source of living. Indeed, women's search for an opportunity to work is an essential characteristic of the informal sector, which seems to be vital and has the most positive side as it is a booster and a creator of employment. Experiences of women participating in the field study in this region of Morocco demonstrate that their participation in the informal workforce is out of necessity as they cannot secure a job in other sectors as well as cannot obtain a diploma to allow them to find a job. For many women who are keen to enter the labor market for survival, employment opportunities in the informal self-employed activities are greater because of the dramatic decline in real incomes (need for revenue to secure basic needs).

The fourth motive suggests that more women seek employment in the informal sector because of the recession and the transfer of skills from one generation to another. This is mostly apparent among women doing artisanal work such as embroiderers and seamstresses. Most importantly, many respondents in the city of Fez engage in self-employed activities because they feel the responsibility for providing subsistence needs for their children and family members. Therefore, one may deduce that the productivity and income generation of those working as self-employed in the informal sector is of paramount importance, especially among women in Fez.

The fifth motive is linked to the way informal work might be performed, especially in terms of flexibility and home-based work. The former has many aspects. Firstly, the data reveal that women may perform reproductive and productive work on the same day. This means that they can manage their time between domestic and self-employment activities. Samira, a married and 38-year-old respondent, points out that:

> in the informal sector work, I cannot count the number of hours I may work per day. My working hours depend on the magnitude of the work. Most of the times, I do the household work in the morning and I do needlework in the afternoon. I sometimes even work for long nights.

However, others confirmed that there is a difficulty in controlling their working hours as a justification because they have to neglect their reproductive responsibilities due to the difficulty in getting the work done on time. Secondly, women's informal work is triggered by the flexibility in the market by quickly adapting to the available conditions of work. A case in point, some micro-enterprises typically use family members as workforce who can perform production and use their homes as a workplace with much ease and absorb some costs needed for production. They encompass costs of rent, electricity among others whenever the production is done within the home space. Khadija even declared that: 'the artisans' work does not demand a lot from them to start their activities.' Most of the workers need small capital sums in order to set up their businesses (e.g. using sewing machines, other tools and equipment) in addition to a substantial amount of learned expertise.

Concerning the choice of home-based work, findings demonstrate that women, performing their income-generating activities in the city of Fez, are not necessarily burdened with heavy overheads in finding a rent or places to perform their informal activities. Into this category falls many craft workers, tailors and seamstresses, and a variety of home-based workers. An exotic example is of a person who might be in an open place to work while others may prefer to sit in a verandah, or even they may create a working space in their own living quarters.[54] Thus, this shows that the informal sector plays a crucial role in creating job opportunities for women because of the flexibility in both the way of performance and workplace.

Figure 13. A woman doing *Takerir*.

54 See Figure 13.

The final motive is related to women's necessity to fulfill the basic needs of their families and their obligations. In this respect, the decision to work as a self-employed is important. It makes it possible for a woman to be a housewife, to raise children and at the same time to generate revenues. A respondent, Rajae, declared: 'I do not neglect my family responsibilities while working. Being a home-based worker allows me more flexibility. I have time for my career without harming my family members.' From the viewpoint, one may understand that if she is a full-time working mother, she may face some constraints that would have a negative impact on the performance of her job as well as for her children who may not have a normal childhood and may not gain a parental care.

In sum, the results are further corroborated by the previous findings relative to women's reasons to end up working in self-employment in the city of Fez. Tables 17 and 18 show that material and non-material factors are reported as reasons and motives, which imply that the informal sector is a source of valuable jobs in the city of Fez. In other words, both economic and non-economic justifications are most important for participation in the informal self-employed activities.

The survey data in the city of Fez by sectors of economic activity have quite significant differences. Indeed, in the textile sector, 27.1% of my respondents choose to practice a self-employed economic activity because they found in it a source of living. This finding corroborates the argument that the creation of an informal unit in the textile sector does not necessitate a higher qualification or training. Additionally, almost similar proportion, 23.7% of workers in this region of Morocco confirm that their family needs are the main reason behind their activity choice while 20.3% of them maintain the need for a source of financial independence. It should be noted that the structure of 'textile' is substantially different to that of sewing and embroidery sector, with a slight difference in the search for a financial independence, search for a living source and in response to family needs as the main reasons for the choice of the activity to be exercised.[55]

55 See Table 24.

However, in the sewing and embroidery as well as service sectors, the survey data revealed a distinct finding from that found in the trade and textile sectors. Many women opted for this work because it affords them a possibility to practice the informal productive work from home 15.6%. 12.4% of workers practice this type of profession because it allows more flexibility while similar rate 12.4% view it as a response to traditions in the trade sector, contrary to other women in the rest of the sectors, who do not exceed 7% as a higher rate found in the service sector. In the trade sector, the survey results show similar findings 9.3% with regard to the two first reasons: in response to the challenges of society and to modern aspirations.

Table 23. Women's Motivations of Work according to Sectors of Activity in Numbers[56]

	Sectors of economic activities				Total
	Sewing and embroidery	Trade	Services	Textile	
In response to the challenges of society	31	9	37	4	81
In response to modern aspirations	24	9	35	1	69
Responding to traditions	26	12	37	2	77
In response to family need	104	16	87	14	221
Search for financial independence	108	15	84	12	219
Living source	102	13	82	16	213
Flexibility in work	96	8	63	5	172
Possibility of home-based work	97	8	64	2	171
Others	32	7	29	3	71
Total	620	97	518	59	1294

Source: Fieldwork Results

56 Fraction of answers (multiple answers allowed).

Table 24. Women's Motivations of Work according to Sectors of Activity[57]

	Sectors of economic activities			
	Sewing and embroidery	Trade	Services	Textile
In response to the challenges of society	5%	9.3%	7.1%	6.8%
In response to modern aspirations	3.9%	9.3%	6.8%	1.7%
Responding to traditions	4.2%	12.4%	7.1%	3.4%
In response to family need	16.8%	16.5%	16.8%	23.7%
Search for financial independence	17.4%	15.5%	16.2%	20.3%
Living source	16.5%	13.4%	15.8%	27.1%
Flexibility in work	15.5%	8.2%	12.2%	8.5%
Possibility of home-based work	15.6%	8.2%	12.4%	3.4%
Others	5.2%	7.2%	5.6%	5.1%
Total	100%	100%	100%	100%

Source: Fieldwork Results

There are clear differences across the distribution of sectors in the view of being in the informal sector. Indeed, tables 19 and 20 break down motivations by sectors of economic activity in the informal sector in the city of Fez. The craft sector, including sewing and embroidery activities, shows the higher discontent with being self-employed due to the family need for financial contribution as well as workers' financial independence in craft, service and trade sectors which is at about 17%.

There are many common motives between respondents across different sectors of informal work in this form of employment. One motive is that self-employment creates opportunities for income generation to vulnerable portions of society. Additionally, perhaps the most important follows from the fact that self-employment becomes an alternative to formal employment or paid employment and, thereby, gives more opportunities for both the potential entrants to the labor market as well as those affected by unemployment.

57 Fraction of answers (multiple answers allowed).

Conclusion

To conclude, the present chapter provided empirical evidence to understand women's employment in the city of Fez. It focused on the analysis of the experiences of female self-employed workers as the main target population of this study. It highlighted two main issues to distinguish between workers in this sector. The first section focused on the analysis of the profiles of women workers via the discussion of their main socio-demographic characteristics. Informal self-employment largely encompasses a variety of adult workers, among whom women, passing their experiences and skills from one generation to another and older illiterate women in small-scale businesses. The majority of these respondents are originally from Fez with some exception of workers who came from other places in the region of Fez-Boulman (i.e. Immouzer, Sefrou, Outat El-Haj, Missour, etc.) Most of them are married and have children in their households. Most of them are not heads of households. This means that they have other members of their immediate family working either in the formal or informal sector.

Education and skills training are important for enhancing the productivity of informal workers. In other words, analysis of the survey data revealed that informal women workers in the city of Fez either did not study or did not reach or trespass primary education while others had few opportunities to continue a formal education because of economic, social or cultural obstacles. However, many highly educated women face up many difficulties to find out suitable careers matching with their diplomas. They end up in the informal sector at a young age. A high percentage of middle or high school leavers consider their qualifications not being adequate to seek a job in the formal sector be it in the public or private occupations. As a result, they opt for employment opportunities in informal economic activities and they compete with illiterate candidates for informal occupational roles, which are substituted for, or complementary to, different forms of employment with a low wage. Hence, one may deduce that the degree of educational attainment comes to be widely recognized as a factor influencing the access to forms of employment in different sectors.

Moreover, the second set of analysis of the first section relied on the professional characteristics of workers. The informal sector generally comprises of self-employed women who have engaged in different income-generating activities. They are semiskilled workers with some professional and technical competencies (e.g. artisans who work as *Mejdoul* makers, traditional button makers, *Makerami* and *Takerir* makers), unskilled workers in precarious jobs. The concentration of women in the modest occupations, such as sewing, embroidery, weaving and service provision, finds the explanation both in blocking employment in certain economic activities, which affect especially the female workforce who are subject to social discrimination. The five industries (sewing, embroidery, trade, textile and services) mentioned previously in this chapter are female dominated and represent the most important ones where women are active in the city of Fez. Moreover, they provide us with some measure of the amount of female participation in the informal sector.

The common characteristics of this type of work are better shown in the availability of opportunities of the income increase as well as recognizable profits without finding oneself in need for a particular capital or storage space. For instance, some informal women workers in the city of Fez who have more experience in their field of work who are old practitioners of such activities, and who may pass on their expertise from one generation to another may make a sizable living as buyers and sellers or even as brokers in business deals with other vendors and purchasers of products. Consequently, women find themselves working in the areas of brokerage and middlemenship. Whether employed or not, the omnipresent purpose is to secure an income opportunity.

The second section of the present chapter focused on the various material and immaterial reasons behind women's participation in the informal sector. The occupations that made up this sector appear to have been chosen by economic and social motivations. The former indicate that women select the shadow segments of work as income opportunities to satisfy their own and family needs. This may mean that women's access to the informal activities has been motivated by economic needs, as many of them feel the urge to escape from poverty. The latter show that most women seek self-independence as a major objective behind their self-employment in the informal sector. Moreover, it is a way to bridge the gap between productive and reproductive responsibilities because of its flexibility and opportunity of home-based work.

In general, the hypothesis developed in the beginning of this study, which stated that the lower the socio-demographic and professional characteristics of women is, the greater the chances they will end up working in an informal activity in its self-employed form is as it represents an important source of absorbing labor force and creating employment opportunities for women, is confirmed by the results of the empirical data provided in this chapter. The significance of studying the relationship between gender and informality also generates additional interests. In this perspective, more focus tends to be relative to the recognition of the links between informality, gender and poverty.

In fact, many studies, whether they focused their inquiries, specifically on the informal economy or undertook a broader analysis of the labor market, clearly indicated the important role played by informal economic activities to fight against poverty.[58] Needless to say that, in most cities of the Moroccan society, the informal sector is primarily devoted to the provision of employment opportunities that importantly offer many women their sole means of earning money, on which they lived along with their families and sometimes even secured a survival source. In other words, there is an increased recognition of the importance of the contribution of the informal sector to the overall economy, as well as its help for many participants to gain a source of employment, which represent a key pathway to reducing poverty within households.

The next chapter revisits the question of the linkages between gender, informality and poverty. In other words, it focuses on investigating the economic contribution of the informal sector as well as the role of women's different economic activities to their household earnings. This means that Chapter 4 will introduce additional evidence exploiting patterns across the business cycle to more fully flesh out the economic nature of informal activities. In this regard, the main economic characteristics of women's

58 For more details, see Abzahd and Labchir (1998), Akesbi (2000), Aksisak (2007), Biadillah (2002), Cairoli (1999), Charmes (1991, 2004).

employment in the informal sector will be investigated and applied to the development of women's sources of income, which in many cases have a crucial link to the contribution to the household needs and the reduction of household poverty.

CHAPTER 4

The Contribution of Women's Self-employment in the City of Fez to Poverty Reduction

ABSTRACT

The focus of the present chapter is to analyze the extent to which women's participation in the self-employed economic activities contributes to the reduction of household poverty. In this regard, I argue that women's income generated from self-employed activities in the city of Fez, though low in most of the cases, contributes to the reduction of poverty at the household level. With this in mind, the question worth rising is: what are the outcomes for women and the household as a result of such participation? The earnings that women generate from their informal work in Fez as well as their contributions to the household are such outcomes. The main purpose of this chapter is to address this question heavily relying on the analyses of survey data collected in the city of Fez, which are relative to different sectors within the informal sector, to illustrate the issues in the content of the research area. Firstly, it aims to discuss the main economic characteristics, which directed the development and the lives of women and those of self-employed workers in the city of Fez in particular. Secondly, the debate around the various initiatives of women to contribute to the needs of the household as well as its impact on the lives of the family members is researched next. This is important to understand and to evaluate the extent to which their incomes can meet the basic human needs of the household, and therefore, to reduce the household poverty. For this reason, the present chapter tries to address the following issues: 1) What are the characteristics of women's work in the self-employment form of the informal sector in Fez? 2) What are women's earnings as informal self-employed workers? 3) Does self-employment in itself imply lower earnings? 4) Do earnings vary according to socioeconomic predictors (period of work, age, education, marital status, etc.)? 5) Do the determinants of earnings vary by sector of employment that women occupy within the informal sector in the city of Fez? 6) What is the contribution of women's incomes, which are generated from self-employment activities, to the household income and expenditure in this particular city?

Economic Characteristics of Women's Employment in the City of Fez

The survey examined in this study of the city of Fez shows that the participation of women in self-employment is mostly characterized as an indoor employment. It is chiefly meant to contribute to meet the needs of the family members and to secure survival for women. Women's employment is characterized by certain economic characteristics that will be presented in the subsequent subsections. They mainly include the duration of work and income and the ways of marketing goods and services.

Duration of Work and Income

In the informal sector, income generation is very much related to the scale of the working duration. It includes the monthly working period, working days per week and working hours per day. In this regard, a general rule is observed, which lies in the fact that the more women work, the more income they may earn. Therefore, one may anticipate that women in the informal sector try to work longer periods to secure more money. This idea will be analyzed based on women's work in the city of Fez per year, days, and hours.

The present investigation of women's informal work in the city of Fez is interested in determining the duration of women's work and income. Indeed, it appears that the majority of the respondents in the sample in Fez exceed the normal working time specified in the labor law.[1] In fact, the

1 According to Article 184 of the Moroccan Labor Code, No. 65–99, promulgated by Dahir (Decree) No. 1–03-194 dated 11 September 2003, the standard legal workweek for non-agricultural activities is reduced from 48 hours to 44 hours, with the daily work period not to exceed 10 hours unless legally stipulated. The annual work period for agricultural workers also has decreased from 2,700 hours to 2,496 hours per year and their daily hours change according to the needs of the crops while the distribution of hours is determined by the governmental authorities. Moreover, employees must receive one full day of rest each week, although this may be suspended in cases

nature of women's economic activities as well as the sector in which they perform their productive work remain the determining factors responsible for the amount of time and the duration of work per year, week and day.

To begin with, the yearly period of work in the informal sector in its self-employed form do not significantly vary among women workers in the city of Fez. The highest work rate is a full year's period time with 64.3% of the total population, generally followed by those who work 11 months a year 10.3%. A similar percentage is witnessed among women who work six months 10.6%. Other categories come as follows: nine months 4.7%, 10 months 3.7%, and below nine months 6%. Interestingly, there are not many differences in these figures when classified by reasons why women do not work a full year.[2]

Table 25. Period of Work per Year[3]

	Frequency	Percentage
3 months	7	2.3%
4 months	4	1.3%
5 months	2	0.7%
6 months	31	10.3%
7 months	1	0.3%
8 months	5	1.7%
9 months	14	4.7%
10 months	11	3.7%
11 months	32	10.7%
12 months	193	64.3%
Total	300	100%

Source: Fieldwork Results

justified by the nature of the company's work, an unexpected increase in the volume of work, the materials used, or the implementation of emergency tasks (see Articles 205, 212 and 215 of the Labor Code).

2 See Table 25.

3 None of the respondents provided one or two months as their period of work per year.

Statistics from Table 25 reveal that employment in such informal activities is not stable and continuous during the year. Self-employed workers in the sample work on average slightly more than six months per year. This means that most of them work non-standard months. In addition, the self-employed women in the informal sector in this investigation are estimated not to work regularly. While there are women who work for 12 months per year, other workers are found to work less. The reasons behind women's irregular work are integrally linked to the following: 32% selected the periodical reasons, 7% chose the lack of financial support, 5.3% preferred high cost of basic needs while 4.3% of informants selected the lack of raw materials. However, the new work activity accounts only for 1% of the total population.

Table 26. Reasons why Women Work Less than 12 Months per Year[4]

	Yes		NO			
	Frequency	Percentage	Frequency	Percentage	Total	Percentage
Periodical reasons	96	32%	11	3.7%	107	35.7%
New work activity	3	1%	104	34.7%	107	35.7%
Lack of raw materials	13	4.3%	94	31.3%	107	35.6%
Costs of basic materials	16	5.3%	91	30.3%	107	35.6%
Lack of financial support	21	7%	86	28.7%	107	35.7%
Others	11	3.7%	96	32%	107	35.7%

Source: Fieldwork Statistics

4 The statistics presented in Table 26 do not include 193 women who work 12 months per year and which represent 64.3% of the whole examined population. Moreover, respondents had the opportunity to select more than one choice to determine the reasons behind their period of work that is less than one year.

Respondents in the city of Fez indicate that most of their work activities are seasonal, irregular, or intermittent. Indeed, seasonality is a major challenge as it is a periodical reason why most workers do not work a full year. Consequently, this results in loss of income during certain periods of the year. For instance, activities in the craftsmanship such as sewing and embroidery, as they represent the main sources of employment in the present study, are seasonal. Some women during the interviews declared that their work flourishes and rises in summer and falls during the winter months. It peaks also during festivals and the wedding seasons. Below are comments made by some female self-employed workers in the city of Fez regarding the irregularity of work during some periods of the year, especially during both summer and winter seasons:

Meriam, a traditional dressmaker, 38 years old, commented on her situation and pointed out that:

> It is well-known to artisans that when it is winter, people do not opt for sewing traditional clothes as in other seasons. There are no ceremonies and feasts. This is a problem we have and business goes very slowly for us as seamstresses. This is very common among other workers such as *Sfifa* makers,[5] *Akaad* maker,[6] *Terazat*[7] and others.

Similarly, Karima, who is an embroiderer and 29 years old, said:

> I know only to embroider fabrics such as the bedspread, clothes, shoes, belts and others. When it is summer, this type of business diminishes because it is the period when brides prepare for their weddings. Tourists also come from all over the world, and there is a market demand at that specific period of the year. But when it is cold, then I do not work that much

From the statements mentioned above, one may conclude that during these periods of the year, workers are busy from dawn to dusk. However, there is little or no work at all for the rest of the year. The researchs results are enhanced by the findings of Chikhaoui who concluded that the expansion

5 A lady who makes borders that decorate any Moroccan traditional clothes like *Jellabas* and *caftans*.

6 A person and mostly a woman who makes traditional buttons to decorate Moroccan traditional clothes.

7 Women who make different types of embroideries.

of the informal sector activities in Tunisia happens during particular times of the year. She said: 'these activities respond so well to consumer's demands that their number and the products they offer vary from one season to another. Ramadan and other religious festivals are times, particularly propitious for the expansion of the invisible economy' (1998: 221). Consequently, many women tend to perform multiple informal activities. The purpose to move from one economic activity to another is to maximize their earnings. For example, the present study reveals that the self-employed in the craft sector, especially seamstresses are most likely to be engaged in multiple market oriented activities across the year. This means that they sometimes perform two or more jobs simultaneously or depending on seasons.[8] For example, some women pointed out that they work in more than one activity in the food industry and craft activities that they may sell in the marker or at home. For example, they may perform activities such as cookies and bakery making in the former category and/or sewing, knitting, weaving or embroidering in the second category. This means that women work in different self-employed activities in a single day and across the year.

There are various reasons for this multiplicity of sources of income. This type of Moroccan women in the city of Fez is more likely to increase their opportunities to generate more income considering the low income generated from each activity. The other reasons reside in their willingness to overcome the problem of the limited market. As an example, Sanae, a married respondent who is working as a seamstress said:

> My main activity is sewing traditional Moroccan costumes such as *Djellabas*, *Caftans* and others. But, when there is no market demand, I prepare cookies to sell to my clients. I am also a member of two cosmetic companies Avon and Oriflam. These beauty companies allow me to do direct selling of different beauty products such as fragrances, accessories, wellness products, among others for the whole year. Nowadays, it is not sufficient to have one source of income, especially with the demands of each family member.

In sum, the investigation in the city of Fez demonstrates that the diversity of the amount of time allocated to the business is interesting to increase the income opportunities. Indeed, the data showed that women are observed to

8 See Beneria, op. cit., 112.

start up a secondary business to supplement income from the main activity. This means that the diversification of jobs offers the female workers several positive impacts. They include additional income opportunities for the workers, overcome of the limited market for many products produced by informal producers, and cash flow from several economic activities can be pooled. This is, in fact, a probable solution to their irregularity of work during the year. Moreover, the more amount of time that a woman may spend on her work might be a predictor of her economic success. In other words, a possible conclusion to draw from the data is that women who worked in the informal sector for longer periods than others may earn more money because their social networks of clients is bigger, their reputation in the labor market becomes more established, which helps them to market their products well, and they are likely to be fluent in entrepreneurial techniques as an outcome of their experience in the business. All in all, the duplication of work sources and the length of time in business represent crucial predictors of income development.

Table 27 shows the distribution of working days among my informants per week. The six days work predominates in the distribution of the female labor force work period in the research area by 55% of the total population. Despite their preoccupation by other tasks, 26.7% allocate seven days per week to their informal activities, followed by five days 12.7%, four days 3.7%, three days 1.7%, and the portion with less working days per week represents only 0.3%.

Table 27. Working Days per Week

	Frequency	Percentage
2 days	1	0.3%
3 days	5	1.7%
4 days	11	3.7%
5 days	38	12.7%
6 days	165	55%
7 days	80	26.7%
Total	300	100%

Source: Fieldwork Results

Most women in the field survey work long days each week with the intention to increase their income level. This idea is maintained by the argument of Budig who found that: 'women may benefit less from self-employment if they invest less time in work' (2006: 731). Needless to say that data also reveal that most of the self-employed workers do not have long working holidays. They may work Fridays and/or Saturdays as well as Sundays, which leave very little time for leisure. Consequently, self-employed female workers in this investigation have less free time in these oppressed schedules due to long working days. Therefore, this situation makes them feel that they are socially deprived and cause harm to their mental and physical health. These circumstances seriously influence the way women in the self-employment view themselves. Latifa, a 45-year-old embroiderer clearly emphasized this point when she rightly noted:

> As a self-employed, I work long days and hours without counting. I feel depersonalized by the nature of my daily work, suffering from a lack of leisure time and low rest periods. The fear of not handing the piece of work to the client on time turned many embroiderers and myself into dependents. I came to the conclusion that the power is in the hands of the client. Consequently, it can be noted that sacrificing the leisure time for the sake of generating additional incomes was a crucial feature to protect ourselves from financial crisis.

Many workers within the population of the city of Fez regularly work long days including evenings and nights while others work regularly during the weekends. Working during the evenings, at night or at the weekend is more common among those women within the craft sector. The research also shows that self-employed women in the adult age are more likely to work regular days than other age groups. Moreover, working at these periods is more common among Moroccan women in Fez who work by pieces.[9] This is because they are constrained by the client who fixes a time to take back his/ her finished work. Thus, one may deduce that working long periods may have negative impacts on the individual's health. This idea is also emphasized by Fatima, a carpet maker who said: 'I spend a lot of hours weaving

9 For example, a seamstress in the craft sector may fabricate an item such as a caftan and may be paid after she hand it to the client.

carpets and I work hard to satisfy the needs of my customers though it is mostly at the expense of my health degradation.'

Concerning the hours of work per day, the findings from the present investigation show that 48.3% of self-employed women in the informal sector in the city of Fez exceed the number of working hours indicated in the labor law. Others go below the average hours of work with 39% of the total population. Only 12.7% of the self-employed women workers in the informal sector who stick to the standard hours mentioned in the labor law.[10]

Table 28. Working Hours per Day

	Frequency	Percentage
Less than 8 hours	117	39%
8 hours	38	12.7%
More than 8 hours	145	48.3%
Total	300	100%

Source: Fieldwork Results

Time is regarded to be a crucial variable interacting with financial resources. Indeed, people prefer to substitute money for time when they look for goods and services performed by others. Women in my case study represent a vivid example of the producers of these goods and services. They work long hours to expend time in order to save money for their livelihood. This idea is stressed by Floro who said: 'by increasing their work day and intensifying their time use, women internalize the costs of

10 Akesebi found that on a national level, in the informal sector, the majority of workers (54.5 %) work seven days per week, and 44.5% work six days per week. Only 2% of these workers engage in work less than six days a week. Of the informal sector workers, 62.5% work between nine and 12 hours a day while 17.5% work more than 13 hours a day. The remaining 20% engage in work between four and eight hours per day. Azeddine Akesbi, 'Analysis of the Labor Market in Morocco: A Segmented Approach,' *Centre d'orientation et de planification de l'Education Morocco*, 3 September 2000, 7; available from <http://www.erf.org.eg/html/blabor1.pdf>. (accessed 23 September 2014).

poverty' with implications for their personal well-being' (1995: 18). In this respect, a close reading of the results stated in Table 28 demonstrates that 48.3% of informal informants involved in the informal self-employed activities work more than the legally specified hours in the labor code.[11] They exceed eight hours of work in hope to guarantee more production and consequently more returns.

Moreover, the nature of women's work among my sample in the city of Fez has an impact on the working day hours. Most respondents do not comply with the eight-hour working day stipulated in the labor law. They feel that the specification of working hours does not apply to them. This might be explained by the nature of their economic activities, which are mostly done on the basis of piece work. In other words, women may increase their working hours beyond the regular hours to augment their earnings levels. In the same line of argument, Akorsu states that: 'since there are times [women] do not have work to do, they have to work as long as there is work to be done. This means that they can only earn enough if they work long enough' (2013: 167). One may deduce that the time spent by women in work converts income into the living standards, which can be enjoyed by family members as far as their needs' attainment is concerned such as food, clothes, shelter and so forth.

Additionally, some informants such as those performing craft and textile work assert that they even may work regardless of the specific hours or limits that the law may require from them. Their working hours are tied to the working piece they have on hand and the different phases of the fabrication process. All these women report that their working hours are not limited. They do not have a fixed schedule of working hours. In most cases, they are the first ones to wake up and the last ones to sleep after a long day of work performance.

Moreover, 12.7% of the respondents claim that their working hours are limited to eight hours per day. This category mainly includes those who are working in shops (e.g. beauty shops, and public baths, known as *Hammams*). They are regulated by the opening and the closing hours set

11 They equal 48 hours a week and eight hours every day.

either by the employer or by the market demand. However, this category of workers reported that they face discriminatory practices with regard to workers' rights. They indicated that their recruitment is not official. Consequently, their work documents are not available; hence, no law can secure their rights and regulate their working hours. However, other respondents 39% reported that their working hours are less than eight hours per day. For example, women working in the food sector (e.g. bakery and cookie makers), *henna* makers, and cosmetic as well as clothes vendors lessens the work time known in the standard working hours due to the nature of the economic activities. Generally speaking, these workers perform their work in the minimum number of hours that most employees should be required to work in a day because of their irregular workday.

In sum, this cluster of results demonstrates that women working in the informal sector have a relatively long working duration. The average working year is 11 months, the working week is highly restricted in six days, and the average working day comes to more than eight hours. In this regard, one may deduce that the informal sector activities require extensive labor time. The extensive long working week might be explained by the fact that the activities women perform are informal and not organized by labor laws in Morocco, which restrict the working hours per week than the average formal sector enterprise, which has 44 hours work per week. Therefore, this leads to larger competition. Hence, informal female workers in this sample in the city of Fez tend to increase their working time to increase their production. Thus, the amount of time that a woman dedicates to her business activity might be an indicator of her economic success.

The relationship between women's incomes and period of work is very important in this study in the city of Fez. Data reveal that the majority of respondents' revenues do not help them secure a thorough economic independence due to their low level returns. This is evident because of the nature of informal employment, which has traditionally been associated with inferior earnings. Opposite to the formal sector, that is regulated by a working period code,[12] and which protects the minimum

12 See articles 184–185, 196-197-199-200 of the Labor Code.

wage for its employees, the informal sector does not do so because entry is not restricted and earnings are not protected by a particular law. This means that activities in the informal sector are distinguished by their easy entry, which makes the revenues from such activities much more flexible due to both the working time and the absence of the law which can protect them. In brief, one may deduce that there is a tight relationship between the low-income and period of work of the engaged women in income-generating activities within the informal sector if compared with the formal one.

Marketing Goods and Services

The marketing phase is a crucial stage in the production cycle for most of the informal workers. Indeed, following the increased output, it is important that self-employed women sell their production. The following cluster of results focuses on the discussion of the various issues of marketing women's outputs. They include places of marketing their productions, types of clients, timing of payment, and levels of income.

In the present investigation, an attempt is therefore made at establishing whether women have an idea as to where they will sell their outputs/products or not. Of the respondents that would resort to individual customers, more than half 60% said they would sell their outputs among relatives and friends; 47% select their homes as a place of work as well as a place of marketing their products; 45% said they would sell in the markets. 6% of the respondents identify themselves as cooperative members claimed that their products must be sold at the same place of production. Only 3.3% of the women in the city of Fez, where this research is conducted, said that they may sell their products either in open areas or send them to other countries through exportation. What emerges here is that individuals would still be considered an important source of marketing. Few women 10.7% reveal that there are other places where they may market their goods and services. They are interested in exploiting many governmental institutions to market their products.

Table 29. Places of Marketing Goods and Services

	Yes		No			
	Frequency	Percentage	Frequency	Percentage	Total	Percentage
Among relatives and friends	180	60%	120	40%	300	100%
In markets	135	45%	165	55%	300	100%
In open places	10	3.3%	290	96.7%	300	100%
At home	141	47%	159	53%	300	100%
Export	10	3.3%	290	96.7%	300	100%
Cooperatives	18	6%	282	94%	300	100%
Others	32	10.7%	268	89.3%	300	100%

Source: Fieldwork Results

There are many axes of differentiation between workers in informal self-employment activities. It is worth pointing out that multiple answers were allowed. For instance, women, basing themselves on the medium used in trading their products and services, may vary in the use of the way commodities are sold. Indeed, data show that some respondents in the sample choose to sell their products to a single buyer or a small group of buyers either because they are their neighbors, relatives, friends or individuals who have knowledge about their economic activities.

Another basic reason is women's inability to reach the market directly. This is mostly available among women working in the textile and craft sectors, especially carpet makers and embroiderers. Many of them require a middleman to help them in marketing their fabrics. Those who prefer to trade their products from their houses are the most common category in the region under study. One may deduce that the participation of women in the informal labor market in Fez does not necessarily take the form of going out to the workshops or to the streets to sell their outputs processed at home. Rather, informal female workers continue to perform their economic activities and sell them at home. Other respondents, however, sell their outputs in market stalls, using a large table or being in a small shop with an open front to sell particular goods in a public space.

This mismatch between the place of production and the customers shows that while the informal sector acts as a provider for many goods and services to different customers, visible and stable places of marketing the productions of informal workers are not available at the same scale. Instead, the informal sector operators depend on their own networking and individual relationships to sell their products. This calls for concerted efforts in order to help workers in the informal sector, in general, and self-employed women, in particular, to access the big business market.

Interestingly, data related to the various types of client show a large proportion 94.3% of workers in the informal sector in the city of Fez who has its customers as individuals, and 32% of respondents have shopkeepers as their main customers and brokers account for 27.7% of the self-employed women. Those working in locals have the opportunity to sell their products to people passing by streets 11.3%, followed by members of cooperatives who use their locals to produce and sell their productions. Recall that most operators in the informal sector use their houses to work, and as will be shown in the table below, 99.3% of respondents do not have the ability to use organized markets as a place for products' sales.

Table 30. Types of Clients[13]

	Yes		No			
	Frequency	Percentage	Frequency	Percentage	Total	Percentage
Persons	283	94.3%	17	5.7%	300	100%
Cooperatives	23	7.7%	277	92.3%	300	100%
Brokers	83	27.7%	217	72.3%	300	100%
Shopkeepers	96	32%	204	68%	300	100%
Organized markets	2	0.7%	298	99.3%	300	100%
Weekly markets	***	***	300	100%	300	100%
Passers-by. streets	34	11.3%	266	88.7%	300	100%
Others	2	0.7%	298	99.3%	300	100%

Source: Fieldwork Results (multiple answers were allowed)

13 *** None of the respondents sell her services/goods in the weekly markets.

Products and services provided through informal economic activities are an integral component of urban economies in Morocco. Self-employed workers, for example, provide different types of consumers with convenient and accessible options. They remain crucial elements of the social and the economic life of the city of Fez. The table above provides different types of the existed clients who benefit from the goods and services provided by women in this present survey.

The empirical evidence of self-employed women commonly shows that individuals are the main consumers and buyers of goods and services produced informally. Women who are an own account workers in urban areas such as the case of the city of Fez usually work in their homes. This category of workers produces various products such as clothes, blankets, carpets, cookies and baked products, etc., which others prefer to buy. For instance, these women in the sample may choose to fabricate clothes and sell them from their homes because they might represent lucrative products than making small arts and crafts as individuals consider clothing as a basic human need and pay for it often, whereas they consider arts and craft purchases as not necessary assets. Others turn their own kitchens into small pastry workplaces to produce and sell Moroccan cookies and baked products. Most of these have customers who are primarily made up of friends and family members, and if they are successful workers, word of mouth brings other customers from all over the city of Fez.

Additionally, 32% of my informants in the present investigation declare that they sell their products to shopkeepers, especially in the textile and craft sectors. In the same sectors, other women prefer to benefit from the skills of brokers to market their products. A broker, as an independent agent, helps female informal workers in arranging transactions between them and the potential clients for a commission when the product is sold. For example, most carpet makers declared that they cannot sell their carpets without the interference of a broker. He functions as a third-person facilitator. His contribution is remarkable since he brings sellers and buyers together to facilitate the sale of a particular product.

Similar to the results of the diversity in places of marketing and the types of clients who benefit from self-employed women's products, the next set of results focuses mainly on the examination of the various timing of payment as well as the level of income. This latter differs on the basis of a multiplicity of variables.

Time of payment refers to the exchange of a particular item produced by women workers in the research area for a potential client after a period of time set between them. The exchange is made for the provision of particular goods or services. Table 31 reveals that the timing of payment is diversified. For instance, data show that the highest rate 55% is allocated to returns gained when a piece of work is given to the potential client. A second class of workers is paid daily 35.7%, followed by those 3.7% who are either paid weekly or each 15 days. The lowest percentage is found among the 1.7% of women who get their payment on a monthly basis or other times 0.3%.[14]

Table 31. Timing of Payment.

		Education Level						
	Illiterate	Illiteracy courses	None finished Primary level	Finished primary level	Secondary level	High school level	University level	Others
Less than 300 dhs	43%	47%	40%	40%	45%	31%	29%	0%
Between 300 and 500 dhs	43%	38%	42%	47%	43%	47%	41%	0%
Between 500 and 1,000 dhs	9%	6%	11%	7%	7%	16%	24%	100%
Above 1,000 dhs	4%	9%	8%	7%	5%	7%	6%	0%
Total	100%	100%	100%	100%	100%	100%	100%	100%

Source: Fieldwork Results.

From the above statistics, it is highly important to observe that most of the workers in the city of Fez perform their work activities on a piece basis.

14 Women who selected this option refer to bartering as a form of payment. It represents a crucial form of the exchange of goods and services.

Though many women spend all of their mental and physical energy to earn a living, their incomes are not obtained on a daily basis. In this perspective, the timing of payment by the piece is also viewed based on the supply of materials and tools. In some cases, self-employed workers own their tools of work (e.g. hairdressers, cosmetologists, seamstresses, carpet makers, etc.). However, in other cases, it is the employer or the client who provides them (e.g. cookie makers, embroiderers, button makers, etc.). Similarly, some workers may buy their raw materials on the market or from the employer and sell the finished work back to him or her.

Moreover, another timing of payment found in the city under study is related to a daily basis. This means that my informants whose timing of payment is on a daily basis, they are paid directly when a potential client receives his/her product. In this respect, the daily payment for a particular product in the informal sector in the city of Fez may give women in the shadow segments of work the opportunity to cover their daily expenses. More importantly, this amount of money can cover part or all of the expenses incurred. For example, it may exclude the expenses of accommodation and only may include food, transportation, health services, etc.

Similar to these findings are those of women who are paid on a weekly, 15 days, or monthly basis. Respondents declared that the payment is made at the start of each working period. It covers the week or the month prior, depending on the timing and the work performed. At this stage, one may deduce that there is a close link between flexible working time and flexible working payment as a critical feature of employment in the informal sector.

As far as the level of income is concerned, the table below reveals that 82.7% of respondents do not exceed the 500 dhs as a revenue for their weekly work period. A second category of workers who earns an amount of money, which ranges between 500 and 1,000 dhs do not exceed 12%, while those who have a weekly income above 1,000 dhs represent only 6%. This means that 82.7% of sampled self-employed producers in the city of Fez fall into the medium and the low categories of income. One may argue that their shallow incomes are strongly related not only to the nature of their economic activities but also to their sector of work. This is also linked to the instability of work performance.

Table 32. Amount of Income per Week

	Frequency	Percentage
Less than 300 dhs	120	40%
Between 300 and 500 dhs	128	42.7%
Between 500 and 1,000 dhs	34	11.3%
Above 1,000 dhs	18	6%
Total	300	100%

Source: Fieldwork Results

There is a clear indication from the data presented in the table above that there is little difference in the earning structures of the two first groups. Indeed, 82.7% of the respondents in self-employment does not exceed the 500 dhs per week. The reasons for this may be related to the fact that most women are home-based workers. They have the same disadvantage of getting more customers because most of them work indoors. Of course, some portion of the sample exceeds this amount, which may be due to certain factors. In the present context, they may include higher level of production and accessibility to market demands. Moreover, the women's levels of income in this category of women workers in the informal sector reveal that the majority of the respondents' revenues do not help them achieve economic independence, which may be justified by the nature of the work's sector as it remains the key element to determine women's socio-economic situation.

As it can be observed from the findings, most of these women are pushed to informally practice their productive work for financial reasons, but their activities remain seasonal. However, many respondents declared that their production process increases in certain months and seasons. The working times for these women, especially seamstresses and embroiderers, increase during the months of March, April, May, June, July and early August as well as during Ramadan and Feasts because of both the demands of the markets and the needs of the clients. Their informal work guarantees for them a source to secure the basic human needs despite of the unfavorable amounts of income they gain for long and hard-working days.

Women who declared that their incomes exceeded the 1000 dhs include clothe vendors, shoes and bag vendors and some members of cooperatives who sell products such as carpets and embroidery. Most of them work on a monthly payment basis. In sum, based on the findings presented in Table 32, it can be concluded that the respondents' incomes are neither equal nor compatible with the amount of tasks they perform within the self-employed sector. Moreover, their profit gained from these activities in the study area is associated mainly with the nature of work as well as the accessibility and reliability of customers of different categories.

What makes this situation more alarming is the fact that all respondents are not officially recognized in the labor law. Indeed, they do not receive an official payment document because most of their transactions are direct with clients. This document has an important role as it provides the worker with detailed information concerning his/her working hours. In this perspective, most women receive their revenues on a piece of work basis or service offered. Concerning this point, Fatiha said: 'I receive my money whenever I finish the work at hand and I hand it down to my client. The payment depends also on the period I took to have the piece done.' This statement shows that women's income generated from informal economic activities is related to the amount of time given to prepare a piece of work. The more concentrated and dedicated the woman is to productive work, the more she increases her chance to increase her income. However, there are other predictions, which may have an impact on the average earnings of workers in the self-employed activities. Most importantly the age of women, their level of education, their marital status, and the sectors of their work activities have been proven to play a key role.

Age is likely to affect the income generation of women in the self-employed activities. The distribution of income is recognized to have links with the age level change. In other words, the distribution of income by age helps the individual to find out the possible links between these two major indicators. So, one may ask: What impact may age have on the economic situation of this category of women workers? The following two tables demonstrate the distribution of the data by income and age.

Table 33. Income and Age in Numbers

	Age			
	20–30	30–45	45–60	+ 60
Less than 300 dhs	32	38	31	19
Between 300 and 500 dhs	29	52	29	18
Between 500 and 1,000 dhs	13	16	3	2
Above 1,000 dhs	5	6	7	0
Total	79	112	70	39

Source: Fieldwork Results

Table 34. Income and Age in Percentages

	Age			
	20–30	30–45	45–60	+ 60
Less than 300 dhs	41%	34%	44%	49%
Between 300 and 500 dhs	37%	46%	41%	46%
Between 500 and 1,000 dhs	16%	14%	4%	5%
Above 1,000 dhs	6%	5%	10%	0%
Total	100%	100%	100%	100%

Source: Fieldwork Results

Readings of the two tables above reveal that women's earnings per week concentrate mostly on the lower income categories. In this respect, it can be noticed that a common thing in all age groups is that the higher the income is the lower is the percentage in the age category. Exceptions are found in the age group 30–45 years old where findings show that the income augments in the category between 300 dhs and 500 dhs. A second exception is found in the age group 45–60 years old where women's incomes increase to above 1,000 dhs with a percentage of 10% as it represents the highest one in the total population. One may deduce that the highest concentration in the low categories of income (less than 300 dhs) and the low representation in the income category above 1,000 dhs per week are determined by various reasons. Firstly, in most cases, women get involved in jobs that are very poor in their returns. For example, they may work in their family businesses, which prohibit their levels to develop. Secondly, it is found that women in both age categories 45–60 and those over 60 have a tendency to choose self-employment towards the end of normal working life as an alternative to retirement in the paid employment.

However, there are also age related choices in connection with employment in this form of informal work, which affects their returns. The old ones are less likely to take risks than younger ones and engage in more activities to gain higher levels of income. This justifies their low representation in the average income between 500 dhs and 1,000 dhs with 4% of share as well as the low presence of those between 45 and 60, who represent 5% in addition to the absence of women over the age of 60 in the income category of above 1,000 dhs. In this perspective, for those women in both categories, income generated from self-employment decreases with the age increase since this does not enable one to maintain the same force and continuity in work activity.

Additionally, another key factor that influences the income of older categories is health problems. Indeed, most respondents in the old group categories revealed the effect of health on their self-employment primarily while talking about their work characteristics. For instance, the longer the hours and the greater the responsibilities are associated with the nature of their economic activities, the less healthy these old women are likely to be. Hence, there is an expectation of a lower production to be associated with lower income generations, which also implies that the older respondents are less likely to take risks than the younger ones.

Furthermore, working in self-employed activities necessitates responsibility and a lot of mental efforts. Then, if approaching an old age, there is increased dislike to mentally demanding work. This means, production can become less obtainable. This point is reinforced by the responses of the interviewees as far as the questions related to health problems are concerned, which designates that poor health significantly decreases the probability of high production in self-employment. This means that physical disadvantages that old-aged women may also confront grant a mental disadvantage in coping with the demand of self-employment and the market in general. Therefore, incomes would be lower.

As previously discussed in Chapter 3, women's educational attainment is a key factor behind their labor force participation decision. Indeed, the results from the sample about the links between income and the educational level are worth mentioning here. In this respect, I expect that the education level will also play a role in the determination of self-employed women's incomes. In this regard, turning to the actual prediction, the effect of lower education standard is to decrease the probability to gain higher incomes. However, greater educational attainment reduces the earning differences. Thus, the findings in the two tables below indicate that the changes in the income levels are due to the direct influence of education.

Table 35. Income and Level of Education in Numbers

	Education Level							
	Illiterate	Illiteracy courses	None finished Primary level	Finished primary level	Secondary level	High school level	University level	Others
Less than 300 dhs	33	16	21	12	19	14	5	0
Between 300 and 500 dhs	33	13	22	14	18	21	7	0
Between 500 and 1,000 dhs	7	2	6	2	3	7	4	3
Above 1,000 dhs	3	3	4	2	2	3	1	0
Total	76	34	53	30	42	45	17	3

Source: Fieldwork Results

Table 36. Income and Level of Education in Percentages

	Education Level							
	Illiterate	Illiteracy courses	None finished Primary level	Finished primary level	Secondary level	High school level	University level	Others
Less than 300 dhs	43%	47%	40%	40%	45%	31%	29%	0%
Between 300 and 500 dhs	43%	38%	42%	47%	43%	47%	41%	0%
Between 500 and 1,000 dhs	9%	6%	11%	7%	7%	16%	24%	100%
Above 1,000 dhs	4%	9%	8%	7%	5%	7%	6%	0%
Total	100%	100%	100%	100%	100%	100%	100%	100%

Source: Fieldwork Results

As it has already been demonstrated in Chapter 3, the education profile of self-employed workers in Fez is generally low. The majority of respondents either did not get access to formal schooling or did not complete primary education. On the one hand, this is related to the economic hardships caused by poverty and financial impediments. Many families are not able to finance their daughters' educational attainment. Moreover, the cultural and social predictors have an impact in this perspective, which place less importance on higher education for daughters. They may include but not restricted to the traditional values, which places women in the private sphere as responsible for gender-based roles. These encompass child rearing, cooking and taking care of the family members. On the other hand, the government and professional organizations reinforce such bias of the lack of women's access to education by providing them with basic trainings instead of encouraging them to get access to education. These trainings are relative to skills that are specific to informal and low paying activities.

Since females are generally seen as future housewives, parents have few incentives to invest in their daughters education. Hence, women are more likely to be affected by high illiteracy rates. Moreover, it affects their access to formal sectors of employment, and, consequently, it explains the low level of income generation in its informal counterpart. An additional explanation is relative to the high levels of drop out from school among females. The most common reasons provided concerning this matter are that girls are needed to perform their traditional gender roles. Additionally, the family would not benefit from investment in girls' education when they are eventually transferred to their husbands households after marriage.

However, a small portion of the sample saw a progress in access to education. Indeed, it has been observed that among the respondents, education and skills that they acquired have no relationship with the skills demanded in their economic activities, and hence their productivity remains low; therefore, their incomes are below what is expected. At this level, given the overall low levels of education among the self-employed workers in Fez and higher incidence of a mismatch between education and skills demanded among educated participants, women are more likely to be confronted with low and irregular incomes.

However, another viewpoint suggests that those women who have a high educational level may earn high income. This is because of their ability to manage a better job in contrast to those women with basic education or those who are illiterate. Similarly, respondents who have an educational level might be able to increase the types of skills needed for an informal worker to assess the extent of the market, and the required products by the customers. This is apparent in the income category between 500 dhs and 1000 dhs where high school and university graduates are able to gain higher-income levels. Additionally, they represent the lowest shares in the income category below 300 dhs as they stand for only 31% and 29% for those who are high school and university graduates. This can imply that higher education may foster earnings. Thus, both education and self-employment can be correlated since the former has an influence on the latter.

As the importance of income in relation to marital status, let's consider the following two tables.

Table 37. Income and Marital Status in Numbers

	Marital Status						
	Single	Married	One of the wives	Divorced	Widow	Single mother	Abandoned woman
Less than 300 dhs	26	38	7	22	15	2	10
Between 300 and 500 dhs	26	46	6	14	21	2	13
Between 500 and 1,000 dhs	9	12	2	5	3	1	2
Above 1,000 dhs	4	7	1	2	2	0	2
Total	65	103	16	43	41	5	27

Source: Fieldwork Results

Table 38. Income and Marital Status in Percentages

	Marital Status						
	Single	Married	One of the wives	Divorced	Widow	Single mother	Abandoned woman
Less than 300 dhs	40%	37%	44%	51%	37%	40%	37%
Between 300 and 500 dhs	40%	45%	38%	33%	51%	40%	48%
Between 500 and 1,000 dhs	14%	12%	13%	12%	7%	20%	7%
Above 1,000 dhs	6%	7%	6%	5%	5%	0%	7%
Total	100%	100%	100%	100%	100%	100%	100%

Source: Fieldwork Results

The suggestion that the marital status predicts differences in earnings is not applicable to the findings reached in my study in the city of Fez. In other words, marriage appears to have no impact, and it may not be taken seriously. This is because it is initially established not to be of direct impact on explaining the changes in gaining revenues in the present book. In fact, although there is little difference between the average of earnings and the marital status of the self-employed, these women are mostly present in low income categories. This indicates that there are other predictors to this concentration.

In general, considering the influence of measured variables on earning, it is apparent that whereas most of the variables are important to determine the entry of women in the informal sector, only age differentials and educational level variables are significant in this respect. In other words, earnings are likely to be affected by observable human capital attributes such as the age, the educational attainment, but certainly other elements may also affect the income of self-employed operators. For example, the sectors of work may provide pertinent knowledge concerning the level of income obtained by female workers in the self-employed sector.

The data from the city of Fez also reveal that women work in survivalist activities since they generate low incomes. These women are mostly omnipresent in traditional sectors of work as previously mentioned in Chapter 3. In the same line of argument, Akorsu argued that: 'women tend to earn lower incomes since they are restricted to survival activities of the informal economy, often extensions of their traditional chores such as dressmaking and food processing' (2013: 166).

Table 39. Income and Sectors of Work in Numbers

	Sectors of economic activities			
	Sewing and embroidery	Trade	Services	Textile
Less than 300 dhs	68	6	32	14
Between 300 and 500 dhs	62	8	52	6
Between 500 and 1,000 dhs	17	4	11	2
Above 1,000 dhs	10	0	8	0
Total	157	18	103	22

Source: Fieldwork Results

Table 40. Income and Sectors of Work in Percentages

	Sectors of economic activities			
	Sewing and embroidery	Trade	Services	Textile
Less than 300 dhs	43%	33%	31%	64%
Between 300 and 500 dhs	39%	44%	50%	27%
Between 500 and 1,000 dhs	11%	22%	11%	9%
Above 1,000 dhs	6%	0%	8%	0%
Total	100%	100%	100%	100%

Source: Fieldwork Results

The incomes generated from self-employment are low both in absolute terms and based on sectors of work. The earnings of women in the textile sector remain the lowest in the research area. Statistics in Table 40 show that 64% earn less than 300 dhs per week, 27% of respondents gain an amount, which ranges between 300 dhs and 500 dhs, 9% do not exceed 1000 dhs, as a return for their production. Both in the textile and trade sectors, women are not able to reach 1,000 dhs per week as an earning for their work. The same pattern of incomes' decrease is noticed in the embroidery and sewing activities. 43% of workers earn less than 300 dhs while women in the trade activities such as those selling cosmetics, clothes, bags, etc. They represent 33% of the total population, which is closer in percentage to those in the service sectors 31%. Moreover, the majority of the respondents in the trade and service work activities are able to practice activities that gain up to 500 dhs per week, which is not the case for workers in the craft sector 39%. 11% of women in both the craft and service sectors are able to secure an income that reaches 1000dhs per week while they could not trespass it as sewing workers. Embroiderers represent 6% and service providers account for 8%.

Despite the diversity in economic activities performed by women in different sectors of the economy, high percentages persist in lower income categories in this region of Morocco. Although the working poor women make up the bulk of the labor in the informal sector in Fez, they are also a significant portion of the workforce in the national economy. Their vulnerability lies in the low and frequently irregular levels of incomes. Developing and increasing chances of high-income opportunities for younger and adult with or without skills remain a challenge.

In sum, informal female workers are proved in the present book to vary their duration of work based on various elements. For instance, they work for long periods of time because of their nature of economic activities. Their extensive working periods in such sector are justified by the willingness of women to augment their opportunities to gain more income. The primary purpose is to secure a survivalist living standard for them and their family members. Moreover, the findings demonstrated that the main obstacle impeding this category of workers to become visible is their place of work and way of marketing products. Indeed, the prevailing place of activity among this portion of society is inside their homes. The latter serve both as a residing place and a workplace for the majority of respondents. This shows the divergence between the place of marketing, as it is generally indoor and/or invisible, and the types of clients who are most of the times individuals who know about these types of productions through word of mouth method. Additionally, the timing of payment remains of important significance in this matter. For instance, the majority of workers are found in this region of Morocco to be paid either per day or when they finish the piece of work they are fabricating. This shows that the shadow sector may allow its workers some flexibility in workplaces and timing of payment.

Concerning the level of income, data demonstrate that women mostly earn low amounts of money as a return for their activities. For instance, as demonstrated previously in this chapter, the amount of time allocated to perform informal self-employed activities is proved to have an impact on the level of income generated. Similarly, other elements are found to have a direct influence. For example, age is also considered as an important determinant of income generation among self-employed workers. It represents a crucial component of human capital. Its effect is pertinent in the older age categories as the income rises at a younger age and decreases towards the end of life.

Education is of great importance as it has a significant role and greater impact on women's earnings. Equally, it raises the probability of gaining higher incomes. However, it can be assumed that education has a double edge effect. Indeed, it could embody two aspects of human capital: one of which is to decrease the choice for self-employment, and the other one is to increase productivity at work, and hence, to increase the income opportunities. Still, there seems to be no concrete evidence for this, and further research is still in need in this respect as I believe that future research should take into account these results and explore in greater depth the diverse range of human capital variables in self-employment choice and income generation. These variables may include race and health, for example. The next cluster of results shifts the focus to the analysis of the financial responsibilities of women and the usage of their income in their daily lives.

Women between Needs and Wants

The section seeks to examine the role of growth of essential human needs and wants. It is divided into three elements. Firstly, it discusses the various financial responsibilities informal women workers hold in the city of Fez. Secondly, it examines the way women's income may contribute to the achievement of human needs. Thirdly, it investigates the various methods women follow to spend their incomes and meet their wants. This division is meant to answer the following questions: (a) On what basis do these women spend their earnings? (b) Do female self-employed maintain financial control and/or ownership of their incomes? (c) What is the contribution of women's work to the household expenditure? (d) How do these women manage to save some of their income?

Women's Financial Responsibilities

In contradiction with our expectation, 51% of respondents assert that they are not heads of households. This is obviously a result of some gender specificities rooted in the Moroccan society. Additionally, one should not ignore the socio-cultural aspects of the Moroccan society as well as the notion of the main breadwinner who should be a male figure. As demonstrated in

Table 41, nearly the same percentage 49% is devoted to women who are the main breadwinners and who devote their incomes to meet the daily expenses of their households including food, shelter, children's schooling, among others.[15]

Table 41. Women as Household Heads within the Family

	Frequency	Percentage
No	153	51%
Yes	147	49%
Total	300	100%

Source: Fieldwork Results

Most respondents in the city of Fez are not the chief earners and heads of households. Before going deeper into this issue, it is obligatory to define the concept of 'head of household'. According to Khan and Khan, the head of the household is:

> a person who bears the chief responsibility of economic maintenance of the household. Alternatively, head of the household is the person who provides most of the needs of the household and is familiar with all the activities of the household. In the absence of any male head of the household, [the] female heads the household. (2009: 74)

This means that women play the role of the head of households in the absence of the male figure who earns money to support others and females are no exception in a patriarchal system. The idea implies that the male should work outside the home, as it represents the public sphere that is dominated by males, while the females are supposed to stay in their private spheres (the home) to perform gender-based roles. The latter include taking care of children and elderly, cooking and doing household chores, among others.

The absence of female-headed household is particularly common among both categories: the married women and one of the wives who

15 See Table 42 for more details on the contribution of women's incomes to the provision of basic needs.

rely mostly on the financial provision of their husbands. One can easily link this finding to the traditional customs that deny women's access to labor market and restrict their movements. In this respect, the Moroccan feminist Mernissi described the traditional image of a woman as: 'an image that confounds virility with economic power and femininity with the passive status of consumer' (1987: 148). This implies the typical image of the socially and culturally good woman. Accordingly, the presence of men in their public sphere as well as the patriarchal system force the male figure to consider himself the sole provider for his own needs and those of his family.[16] So, the spatial immobility is considered as a constraining element of women's opportunities of household headship.

Although statistics show that 51% of the respondents are not the heads of households, the majority of them are the main responsible for the divisions of income for household needs. A case in point is the situation of Saida who talked about her husband's practices each month:

> My husband comes to me at the beginning of each month with an amount of money he devotes to the expenditure of the household and tells me that I have to take it and divide it on the payment of electricity, water, food and other basic needs. I have to go through a miracle so as to keep the amount of the money till the beginning of the next month.

This testimony shows that some women are bearing an undue responsibility for household survival in a situation that is often highly exploitative by male partners. In most cases, men detach themselves from their obligations within the household and give women the whole responsibility. As maintained out by Ouafae: 'women are responsible for taking care of their children as well as bearing the responsibility of management of the husband's income reserved for family expenses.' This means that the low presence of female heads of households in the city of Fez may be more justified by socio-cultural than economic factors.

Furthermore, the socio-demographic characteristics of the husband may be of great importance in determining a woman's position as a female

16 Mernissi (1987): 148.

head of household. Indeed, in a society like Morocco, a husband or a father usually has the culturally and the socially assumed role of the main breadwinner. He is always assumed to be the main chief earner. He is actually the head of the household and steers the activities of the family members. However, the educational attainment of the husband may affect the contribution of women. One may presume that educated husbands are likely to encourage their wives' participation in the labor market to enhance the financial status and the welfare of the family members. In the case of informal employment, where women are also included, the households are primarily characterized by women's low level of educational attainment, poverty, vulnerability and socio-economic difficulties. When the male partner or husband is likely to secure more income due to his education and regularity of work, it results into comparatively an acceptable economic status of the household. Therefore, the wife's contribution to the budget remains low and heading the household is not tolerated.

Female heads of households in this sample in the city of Fez, as responsible for the household headership because of the absence of a stable male breadwinner, represent those females who rely on the absence of the male partner, ex-partner or male relatives in the up-bringing of children. This situation demonstrates the absence and invisibility of a gendered responsibility and dependency. Female household headship indicates positive aspects of their situations within the household. For instance, findings show that women, as heads of household, contribute more to the family expenditure as well as to the household budget. One may foreground an important and clear explanation that nobody other than children and old-age members who are available in the same household, specifically siblings compel women to provide extra income to support the household financial resources. This is confirmed by the following statement made by Khajida:

> I am a widow and a mother of four children. My situation became worse off when I lost my husband. With the absence of the breadwinning partner, life gets more complicated … I did not only lose the source of finance, but I have relatively more persons depending on me to support and secure their survival.

In the sample of this study, 49% of the respondents are heads of the household, and they play the role of the main breadwinners. As it will be demonstrated later on, greater contribution by the women in the household stands for their good status within their families. There are many reasons responsible for having households headed by females. They include immigration, single parenthood, and patriarchal authority of the male figure.

Firstly, long term or permanent immigration processes from Morocco to other countries have traditionally left women behind, largely because of their partners' intentions to seek employment opportunities abroad.[17] Secondly, single parenthood is an important factor behind women's headship in households. 1.6% of women in the sample are single mothers and responsible for their financial resources provisions. For instance, despite mounting awareness about the use of contraception, there is an increase in single mothers' issue in Morocco. Consequently, out of wedlock pregnancies represent a motive for many women to seek employment in informal activities, especially because they experience motherhood at early age added to family and society's rejection to them and their babies.

Thirdly, informants demonstrate that they are less constrained by the patriarchal authority of the male figure at the domestic level. Their main reason is relative to the income they provide for the survival of the family members. They are better off than they would have been if they stayed unemployed. Beneria and Roldan, based on their study of '*maquila*' industrial home workers in Mexico, suggested that enlarging household income through women workers' participation in the labor market gave women opportunities to mitigate husband's control over their lives.[18] Generally, these reasons are crucial to determine the headership of households by women. As a result, there are many positive aspects of female-headed households. They encompass submittal to marital authority where women gain more self-esteem, more personal freedom to manage and spend their incomes, more flexibility in having more than one job, reduction or elimination of gender-based violence and psychological abuse of resources by

17 See Moha Ennaji and Fatima Sadiqi. *Migration and Gender in Morocco: the Impact of Migration on the Women left Behind.* Trenton, NJ: Red Sea Press, 2008.

18 See Lourdes Beneria and Martha Roldan. *The Crossroads of Class and Gender: Industrial Home work, Subcontracting and Household Dynamics in Mexico City.* Chicago: University of Chicago Press, 1987.

the husband or male figure in the household, among other things. These positive aspects are good ones to reject the traditional view about women's headership as synonymous with poverty.

Additionally, many respondents in the present investigation declared that they are both the heads of the household and the chief earners. For instance, most of them contribute to the household expenses if not to say that they are the main providers and the principal earners. Almost all of them declared that they could not benefit from a break whenever they want. This is because they need to keep the machine working and they are obliged 'to earn their piece of bread' as postulated by some interviewees. Consequently, to earn their living caused them periods of anxiety and tension between their need to earn money for survival and cherish some time for leisure and family.

Women's Income and Contribution to Human Needs

Both single and married women devote a part, be it large or small, of their incomes to contribute to the household's financial expenses. Women's participation in the household income as Sadiqi writes: 'is a way of negotiating more gender equity in the family in the sense that their doing so lessens the authority, power, influence and prestige of the husband' (2003: 77). The data retrieved from the sample reveal that most respondents 89.67% contribute to the household expenses, in contrast to only 10.33% who do not find a driving force to enable them to participate in the household budget.

Table 42. Women's Contribution to Household Financial Expenses

	Percentage
Yes	89.67%
No	10.33%

As concerns the case of married women, the husband's employment status may be a crucial factor to determine a woman's contribution to the household budget. In the Moroccan society, women's contribution is generally determined by the household's economic status. The latter mostly depends on the position of the husband within the labor market, who is culturally and socially assumed to be the head of the household and the chief bread earner. For women informal self-employment in the city of Fez, the unemployed husbands often rely on their women to meet the family needs. Some interviewees argue that men even do not bother themselves to find work and remain unemployed. Accordingly, their participation in the labor force is considered as a replacement of their husbands' own employment.

Moreover, the educational attainment of the husband has an important role in determining women's contribution to the household budget. Indeed, husbands with lower educational levels or illiterate situations are assumed to have low productivity in the labor market; therefore, the income level of their households remains insufficient, which urges women in the family to contribute to the household budget. The situation of this category of households may also be aggravated by the availability of children. Consequently, the household might be affected more by poverty. Thus, the low educational attainments of the household, the underemployment as well as the presence of children are crucial factors characterizing poor households. In this perspective, poverty of the household is the main factor behind women's participation in informal economic activities. It also has a great role in boosting a self-employed worker to contribute more in the household budget as well as to devote more time to secure a financial status of the household.

The structure of the household has an important role in determining a woman's contribution to the household budget. Indeed, the size of the household represents either the nuclear system or the larger extended family system. The former refers to a family encompassing only parents and their children. The latter represents a joint family where a woman lives with a family that extends beyond the nuclear, consisting of other members apart from husband, wife and children. They may be parents, grandparents, brothers, sisters, uncles, among others. More precisely, on the one hand, for most women in the city of Fez, the nuclear family has negative impacts, particularly in relation to their child-rearing, household management, and care for domestic labor. On the other hand, living in an extended family system represents an additional burden to women informal workers. In this respect, Somia pointed out: 'the income of my husband is not sufficient to serve the needs of the big and the small family, we leave with my parents in law so we need assistance and my contribution to the family expenses is obligatory.' This means that these women are not able to save some money from their incomes due to extra expenditures. In other words, the larger household is taking more contributions of women than the smaller one. Another explanation shows that the presence of adults in a household, other than the woman who is working, may participate in the household labor and substitute the working woman as child-care providers, especially when this woman is doing her productive tasks.

Additionally, the contribution of women to the household budget may be influenced by demographic characteristics such as availability of children, their number, age as well as their activities. For instance, women having infants and school-age children are likely to contribute less to the household budget as both types need different tasks of child caring that require more time. Babies require the availability of their mothers with them in the absence of other family members as they require full-time care while school age children comparatively need less time dedication from their mothers. However, households with school age children necessitate from women additional financial resources as they consume a majority of these resources on food, clothes, and more particularly, on education expenses. In this respect, mothers may increase their household resources by contributing to the household budget. In contrast, the availability of prime-age children (16 years or above) in the household may have a different impact on the contribution of women in the household budget as compared to infants and school age children. In fact, some interviewees reveal that their prime-age children who have either finished their schooling or those who dropped out from school joined the labor force. Consequently, they represent additional financial sources. Therefore, they may reduce the contribution of a woman to the household estimate of income and expenditure for a period of time.

However, women who are chief earners are automatically contributing to the household expenditures. They are generally more common among widows, single mothers, divorcees as well as abandoned women. They suffer from difficulties, which are not only related to prejudices, but also linked to social stigma. They have far more difficulties in maintaining their families because of their sole source of financing. In Morocco, social norms discourage the second marriage of widow and divorced women, particularly with the availability of children, which may secure a male financial support. However, relatives and family members care for these women thought their economic circumstances are not so good at large.

Most respondents 64% point that they are obliged to financially contribute to the daily expenses of the household. Their socio-demographic profile reveals that the majority of respondents are generally from lower class households. Consequently, they suffer from high rates of male unemployment or low income. Moreover, never married and divorced women also live in their parents' house.[19] They report the use of small or big amounts from their incomes. The aim is to secure the basic needs of the members of the family. This strategy is adopted in most households where men find difficulties in securing a stable work. During the survey, interviewees complained that their husbands do not contribute their entire income in their families, which obliged women to be sometimes the full responsible for the household expenditures. However, the common feature among them is that their income is not regular and not monthly stable. This is emphasized by the following statement by khadija: 'my husband is also a traditional tailor. His income is not stable. So, he contributes with a little portion to the family needs. Hence, to give a certain financial stability to our family, I am obliged to work and to contribute to the household expenditures.' This means that, in a way or another, women are obliged to contribute to the household expenses. This assumption is confirmed by the next cluster of findings.

Table 43. Obligation of Contribution to Household Expenses

	Frequency	Percentage
No	108	36%
Yes	192	64%
Total	300	100%

Source: Fieldwork Results

19 In the Moroccan society, divorced women return to their parents' households when possible.

The investigation reveals that most respondents who contribute to the family expenses either take the responsibility to spend the income themselves and/or hand it over to one of the family members, mostly parents or husbands to pay for the household necessities. However, their contributions are not recognized and considered as not necessary. Rassam wrote:

> Formal economists here, as elsewhere in the Third World, tend to dismiss domestic production and home industries as marginal, and they consequently devalue women's contribution to the economy. In fact, these women [...] would normally appear in the official census as 'inactive' or 'unproductive' since they are not directly involved in wage labor. But the fact remains that women are actively participating in the economy, and their labor is being converted into real goods, whether these be destined for the auto consumption of the household itself or for sale at the market. (1980: 65)

In contrast, only 36% of respondents declare that they do not contribute to the household expenses. Their main justification is based on the presence of a male figure in the household who is in charge of providing money to pay the necessities of the household. Generally speaking, the male figure is either the father or the husband. This category of the informants is socially and culturally not assumed to contribute to the family economy. Moreover, this category of female workers admits the availability of several features in the informal sector that ensure that the worker's income does not help in securing a stable working status, which may allow the woman the role of the breadwinner. The income of these women is not stable and regular. It makes families not able to rely on it on a regular basis because of its seasonal nature and task accomplishment based payment (payment is given after the piece of work is handed over to the client).

Women's participation in shadow segments of work, as it was already demonstrated, is mainly motivated by economic necessities and, hence, used as a means to resist the daily household expenditures. In this respect, income from the informal economic activities is commonly regarded as a source to overcome the needs of the family. Self-employed women were requested to give their viewpoints on the contribution of their incomes to the following: food, health services, clothing, housing, education services, household equipment and transport.

The following table shows that almost all women in the research area contribute to the provision of food after engaging in self-employed activities. Data reveal that almost all participants 82% contribute to the provision of this human need for their family members while only 7.7% of the total population does not help in providing food.

Table 44. Food Accessibility[20]

	Frequency	Percentage
No	23	7.7%
Yes	246	82%
Total	269	89.7%

Source: Fieldwork Results

The data reveal that the purpose of women's contribution to food expenses is to secure a healthy eating and nutrition to their family members. Indeed, women increase their contribution to food security because they are forced by necessity. Their main objective is to achieve and maintain sufficient food accessibility and provision to feed themselves and their family members. Fatiha commented on her situation and said: 'my husband was working, but after a traffic accident, he becomes a victim of a physical handicap and he is no more able to move and work. I found myself obliged to work more and more to support my family needs.' This demonstrates that when women have an income, substantial evidence shows that their earnings are more likely to be spent on the provision of food, children's needs and other human basic needs. Since women are generally assumed to be the responsible for the household management, they are assumed to be not only responsible for food selection, preparation, but they are also supposed to spend their money on the feeding of their family members.

The next table below indicates the proportion of sample respondents who reported their contribution of their income accrued from self-employment to the ability of the household to sustain the health service costs. As demonstrated in the case of food accessibility, it can be equally argued that most women working informally in the city of Fez have the ability to meet at least the minimum requirement of having access to health

20 These data exclude 31 women who do not contribute to family expenses.

services while working in self-employed activities. Data reveal that 74.3% contribute to the health services whereas 15.3% show the opposite.

Table 45. Costs of Health Services[21]

	Frequency	Percentage
No	46	15.3%
Yes	223	74.3%
Total	269	89.7%

Source: Fieldwork Results

It is generally recognized that access to health care services is important for increasing the quality of a healthy life for women in this region of Morocco. In this respect, respondents reserve an amount of their incomes to sustain the expenses to access the health services though they face some barriers to benefit from these services. For example, they are confronted with high costs, lack of insurance coverage, and lack of availability of adequate and emergency services. Consequently, their contribution remains minimal and serves only to secure access to the public health care system since the private one is very expensive for most of the participants. Therefore, the obstacles to get access to quality health care may lead in most cases to delay in receiving appropriate care, inability to get preventive services, greater possibility to have poor health status.

Similar to the results stated in the table above, Table 46 indicates the portion of the sample's respondents who contribute to the clothing needs. As is the case with the other two indicators of poverty already debated above, it appears that most participants in the study area are able to contribute to the costs of clothes' provision for themselves and for their family members. Along the same line of reasoning, Safia said: 'my husband's income is not sufficient and I have to help with the house income to keep the family survival. I always buy clothes for myself and my children.' Like Safia, 73.3% of my informants in the sample contribute to the purchase of clothes mainly to children, whereas 16.3% do not consider the clothing provision as their priority to spend their own incomes.

21 These data exclude 31 women who do not contribute to family expenses.

Table 46. Clothing Provision[22]

	Frequency	Percentage
No	49	16.3%
Yes	220	73.3%
Total	269	89.7%

Source: Fieldwork Results

Another surviving strategy of self-employed women is the provision of clothes for different family members, especially children. Indeed, most women maintained that they insist on providing suitable clothing depending on the situation and the seasons. In this perspective, the contribution of women's income to the provision of clothing as a human basic need is believed to be an undeniable key element to reduce household poverty. Another different issue of self-employed female workers is the contribution of incomes accrued from self-employment to the ability to sustain household availability and to meet its costs. Table 47 indicates that most women 53.3% do not contribute to this human need. This may be explained by the fact that most of them, as previously indicated in Chapter 3, either live with other family members or with their husbands who are the main providers of the place of residence. 36.3% of respondents who contribute to the housing expenses are in large part women living in single parental households, particularly in the cases of single mothers, widows, and divorcees.

Table 47. Housing Availability[23]

	Frequency	Percentage
No	160	53.3%
Yes	109	36.3%
Total	269	89.7%

Source: Fieldwork Results

22 These data exclude 31 women who do not contribute to family expenses.

23 These data exclude 31 women who do not contribute to family expenses.

Similarly, the next table indicates the proportion of sample respondents who contribute to the costs of education services. The contradiction seems, in the case of other indicators previously demonstrated, that 66.7% of self-employed women in the city of Fez are not able to meet the costs of education services. This may be explained by the fact that most women with children are not in the age of schooling. Others reveal that they are obliged to push their children to drop out of school in order to join the labor market to increase the opportunities of income generation.

Table 48. Costs of Education Services[24]

	Frequency	Percentage
No	200	66.7%
Yes	69	23%
Total	269	89.7%

Source: Fieldwork Results

This study reveals that most households with children know the participation of women in the education costs with a rate of 23%. These women have their children study in public schools. Their contribution includes different costs such as purchase of school materials (books, pens ...) as well as paying extra hours courses for kids in some cases. These categories of women believe in the importance of education for their children. They survive the hardships of work in order to secure a minimal amount of income to pay for the costs of education services, as they are convinced it is an individual's human right from which most of them are deprived.

Concerning the next table, data indicate that the portion of respondents who reported their contribution to the payment of transportation costs is nearly similar. Indeed, statistics show that 48.7% are responsible for the payment for this service. This is mostly among women who have children studying and they need to take public transportations to reach their schools. Others reveal that their work obliges them to move from one place to another, either to buy raw materials, to meet their clients or

24 These data exclude 31 women who do not contribute to family expenses.

to sell their products. So, there is a need to reserve an amount of money to transport costs.

Table 49. Transportation Costs[25]

	Frequency	Percentage
No	123	41%
Yes	146	48.7%
Total	269	89.7%

Source: Fieldwork Results

The last element that self-employed female workers may contribute to is related to household equipment. Indeed, the table below shows that the average contribution is seen to be 58.7%. Other respondents claim that the household equipment is not their primary interest where they can spend amounts of their income. For instance, 31% do not find it as a necessity

Table 50. Purchase of Household Equipment[26]

	Frequency	Percentage
No	93	31%
Yes	176	58.7%
Total	269	89.7%

Source: Fieldwork Results

Many women in the study area do not consider that purchasing household equipment as a necessity while others view it as an important thing. Accordingly, many respondents buy different indoor household tools. They mostly do not pay the household appliances at once. They rather prefer to finance the purchase through monthly payment and sometimes for extended periods of time.

It can clearly be concluded from the above discussion that women's income accumulated from self-employed activities has a positive impact

25 These data exclude 31 women who do not contribute to family expenses.

26 These data exclude 31 women who do not contribute to family expenses.

on the households. Indeed, many women in the city of Fez indicate that their incomes help them contribute to most human needs. It also has an important role in contributing to the household poverty reduction in terms of ensuring household food accessibility, the ability to meet the costs of health services, ability to secure the need of clothing as well as the ability of the household to meet the costs of purchasing household equipment. However, housing costs and education services remain of less interest to most self-employed workers.

However, many interviewees emphasized that their contribution is for daily consumption and not for long periods of time. Accordingly, this argument enhances the idea that the participation of women in meeting the basic needs only allows them to secure a survivalist level and sometimes to trespass the poverty line. Moreover, the contribution of women to the household expenditure makes their place in their families and society at large very important. In fact, it makes them more confident, more assertive, and better able to face and handle systematic gender inequalities. Despite the low income earned by women in the shadow self-employed activities, their work enables most of them to become economic agents of change. This happens through the increase of employment opportunities, development of productivity, access to markets, and ability of decision making in their lives. However, in certain cases of inability to work, women face income insecurity. For instance, a brief period of incapacity can leave the woman worker and her family without enough income to live on. Moreover, the sickness of a member of the family or the woman herself can result in extra costs, which may cause a kind of destroy to the balance of the household budget.

Further, women are rather very reluctant to divulge their approximate earnings on a monthly basis. For example, it has been shown through personal interviews with female self-employed workers that they control their own finances. Women generally spend most of their income to sustain their basic needs expenses. They spent most of their money on food, education, clothes and had very little to spend on themselves. On the opposite, the vast majority lamented the low earnings, which did not always cover their household and living expenses. Below are some of the comments from the females who contribute to their household needs.

Naima mentioned that: 'I buy the necessities of the household. If I have extra money, I make some savings, but not regularly.'

Amal further noted that: 'Because I am the only breadwinner of the family, I have to buy everything for my kids such as food, clothes and the payment of school fees. I used to buy necessary things for myself like a Jellaba in Ramadan and sometimes I do not buy for myself. I prefer to invest most of my money on my kids' schools and food security.'

Opposing the argument of Lister that: 'access to an independent income strengthens women's economic position within couples as well as providing them with the capacity to establish autonomous households' (2004: 61). The findings of this research reveal that some women are not satisfied with their incomes. They declare that their earnings, particularly when they work seasonally or temporarily, are frequently not sufficient to provide genuine economic independence in terms of economic balance within the household or the ability to maintain an independent poverty free household. This is due to the fact that in most households, families in fact rely on more than one income providers. The next set of results deals with the ways of the use of personal income.

Women and the Spending of Income

The present section attempts to examine the ways women in the city of Fez make use of their incomes generated from self-employed activities on a more personal level. It encompasses a discussion of whether women in this region of Morocco have the freedom to personally manage their incomes or they know the intervention of some family members when referring to their income use. Moreover, this section attempts to provide analysis of women's possibilities to reserve a part of their incomes to spend it on their personal necessities. This will be followed by an examination of women's saving opportunities while working in the shadow sector.

Despite the fact that women earn a reasonable amount of money via their productive activities, they are not fully responsible for its management. In other words, women may not have the ability to gain personal benefits because of their little control over the household resources. On the one hand, this is due to their earnings, which are appropriated by the males in the family (either the husband, or the father, or the brother). On the other hand, they are diverted to expenditure on others. In the same perspective, Bradshaw and Linneker provided three fairly generalized patterns:

> namely, that women have fewer possibilities to translate the work into income; that when women do have the income they find it more difficult to transform this into decision making capacity, and that when women do make decisions these are less likely to enhance their own well-being as that of others. (2003: 9)

In the present investigation, statistics reveal that 80% of respondents have the freedom of income use, whereas only 20% of workers have limits in dealing freely with their revenues generated from the self-employed activities in the shadow sector in the city of Fez.

Table 51. Freedom of Income Use

	Frequency	Percentage
No	60	20%
Yes	240	80%
Total	300	100%

Source: Fieldwork Results

80% of respondents of the questionnaires claim that they have changed the traditional practice of handing over their income to their husbands or fathers, which has, therefore, created a change and imbalance in power structures within households. For instance, some married women declare that the disapproval of their male partners concerning their status as the main breadwinners. This is maintained by Chant who argued that masculinity is so much bound with household headership and that in order to earn respect as 'men', males have to exert authority over women as households' heads.[27]

The majority of females in this study have full control of their finances. In other words, they have their freedom to spend their income and to take control of it without the intervention of their male counterparts. This means that their decision making is not affected. This finding reveals that

27 See Chant, (1997a).

as most of these women are running survivalist economic activities, their earnings are spent on basic human needs as mentioned previously in this chapter with little money left to spend on themselves.[28]

Moreover, interviewees report that there has been an improvement for them in terms of freedom of income management. This is mainly pertinent in the case of single women and women without partners such as divorcees, widows and abandoned women. However, many women involved in a marital union report that it is the husband who takes control and decisions of the household. In this regard, female heads of households express their advantageous position with respect to married women. This is mainly due to different key factors such as the fact that they feel better off, they have relatively felt independent of male domination, and they do not experience gender inequality at the household, where they can make their own decisions.

As far as these women's incomes and self-use is concerned, data reveal that women's participation in the expenses of the household gives them the ability to make self-sacrifice and not use an amount for themselves. In this connection, the results of quantitative data demonstrate that 18% of the informants frequently prefer to contribute to the family needs (i.e. food, warmth, and clothes.) Their aim is to protect other family members, especially children as it was maintained by khadija who is a married baker and a mother of four children. This means that women experience a lot of stress as they generally act as the responsible for money management in low-income families. Hence, this stress can result in damaging effects related to physical and mental health although some informants declare that they have proudly done this for their family members.

Table 52. Income and Self-use

	Frequency	Percentage
No	54	18%
Yes	246	82%
Total	300	100%

Source: Fieldwork Results

28 See Table 52.

As demonstrated previously in this chapter, on the one hand, many women revealed that they devote their incomes to meet the daily different expenses of their families and their households. On the other hand, those who are able to devote a part of their incomes, be it large or small, to cover their personal expenses are really considered as an important category. Table 52 reveals that 82% of respondents retain a small part of their revenues to satisfy their personal expenses. In this regard, Safae explained that:

> the money I earn from vending clothes is mainly needed to contribute to the family expenditures and to buy the children's clothes and school supplies. Sometimes, I use my money for my personal needs. I actually spend it on clothes for myself, makeup, and I save a small amount for crisis time.

In this regard, Table 53 shows the various things women may spend their money on. They encompass 80% of women who spend money on their personal care such as buying clothes, cosmetics, hairdressing, shopping, etc. 36% of women prefer to go on excursions with their families, followed by 14% of women who visit their parents to help them or help their sisters and brothers who are still in school age as well as those who are still unemployed. 9.3% of women prefer to save their money on buying jewelries. The 4.7% as the rest of the sample prefers to spend money on other things.

Table 53. Things on which Women Spend their Incomes[29]

	Yes	No
Personal care	80	2
Excursions	36	46
Parents visits	14	68
Jewelry Purchase	9	73
Others	5	77

In connection with the income generated by self-employed women and their personal savings, the results of the research demonstrate that most

29 These data include answers of 246 respondents who spend some of their income on self-use (82%).

women 62.7% in the study are able to save some of their income although they spend on household expenditure. They are more likely to have disposable income and have savings accounts in financial institutions. Even though many women are own account workers, they have larger opportunities to keep small amounts of their earnings for future need as it was confirmed by Hassania: 'al dirham al abyad liyawmi asewad' 'the white Dirham is for the black day.' Farida, another interviewee further pointed out: 'yes, I save some money aside. My parents do not know about it. I always keep an amount of money from my work at a post account. I have always to be prepared for all kinds of future crises.' From this statement, one may suggest that by saving some amounts of money from their incomes, women lessen the risk of financial insecurity and their dependence on others including their husbands or the employed family members. In other words, saving money is a strategy by which women become able to take some control over their personal lives.

It should also be noted that most respondents who have the saving ability generally report improvement in the standards of living of their family members. Using the saved amounts of money in times of necessity, being able to buy household needs and to meet the children's needs of schooling are stated to be some of the justifications regarding the benefits of saving some money.

Table 54. Income and Personal Savings

	Frequency	Percentage
No	112	37.3%
Yes	188	62.7%
Total	300	100%

Source: Fieldwork Results

On the other hand, 37.3% declare that they do not earn enough to keep aside money. The overall argument is that they run small businesses and most of their income is spent on necessities and daily needs. At the time of the interview, Loubna, a divorced and illiterate embroiderer aged 36 years had school aged children and she was divorced a couple of years earlier, after which she moved to live with her parents. She had been divorced twice, and both times had to move into her parent's house with her children and re-establish herself. Loubna has irregular income to spend on human basic needs such as contributing to food, clothes, and education as well as health service costs. After participating to the daily family expenditures and other fixed expenses, she has nothing left from her income to be saved. She commented on her economic situation and said: 'I work from hand to mouth. It is impossible for me to save a Dirham.'

Other respondents also expressed similar feelings. Aicha gave the following reason for her inability to save money: 'Sometimes, people come to insist on you to take clothes on credit, but they never come back to pay you. Then I have to take the money I am saving to pay in his/her place.' Consequently, this shows that it is no way to keep an amount of money saved for periods of crisis. It is worth noting that even with low incomes, those who report that are able to save some money, they use different saving places, as is clear from Table 55.

Table 55. Places of Income Saving[30]

	Percentage
Bank account	15%
Post account	21%
Group saving	9.30%
Jewelry purshase	0.70%
Others	16.70%

An important strategy used by women to save some amount of their income is via group savings schemes or as it is named *dart*, as these are named in the Moroccan dialect. Aksikas provides a summary of this process of saving money as the following:

> The most important communal element is displayed through their 'loan' system, known in certain regions of the country as *dart* 'rotation', and in others as *qur'a* 'lottery'. *Dart*, or *qur'a*, is a network of people who contribute an equal sum of money, but with only one person taking the total sum of money at once, usually on a weekly or monthly basis. All the members of the loan network rotate or take

30 These data are based on the answers of 188 women who save some of their income (62.7%).

> turns (and from here the term dart) in getting the money contributed by all the members of the community; the decision of the exact order in which each of the members receives the total sum usually depends on pure chance (and from here the term *qur'a*). Most often, a lottery is held to decide the order in which each of the members would receive the total sum of money. However, the whole group might also decide to give priority to someone in dire need of the money, and in a number of cases, these lotteries or networks are precisely initiated to help a friend, relative or neighbor in need. (2007: 259)

One may deduce from the above discussion that the increase in women's participation in the shadow sector is mostly enhanced by the limited opportunities for employment in the organized sector, which is covered by regular financial returns and social protection schemes. In Morocco, formal wage employment is generally not dominant among a big portion of this society. It does not present a predominant mode of employment. Instead, as it was found in the investigation, the majority of the labor force opts for self-employed activities in the informal sector as a source of survival. It has obviously been noticed that there is significant under-utilization of labor as well as the returns to work, which are found to insufficiently contribute to the overall poverty reduction.

Conclusion

By way of conclusion, it should be noted that the lives of self-employed women in the city of Fez reflect the importance of development thinking over the decades. The investigatory journey above, from the so-called effect of women's main economic characteristics of their employment, through the exploitative situation of women's financial responsibilities to the shifting emphasis from basic human needs for the use of income provide sufficient evidence in support of the assumption that women's informal employment contributes to household poverty reduction.

Equally important, the findings have crucial economic and policy implications. The main results of the analysis are that the economic contribution of self-employed women to the household increases by all aspects of poverty, i.e. unemployment and lower educational status of the husband, availability of children, structure and size of the family, among others. It is obvious that the majority of the respondents are mainly contributing to the household financial expenditure due to the pressure of an insufficient household budget. Accordingly, they are struggling to secure a source of livelihood for family survival. As a result, an increase in productivity and income of informally employed women may have trickled down the effects on reducing the household poverty.

Moreover, it is worth noting that the correlation between the shadow sector and poverty reduction challenge is more than a coincidence. The empirical evidence showed that there is a positive link between women's work in this sector and the contribution to the reduction of the household poverty. Hence, the alleviation of poverty, which the Moroccan government grapples with, cannot be achieved without having a comprehensive policy for the shadow sector and its workers. For instance, addressing the needs of most workers can result into two issues at the same time: the needs of the persons working in the informal sector and those of the people affected by poverty. In this regard, given the crucial overlap between the two variables, most strategies and development programs can be jointly developed and implemented to ensure a sustainable development of the impoverished categories.

It is, however, important to emphasize here that the development and emancipation of the vulnerable categories of the Moroccan society are enhanced through the inclusion of women in political and social life. Chapter 5 will focus on examining the linkages between women's informal employment and their engagement in political, social and domestic spheres.

CHAPTER 5

Women's Self-employment and Emancipation

Abstract

In most developing countries, women are viewed among the vulnerable segments of society. Having reviewed their economic participation in the previous chapters, the present one tackles the political and social dimensions of self-employed women emancipation. Indeed, participation in political life and community-based activism as well as cooperatives can be used as breeding grounds for their empowerment[1] by enhancing their specific knowledge and capacities. In this respect, 'promoting women's empowerment is essential because in most cases women are responsible for their children and for their family, thus empowering women is empowering the society in large' (World Bank: 2001). The aim of this chapter is to develop a framework to serve as an instrument for establishing the extent to which women participate in other activities without economic features. It is divided into two general sections. The first one develops an understanding of women's participation in politics and community based activism. The focus of this section is to provide justification about the participation of self-employed women in the political sphere, their involvement in cooperatives as well as their associative activism. The second section examines the link between women's shadow work and the private sphere responsibilities. It establishes a discussion about their participation in domestic labor, which is followed by analysis of data concerning perception of housework. The chapter closes up with a discussion of women's reconciliation between productive and reproductive responsibilities.

1 For the purpose of the present book, the term empowerment implies that women have the right to participate in all disciplines and to take decisions. Individuals have to work together and all take advantage from the extensive influence one individual could not achieve singly. Empowerment further means a process of personal development that is sped up by external support.

Women's Political and Community-Based Activism

The present section attempts to discuss the results of the fieldwork concerning women's participation in the political sphere as well as community based activism in the city of Fez. The former has a very wide meaning. In the present book, it is linked to women's participation in political parties, their types of membership as well as their negative political consciousness linked to this participation. The latter concentrates on the provision of findings about development based activisms through the participation of women in cooperative and associative work within their communities.

Political Participation of Women

Nowadays, Morocco is characterized by democratic and social movements which seek to achieve equal opportunities to all its citizens. Indeed, the Moroccan government established certain initiatives to end up women's marginalization from politics. In this respect, the political arena in Morocco becomes open to both men and women. However, opposite to my expectations, the findings of the present study confirm the low participation of women in politics. In other words, the majority of respondents do not exhibit their interest to join the political field.

The results in Table 56 below demonstrate that the political participation of women is low. They reveal that 81% of women in the city of Fez are not officially affiliated to any political party. Their absence is justified by various reasons: the first cause is linked to women's lack of trust in the Moroccan political system. My respondents confirm that the political sphere in the history of Morocco is full of unforgettable events, which include oppression, corruption, violation of human rights, barbaric practices against people who wanted to break the silence. Morocco has equally witnessed various discriminatory practices against people who attempted to make their voices heard publicly over several decades; therefore, such unfair behaviors demonstrate women's strong fear of this vicious past, which creates their negative perceptions of the world of politics and reinforces the absence of trust into politicians and their discourses.

Table 56. Women's Political Participation

	Frequency	Percentage
No	243	81%
Yes	57	19%
Total	300	100%

Source: Fieldwork Results

Other respondents reveal that their absence from the political sphere is linked to their lack of knowledge about the available political parties. A case in point is Fatiha, a 28-year-old young seamstress, who ironically said: 'I do not know how many political parties we have in Morocco. All that I know is that I have to go the day of the elections and vote for a sign, which I ignore which party it represents.' This demonstrates that women's ignorance about the availability of parties distances them from politics. Instead, their voices are only used during elections as voters. This might justify women's lack of interest in how public affairs are structured. Generally, women's lack of awareness about the political parties puts them at risk of low participation in the political sphere.[2]

In spite of the fact that this category of respondents speaks about politics with irony, others provide various issues explaining their absence from the political sphere. Firstly, women's low level of the educational attainment represents a constraint to invade the political arena. Indeed, more than 64.3% of illiterate women and those who did not trespass the primary level of education declare that they are not happy because they were deprived from having access to education services. Accordingly, they were deprived of their right of being full citizens, and consequently, from their full participation in the social and political arenas. Thus, they are

2 See Sadiqi (2003), op. cit., 92 for detailed discussion about women's negative attitudes towards politics.

unable to deconstruct the stereotypical images about women as passive consumers and inactive participants. This is emphasized in the statement by Fatiha: 'women may not be in political parties because they are mostly illiterate or have low education. Moreover, they cannot go through the systems of political parties.' Moreover, if educated women are under-represented in the political sphere, then illiterate women are near to invisible. Saida declared that: 'Unfortunately, I am not eligible to be a politician. I do not have the educational level that allows me to be a member of a political party like other females who have degrees from schools or universities.' This indicates that education of women still lagged behind that of men. Thus, Morocco could not develop if it fails to tap women's talent for full participation in society. This is emphasized by the saying: 'if you educate a man, you educate an individual, but if you educate a woman, you educate the nation.'

Secondly, the patriarchal structure of society strengthens the lack of women's engagement in politics. It operates at all levels to degrade women and allocate them to lower positions than their male counterparts. Historically speaking, it was regular that it is the men who get access to the public sphere and decision-making positions while women are culturally allocated to the private sphere, especially when their sources of income are guaranteed by others within the household. Moreover, the patriarchal system maintains the tradition of males holding primary power posts, which keep them predominating in roles of political leadership; therefore, this situation allows them social privilege and more control in the private sphere. Safia, a wife and a mother of four children, pointed out that: 'politics and elections are for men. I have kids at home who need my presence, and it is not of my priorities to be in a political party.' This statement demonstrates an example of comments, which categorize the areas to which men or women best attribute themselves.

Thirdly, the nature of the political sphere represents a major constraint to women's access to politics. It is assumed to be a male sphere par excellence, which has denied women not only equal participation before the law, but also equal access, control over resources and support.

Khadija, a young graduate student, speaks about her experience in this male-dominated field:

> politics are the males' professions. I will never participate in political life because there are no female role models to look up to in this area. All that I see is men who have more power and control while women are less likely to enter into politics and to see it as a viable option.

From this statement, one may deduce that this category of women would not struggle to get heard in political life because of the negative attitudes about the nature of the political arena over generations. The above mentioned are important social indicators that have a direct bearing on the incidence of female absence from the political sphere. They reflect the levels of social exclusion that is produced, justified and perpetuated in the city of Fez and the Moroccan society at large.

It is worth mentioning that the message of women's negative perception about the political field in Morocco is transmitted through their non-verbal communication. Many informants' dissatisfaction about politics through their facial expressions is also explicitly echoed through their voice tone. Fatiha, a middle age carpet maker, expressed her negative experience with politics as follows: 'I don't want to talk about politics. I did not earn from it except troubles and sufferings. My husband is in jail because of politics, and I am now working to earn a living for my children.' However, these negative attitudes towards women's participation in the political sphere do not seem to exclude other women to invade the political arena, which is culturally fabricated to serve as an authoritarian male domain par excellence.

Data revealed that 19% of respondents actively participate in the political field. These women are the highly educated ones and mostly have a male relative who is already a member in these institutions. Merriam pointed out that: 'my father has a good position in the Istiklal Party, which made my entrance very easy and equitable participation is no more a challenge.' These respondents were asked to describe their positions within political parties and Table 57 depicts that 18.3% of the respondents are ordinary members, with lower participation in board positions which account for 0.7%.

Table 57. Types of Women's Membership within Political Parties[3]

	Percentage
Member	0.7%
Member within offices	18.3%

The more women are participating in politics, the more they are personally empowered. However, the above results show that 18.3% of the respondents are politically active. This is consistent with the reality of politics in the Moroccan society which shows that the Moroccan political sphere largely remains a male domain and restricted to individuals with a (relatively high) level of education. Although women's participation has increased in the last few years, it was shown that only a few women are members of political parties. Their presence remains shallow and limited by various social, cultural and economic constraints. This may be justified by the lack of commitment or know-how of participation to break the beliefs and customs of the society that hinder women's participation in political and social life.

Cooperative Involvement

Membership in cooperatives does not seem to be popular among self-employed workers in the city of Fez. In fact, only 10% of the respondents are members of cooperatives. The percentage is relative to those who both practice their activities at home and market their products in cooperatives, or those who work within the locals of cooperatives themselves. The participation in these solidarity and cooperation institutes help to dramatically uplift the income of indigenous women in the city of Fez.

Women's organization into small cooperatives helps them produce and sell manual products using their skills relying on a mixture of traditional and modern methods. At the same time, they connect with other social actors to keep their businesses active and operating. 'Being a member of a

3 These data are concerned with 57 women who participate in the political arena (19%).

carpet cooperative has brought me many benefits,' said Halima, 45-year-old single woman and a member of one of the oldest carpet cooperatives in the city of Fez. She further added:

> I have been able to collaborate with other women to develop our artistic skills and produce wonderful pieces. When I enrolled in the cooperative, I became able to organize myself into work, to be trained to use the new technology, and also to be trained to run the cooperative, administration, management, marketing and all aspects ...

Table 58. Women's Cooperative Membership

	Frequency	Percentage
No	270	90%
Yes	30	10%
Total	300	100%

Source: Fieldwork Results

Despite the economic aspect linked to cooperatives, they also have a crucial role to promote social interests of its members. Firstly, members of cooperatives live in harmony. For instance, all the members agree that their engagement in cooperative work is driven by the nature of their enterprises. This means that they are a member driven business enterprises in which decisions balance in a harmonious manner the pursuit of profit with the needs of all members. They establish a social order based on the spirit of sharing and cooperating. Secondly, cooperatives are essential in developing the self-esteem of its members. For example, through both the promotion of the economic interests of the cooperative's members and the creation of better conditions for sustainable businesses, women in the study area are able to develop. Samira, a member of the embroidery cooperative, said: 'when I enrolled in the cooperative, I did not have the economic profit as a primary objective. I was much more interested in the human growth and the personal development.' In the same line of argument, Tesfay and Tadele provided some aspects of the role of cooperatives in promoting social empowerment of women:

> cooperatives have a role to play in alleviating different shocks, and paving the way towards recovery that is socially and economically sound and sustainable. Ultimately, cooperatives can create a safe environment where women increase their self-confidence, identify their own challenges, take decisions and manage risks. As a result, women are empowered and become active agents of change, entrepreneurs and promoters of social transformation who can improve their own lives and those of the community. (2013: 2)

Thus, cooperatives are very crucial business entities in enhancing the social and economic situation of self-employed women in the city of Fez. The latter is guaranteed to members by improving their power and income. The results of the present study correlate with the findings of Ghebremichael who investigated the role of cooperatives in empowering women:

> On an overall assessment, it can be concluded that cooperatives are rendering fruitful services to the society concerned especially to women. The survey reveals that the women are able to enrich their lives. They are fully satisfied with the services rendered by these cooperative societies. They got recognition in the society and also economic interdependence in the family. Hence, it is needless to say that cooperatives are playing a very important role in the empowerment of women through various schemes. (2013: 53)

Because of their economic nature, cooperatives, as enterprises, play an interesting role in enhancing the economic well-being of their members. For instance, respondents declare that one of the economic features of being a member of a cooperative does not contribute to the improvement of their income since the sum must be divided accordingly among its members. Thus, the little revenue they may gain does not allow them to secure a regular income to meet continuously their expenditure on food, clothing, transport, education and others.

In contrast, 90% of respondents in the sample do not belong to any of these cooperatives for two main factors. Firstly, the structure of the Moroccan society, especially the nature of Fez, as a traditional city, impedes the mobility of women. Many conservative families do not support loosening traditional gender roles and restrictions on the grounds that women in the city of Fez are required to conform to the norms of the traditional society. For example, Hassania, a mother of four children and a seamstress, said: 'restricting females' mobility has no basis in Islam. It is related to our culture and traditions.' Meanwhile, Safia, another seamstress and a widow, confirmed that: 'the interpretation of religious texts and the strict customs, as they are transmitted from one generation to another, are the key factors that curtail women's mobility and rights in Fez in particular and Morocco in general.' Therefore, the variety of interpretation confirms that it is due to culture and customary law, which are considered central. Safia further points out that: 'if all women were not restricted by the traditions and were not supplanted by conservatist customs, then the issue of whether Moroccan women have equal access to the labor market would be solved.' One may deduce from the above statements that the restriction of women's mobility is derived from the extreme concern for female purity and family honor. Women who may socialize in public spaces and may have contact with men who are not relatives can be harassed. This implies that women must have no contact or interaction with the opposite gender.

Secondly, the patriarchal system, which is dominant in almost all families, limits women's access to the public sphere. Since the public sphere of life is male dominated, women are expected to stay in the secluded areas of their homes. They are assumed to minimize social interactions. In this respect, Khadija said: 'the restriction of women's employment in cooperatives is linked to the patriarchal system, which confirms that the best place for a woman to serve is in her own home.' This shows that a woman may not be allowed to get access to the public sphere and be employed without the approval of a male guardian.

Moreover, a woman's work outside the home is also prohibited as it may interfere with her traditional gender-based roles, or with her eternal duty of child rearing. As a consequence, this segment of women is generally discouraged from getting access to the public sphere. Commonly given reasons for the discouragement of women include, on the one hand, that working in cooperatives needs a woman to go out of the house for the whole day. On the other hand, the family responsibilities are the first obstacles restricting women's access to public life. Additionally, in a patriarchal society, men are the center of activity. All that they do is considered important for the progression of society. This means that men living in a patriarchal system must be in control of all social and familial situations. For example, Karima describes her situation as follows:

> I live in a system which still operates under the patriarchal influence not only in my parents' house but also in my conjugal house. I wasn't allowed to work when I was living with my parents because my father did not believe in women's employment outside the house. When I moved to my husband's house, I thought I would have a chance to gain my own income. Unfortunately, I discovered that the subordination of women to men is still prevalent. I discovered that women are not only treated as subordinate to men, but also they are subject to various discriminatory practices if they want equal treatment in terms of access to public spheres.

This statement demonstrates that the exploitation and oppression women experience may be related not only to their biological differences or sex, which is natural, but also to their gender differences which is a social construction.[4] Thus, it is important to reconsider this social and ideological construct.

To this end, government initiatives and non-government organizations are representing crucial work to promote the situation of women and their empowerment. For instance, though I am aware that it will take many generations in order to make men and women be themselves without society dictating their roles, changing gender roles may be something enlightening and allowing each individual to benefit from equal resources. As a result, considerable awareness creation should be derived by the appropriate stakeholders through advocacy campaigns and policies. These techniques may be about sensitizing people about various issues which may include the following: women's necessity to attain education, the change of women's actual position in terms of their capacity to make decisions and

4 The traditional linguistic distinction between gender and sex differentiates gender as the linguistic description of words as feminine, masculine or neuter, from sex, as a designation of biological differences. Gender denotes women and men depending on social and cultural factors, as social role or identity, which has been confirmed by many scholars. Humm, for instance, defines gender as 'a culturally-shaped group of attributes and behaviors given to the female or to the male' (Humm, 1989: 84). West and Zimmerman confirm that 'It is individuals who do gender' (1998: 112). In contrast, sex denotes human males and females depending on biological features.

be independent, increase women's chances of changing their position of housekeeper and be financially independent of their husbands, etc. Thus, trying to take a step forward in securing these elements may be an important contribution to women in the city of Fez in particular and Morocco in general. This initiative may help them to reduce the opportunities of facing obstacles and to get access to public life like men.

Activism within Associations

Associations make a valuable contribution to the development of communities. Most of the times, they closely link with the community as they serve in a consultative manner and work from a basic needs perspective. Cited in Skalli's prominent article, Belarbi describes associations as the following:

> On the non-governmental side, women's groups and NGOs with the development objective proved to be effective instruments in breaking the cycle of vulnerability and social exclusions of women. With the help of national and international funds as well as expertise, NGOs operate as useful entry points for initiating pertinent strategies, and developing activities aimed at reaching poor households. Such actions range from literacy classes offered to women of all age groups, consciousness-raising and initiations, to legal and health issues, counseling and assistance in the development of income-generating activities. (Skalli, 2001: 85)

The role of associations and women's NGOs is to work on the promotion of women's rights, emancipation, participation in different scopes of life, which encourages a culture of responsible members of society and not passive subjects. Ennaji, in his prominent study on the role of women's NGOs in the Moroccan society, distinguished between two types of these institutions. The first type of feminine NGOs targets community based activism since it 'focuses on the service provision, filling the gap left by the deficient state structures in terms of economic and social development'. (Ennaji, 2005: 83) These associations focus their work on areas of human rights, social and economic development of citizens, access to human services such as education and health. Additionally, they do advocacy work to fight discrimination against women, combat violence and eradicate poverty. The second type of associations according to Ennaji 'focuses on advocacy and lobbying with the objective of defending a democratic vision of society. Human rights groups are the most prominent examples of this second type' (2005: 83).

In fact, 75.7% of women in the city of Fez show low level of adherence to associations. Almost all of them indicate that if they have more time left, they would not spend it on their social life through membership in associations. For example, Sanae, a traditional button maker and at the same time an embroiderer, points out that: 'with the lower quality employment opportunities, adherence to associations is not one of my priorities. I prefer to maximize my opportunities of income instead of becoming a member of an association.' This may demonstrate that their work as self-employed would have more importance for the majority of respondents. Similarly, Rachida, a traditional clothes maker claims that there are various factors behind women's interest in working more than associative participation. She said: 'I prefer to focus on my economic activity instead of enrolling in an association. This is aggravated by the presence of children at home, family life responsibilities, daily necessities, etc.'

Furthermore, the low participation is relative to the negative attitudes towards these organizations. A vivid example is the comments made by Salwa, a young cookies maker and a mother of three children, who said:

> cultural barriers and negative attitudes concerning associations impede an equitable inclusion of women in social activism ... It is recognized that access to these organizations is consistently difficult because of their nature as mixed sex institutions, they do not allow women to make decisions on their own, and for their best interests. They may be spaces where women may experience unequal treatment in services.

Hence, one may estimate that the negative attitudes and stereotypes can lead to women's exclusion from public life in the form of negative comments and social isolation. Fear of being discriminated against based on gender can also mean that women do not seek guidance for development. In this regard, I may suggest that organizations can address negative attitudes to make sure that both men and women take part in their activities through various elements. They include education on human rights, which works best to change the mentalities alongside a strong proactive strategy to prevent unequal participation. This can be achieved through provision of education and training programs, anti-harassment and anti-discrimination policies, and awareness campaigns, etc.

Table 59. Women's Associative Membership

	Frequency	Percentage
No	227	75.7%
Yes	73	24.3%
Total	300	100%

Source: Fieldwork Results

Almost all women in the city under investigation linked their adherence to associations with rest and free time. Women working in self-employment activities often have no time for social life. They are mainly interested in their self-development often through their work. Fatima, a home-based *mâalma* (i.e. a person who works as a traditional clothes maker and a teacher for other young apprentices), points out:

> I want to focus on other things instead of enrolling in an association. I want to meet new people, keep developing, and be updated about what's happening around me. However, I do not have time to waste. While working, I keep track of things and I meet a lot of clients, whereby I discover a lot ... So, I do not need to be in an association. My job is sufficient for my personal development.

While one may assume that work and private life are intertwined, enrolling in an association does not allow these women to find a deeper meaning in their lives. Based on the interviews conducted with the heads and members of some professional associations, it was reported that these institutions have a crucial role in developing women's skills. Put differently, it correlates with their main objectives to train girls and women as well as to qualify them to get access to the labor market. Most importantly, these associations make important efforts to reduce females' unemployment in the city of Fez.

Along the same line of reasoning, women working in the service sector such as clothes, cosmetic and shoes vendors indicate that their work is their sole source of personal development. Their participation in associations is not considered a source of emancipation. They consider that spending more time on going inwards to develop their businesses, to know which choices to make and to feel how to deal with failure experiences is of great importance. Others reveal that reserving a personal time to enroll into an association is not important. They rather prefer to take care of their children and work on the development of their careers. For that reason, many women look for opportunities to expand their economic activities through trainings and work related sessions. In sum, the results presented in this regard stress the importance of maintaining a subjective definition of a work development perspective instead of participating in social life via association enrollment. Self-employed women are more interested in meeting their personal economic goals through work expansion instead of being part of the associative tissue, which is mainly a social practice.

However, Table 59 shows that only a small number of the respondents, 24.3% who are official members of associations. Their affiliation is mainly in professional associations, which provide different services to the community, namely '*Point de Depart*' '*Starting Point*' (ESPOD) to which most seamstresses, embroiders, cookie makers, decorators belong. Other associations provide exclusive skills trainings in bakery, drawing on glass, knitting and others. For example, the *Association Feminine al ɛahd El-Jadid* [The Feminine Association of the New Era] is prominent in promoting young girls and women's skills in various domains. Most of the respondents affiliated to this association are future informal workers. Their participation in associative work may allow them more visibility in social organization at the local level. It may also change the traditional attitudes about women. Kaoutar, a young graduate student and an embroiderer declares that: 'my participation in an association allows me more revaluation of myself and gives me more self-confidence.'

Moreover, other respondents view that social empowerment of women is a continuous process whereby they are able to freely exercise their rights and duties with confidence. Their membership in associations is a crucial element to serve this purpose. In the interview I conducted with the head of the *Association Feminine al ɛahd El-Jadid*, which is an association of human development in the city of Fez, she believes that women must have the right to be members of society-based activities. They should share their ideas and receive others' ideas to develop their opportunities of freedom of expression and impression. She further explains that women in the shadow sector need to be involved in social activities and to contribute not only to their own existence, but also to the future of their community, in particular, and to their society at large. Finally, she claims that women's emancipation implies the right to externalize their skills and share their personal experiences through civil society activism.

In conclusion, the research on self-employed women in the informal sector suggests that many of them are not members of associations. Given the importance of collective action to inclusive planning, these low numbers of adherence of women constitute a challenge to both existing associations and local authorities. Further work is needed on how to motivate women to be active participants in these organizations, and how the state can create a suitable environment conducive to the development of associations. Hence, one may deduce that women's active membership in associations is an important means to pave the way for women's empowerment mechanisms to take place. The empirical evidence provided here suggests that women should be added to the list of participants in the associative work, which in turn necessitates future research to interrogate the reasons behind who is included and who is excluded in the current formation of civil society organizations. Nevertheless, one may assume, based on the results of the present fieldwork, that the low participation of women in the research area in these institutions is limited by the nature of their work as well as their socio-demographic characteristics.

In general, the absence of respondents from the political field, cooperatives as well as associations is obvious in the study area. This idea confirms the hypothesis developed previously in this study, which maintains that the participation of women in the informal sector activities is a stumbling block impeding informal women workers from being active participants in political and community-based activities. Their work is more a source of income and perception of goals pertaining to self-respect, self-esteem and power within their families, rather than visibility in the political and social fields. In this respect, the limited access of women into these areas is explained by the burden of the socio-cultural barriers and patriarchal system that prove to be significant in this regard. Consequently, this hampers their development and weakens their opportunities of empowerment as well as participation in decision-making positions and, hence, hinders their active participation as full citizens as well as limits their full integration in sustainable development.

In summary, a general assumption may be put forward to describe women's absence from the political and social life in order to be able to compare them across women working in different informal sectors. Looking at the similarities first, all women in this study find development important in their work, which refers to secure a livelihood for their children, stability, and relaxation. This means that practicing politics or community-based activism is not the top priority for them. Furthermore, from a sociological standpoint, one might notice that self-employed women's goals in life are reflected in their jobs and nothing else. In this respect, analyzing women's emancipation per sector is essential at this level.

To begin with, women working in craft and service sectors are looking for self-development in their personal domain as well as their work domain. Most women working in these sectors find inspiration in their contacts with other people. They show enjoyable moments in depth conversations and reflections with clients on things they encounter in their daily experiences and work, especially women working as seamstresses, embroiderers, hairdressers and cosmetologists, as well as weavers, among others. Therefore, they use insight from their connections in their work with others.

For women in the trade sector, spending time on their commercial services is essential. Indeed, women traders reveal that their main aim is to find security and success in their economic activities, by which they might ensure additional financial rewards and achievements in their careers to be proud of. To achieve this purpose, most of them indicated the importance of working hard. Some of them add that they prefer their free time to spend it with their family members instead of involving themselves in things they do not know about.

As far as women in the textile sector are concerned, adapting themselves to political and social life is not stated to be of their priorities. They establish a connection with themselves and rely on their self-development. This provides them with inspiration to develop their productions. For most of them, it is difficult to enroll in political parties or associations because of their irregular period of work. Additionally, these women take that they are the only person often responsible for different roles and tasks within the family. For this reason, they value spending more time at work. In the sense that work for them is an extension of their personalities. This is different from those who tolerate being active in political and social life who have adapted to the organization's culture, including behaviors, rules, and various thought patterns.

Therefore, these limitations need improvements in women's educational attainment, trainings and the awareness of citizens based on different perspectives to encourage women's access to politics, cooperatives and associations. This absence is gradually enhanced by women's responsibilities in their domestic sphere. For self-employed women, to have domestic responsibilities has many effects on their daily lives. This issue will be taken up in the following section.

Women's Informal Work and Private Sphere Responsibilities

This section seeks to answer how women create a sense of balance in the midst of enormous family and work related responsibilities. Insight into how self-employed women, especially in a couple of situations, successfully create a balance between productive and reproductive tasks is important to self-employed workers. The present section discusses three main elements. Firstly, it starts with an examination of women's participation in domestic labor. Secondly, it demonstrates the various ways women perceive their housework. Thirdly, it provides an analysis of the strategies women follow to reconciliate between their work and domestic responsibilities.

Women and Domestic Labor

In order to determine the effect of women's informal work on their lives, this section examines women's responses and comments on several questions related to this issue. Respondents were questioned regarding their participation in domestic work, the availability of a helper and the support of their husbands with regard to sharing housework.

The present research demonstrates that most informants 94% perform domestic tasks in addition to their daily economic work. Self-employed women in this study do usually care for children and household responsibilities at the same time as they perform their economic activities. The flexibility in their work has very important implications for the ways they can manage their time and responsibilities. However, only 6% of the respondents declared that they do not do domestic labor; they either have some relatives or domestics to help them.

Table 60. Women and Domestic Labor

	Frequency	Percent
No	18	6%
Yes	282	94%
Total	300	100%

Source: Fieldwork Results

Domestic labor in the present investigation refers to the workloads performed within the household. It is described in the Arab world on the basis of gender. In Morocco, the situation is not different. In other words, the household labor mostly performed by women consists of many activities. They encompass tasks relative to maintaining and running a household. They are a set of activities provided to members of a household encompassing food and other services. However, these forms of work are performed without a financial return. In the same line of argument, Hoyman cited Berch's viewpoint on the nature of housework: 'it is safe to say that housework is an unpaid job' (1987: 70). At the same time, women's domestic workloads have not changed for generations. For instance, women continue to be primarily responsible for their traditional gender roles. In line with this argument, Rassam said: 'childrearing and housekeeping were considered the proper and exclusive domains of women and, for the less wealthy, must be added the production of most household goods among which weaving was probably the premier activity' (1980: 65).

Women who maintain the household frequently experience a double burden. Indeed, they experience a dual responsibility within households with the availability of children. In other words, female household heads in the survey area have double duties in the sense that they take on an increasing domestic reproductive burden whilst they are also the providers of the income within the family. Data of the present study reveal that divorced women who have children, for example, become responsible for rearing children and providing financial resources for their survival. It implies that 'when a couple with children breaks up, frequently the man becomes single, while the woman becomes a single parent,' as observed by Pearce in her prominent piece of work on the feminization of poverty (1990: 267.) The same argument holds true in the case of single mothers, widows and abandoned women. Hence, the complete economic dependence on a male partner is now absent and women's earnings play a crucial role in keeping families and the households out of poverty.

In this connection, one may assume that gender is a crucial dimension in understanding the costs of being a self-employed worker. Indeed, the participation of women in the labor force can prompt changes in gender relations in the household. Nevertheless, those changes may not always be in the positive interest of women. The empirical data demonstrated that women who are working from their homes are not likely to improve their bargaining power within or outside the household compared to their counterparts who are working outside the home. However, for both groups of women, it is not surprising that they continue to perform most of the household chores, ending up with multiple burdens of productive, housework and reproductive work. Furthermore, the examined data in this piece of research reveal that women tend to follow a path of combination of these tasks in compatible manners. This combination appears as a deviation from the norm common in the Moroccan society. The latter confirms the absence of maids in the households under scrutiny.

The 94.3% of respondents assert that they do not have a maid in the household to help them in their daily domestic labor. Rather, they declare that they are the first ones to wake up and the last ones to sleep after a long working day of productive and reproductive tasks. For example, many of my married participants specifically argue that they have to wake up early to prepare breakfast, to wake up and help their kids get prepared to school and prepare lunch before starting their economic activity. These daily tasks become a routine for most of them. However, less than 6% of my respondents stated that they have a maid helping them in their daily household labor.

Table 61. Availability of a Maid

	Frequency	Percentage
No	283	94.3%
Yes	17	5.7%
Total	300	100%

Source: Fieldwork Results

The present research emphasizes the negative influence of family support on women's small business success. The majority of respondents reveal that they are solely responsible for household chores. As for the data in the next table, 24.3% of married women do not receive help from their husbands neither in the absence of other people nor in urgent cases. A predominant judgment is related to cultural beliefs. This means that husbands claim that the housework is a woman's responsibility par excellence. In other words, the married women, no matter how committed to their economic activities as a money making source, they are unlikely to receive substantial help from their spouses. Asmae said: 'my husband thinks it is a humiliation to do household chores. For him, it is no question to do women's work.' This is obviously an indication of the traditional principles, which are related to gender inequalities and which are for many feminists a reflection of the men's patriarchal position within the family as well as the gender-based division of labor. The latter allocates productive roles to men and reproductive tasks to women. In this respect, some respondents maintain this principle by their own traditional beliefs of socially appropriate roles as wives.

Consequently, women's consideration of the housework is relative to wifely duties par excellence. As a matter of fact, it is an essential part of being a good responsible wife and a mother. Some interviewees even take pride in performing domestic chores without the help of their husbands.

This may probably be explained by the all-pervading patriarchal system in the Moroccan society. This view considers women as socially and culturally positioned in subordinate positions to men. They are seen as good wives who respect their husbands, and serve them in every way possible. This is an outcome of the socialization process, as is stressed in the literature, where the wives are taught to demonstrate worship attitudes to their partners.

Table 62. Husband's Help in Domestic Labor[5]

	Frequency	Percentage
No	73	24.3%
Yes	42	14%
Total	115	38.3%

Source: Fieldwork Results

Unlike single or divorced women who are living with others and who often share their responsibilities with them, married women stress that they do not receive the practical support of the spouse in the domestic chores. This is again a reflection of the socialization process, which taught them that the responsibility of housework is a part of their legitimate gender roles. For example, a young respondent said: 'I personally would never let my husband stand in the kitchen or do the cleaning. This is my duty and I was educated that women are the responsible for housework.'

On the contrary, only 14% of the informants assert that they receive help from their husbands in performing household tasks. Along this line of reasoning, regarding of the most obvious observations is that there are moves in the gendering of domestic work and to more changes in its performance within heterosexual couples. In a range of societies, it has been argued that there is some optimism on the moves towards more gender change in domestic work. To explain this, Gershuny, et al., as cited in Strangleman and Warren, write: 'over extended periods of time, the division of domestic

5 These statistics are concerned with both categories of women in the sample. Those who are either married and those who are living in a situation of polygamy (she is one of the wives).

work is adapting to changing circumstances …; in other words, men who are brought up in more equal homes as children and who live as adults with women who demand equality learn to share domestic tasks' (2008: 237).

It follows from this that in almost all cases, the husband has flexible work hours either because of being an informal worker or organizationally employed. Amina reflected on her experience when she was asked about her husband's contribution to the domestic labor by saying that: 'my husband helps me from time to time in the kitchen. When he has free time, he prepares dinner. For me, that's already a very big thing that I appreciate, especially for someone who lived under mother's wings.' This means that the female partner in heterosexual couples demonstrates admiration to the husband's help. Because many women are very grateful for the little domestic work performed by husbands, Hochschild suggests the term 'economy of gratitude' to indicate the extent to which women accept and appreciate their partners' far less contribution to domestic work.'[6]

Nevertheless, the spouse's contribution to the domestic labor is only provided in cases of emergency as it was asserted by many women in the couples' situation. More specifically, many women justify their husbands' participation in housework as not regular. This is due to their need to maintain the public image of a socially acceptable male role within the family despite of their egalitarian beliefs. Thus, men's help remains secondary and not regular. This idea is enhanced by the argument advanced by Belarbi:

> L'aide du mari n'est pas permanent, il intervient quand la femme est incapable d'agir ou ne peut à elle seul accomplir toutes les tâches domestiques … En cas de maladie grave, il recourt à une parente, à un substitut de femme pour prendre en main le travail qu'elle accomplissait. (1988 : 88)
>
> [The husband's help is not permanent. He intervenes only when the wife is incapable to act or cannot undertake all the domestic tasks alone … in case of her illness, he resorts to a parent or a substitute in order to do the work she used to accomplish.][7]

6 Cited in Strangleman and Warren, op. cit., 239.

7 The translation is mine.

This quotation demonstrates that men's participation in the domestic work is of casual help or assistance. Regardless of the fact that husbands do not show disapproval to participate in domestic labor, they refrain from doing so. This is because they do not want to lose their socialized image in front of members of the extended family who would view the male's participation in the housework as' inappropriate'. In this perspective, one may deduce that the exclusion of men from household chores is a socio-cultural tradition from one generation to another. The following observation by Safia, a married woman and a crochet maker, who clearly illustrates this issue as she reports:

> I do all the household chores that a woman is supposed to do. I clean, I wash dishes, I prepare food, and I take care of children ... I can ask my husband to help me, but it is not his tasks. In our society, a man is not supposed to be in the kitchen or take care of the kids.

Similarly, another explanation is given by a head of a professional association who reported that in spite of her workload and responsibilities of the household and the market, her husband always rejects to help her doing household chores, especially with the presence of his family members. As made clear in the previous statement, the husband avoids domestic work, not because he is against the engagement of men in housework, but because he mainly does not want to be perceived as doing 'women's work'.

The above testimonies stress the fact that not only are most unpaid activities performed by women as their traditional gender roles, but they also confirm that these roles are accepted and not questioned by the woman. Accordingly, it is the task of women to be responsible for domestic work. In the same line of argument, Hoyman cited Pahl's analysis of historical examination of the division of labor: 'women are put in the position of having multiple ties – to work, to husband or partner, and to family – and they adjust in pragmatic ways to changes in their marital status and status as mothers' (1987: 70). This means that men are more appropriate to be the breadwinners or in the words of Pahl the 'chief earners,' and women the 'chief workers' (Hoyman, 1987: 70–71).

Women's Perception of Housework

The present investigation reveals that women's perception of housework within their families is more essentially determined by the socio-economic and cultural aspects. They are intersecting variables representing the most important factors behind women's conceptions, and they are also the main reasons that shape their gender. This idea correlates with the argument of Saginak and Saginak as concerns the issue of balancing work and family responsibilities which claims that: 'men and women tend to divide household and domestic labor based on what they perceive to be gender appropriate' (2005: 163). In this respect, 56.7% of my respondents in the sample disagree with the traditional social stereotype that women's first responsibilities are related to doing housework and childcare. This is declared by Fatiha. She is one of the respondents who work as a crochet maker: 'I disagree with these social stereotypes and traditional beliefs that allocate the woman to the private sphere, where she must be the good wife, the good mother and the good cook as well. It is high time for us to be equal and to apply the egalitarian model in our marital relationships.' Along this perspective, one may deduce that women did not believe that housework is an exclusive role of women and that they certainly expect to get help from their partners.

Data in Table 63 reveal that the majority of women do no more agree with the traditional gender-based roles attributed to women by social and cultural norms. According to the latter, a woman's position is basically in the private sphere and it is of a non-economic nature. This idea is emphasized by the following states by some interviewees. For example, Khadija said: 'women are the main mainstay of the house in the Moroccan culture.' Similarly, Sanae stated: 'every one has his/her own responsibilities and those of women are relative to household responsibilities.' In this respect, from these explanations, one may assume that women are conceived as being economically dependent, subordinate and irresponsible creatures.

The traditional main roles of a female in the Moroccan society are to be a good housewife and mother. Related to this idea, Sadiqi pointed out: 'gender asymmetries in the Moroccan context are rooted in the fact that women are responsible for domestic reproduction (child rearing and domestic labor)' (2003: 65). However, some of my respondents state the oppose of this statement. For example, Latifa said: 'nowadays, women are like men. They are no more considered as the only responsible for being good wives and mothers. Everyone needs to work and get revenue, because it is difficult to support family only from one income.'

Table 63. Perception of Housework and Child-rearing as the First Responsibility of Women

	Frequency	Percentage
Agree	105	35%
Disagree	170	56.7%
No idea	25	8.3%
Total	300	100%

Source: Fieldwork Results

However, 35% of the respondents agree about the traditional division of household responsibilities, which allocates women to housekeeping, child rearing and cooking among other tasks. They justify their choices by the fact that women should be the only responsible for the domestic work and men should have the responsibility for bringing the money into the house and being the main breadwinners. In other words, this category of respondents confirms that housework is their main duty and perceives it as their primary responsibility. This might be interpreted as if women are the main house responsible and men as breadwinners. This idea emphasizes the argument advanced by Sadiqi about hardworking women: 'the concept of lhadga "extremely hard-working woman" has been strongly appreciated in Moroccan culture' (2003: 180).[8] In the same line of argument, Saginak and Saginak referred to Coltrane's finding:

> discussions about family values often suggest that these notions of work and family divisions are strongly grounded in present-day, traditional gender perceptions in which women are viewed as being more naturally suited for work in the home, and

8 Also see Bourqia, et al., *Femmes, culture et société au Maghreb: Culture, femmes et famille*. Afrique Orient, 1996.

> men are seen as contributing more by fulfilling the role of outside wage earners. (2005: 163)

This quotation confirms the labor division between men and women that is at the same time a division between public and private spheres. Respondents' perceptions on housework reflect their traditional beliefs on different gender-based roles as well as indicate the way they internalize the responsibility of housework as part of their legitimate gender sphere. A case in point is the declaration of Fatima who is a crochet maker. She said: 'my mother told me that my husband is responsible for bringing the money to the household. Being a woman, it is my duty and responsibility to do all the household chores.' One may suggest that these perceptions are mediated by various factors such as the low level of education, class positions, patriarchal system, beliefs about gender roles, and women's considerations about wifely appropriate roles. This view is not just maintained by women who are primarily chief earners in the household, but it also extends to other women in the study area.

Finally, 8.3% of my respondents in the research area remained neutral. It is apparent that they are aware of the socially and culturally division of labor between men and women, but they decide to choose the 'I do not know' answer as an option. A probable explanation may be that these women declare their ignorance with the stereotypical attitudes, but they act according to the socially created rules. In this perspective, I may venture to say that for this category of women, they are aware of the unequal gender relations as well as the gender division of labor, but they choose to show that they know nothing, and there is nothing wrong about the situation. They seem to take these behaviors as being the normal conducts.

Women's Reconciliation between Informal Work and Housework

From the data presented in the table below, it can be noticed that 76.7% of self-employed women in the informal sector in the city of Fez are able to fulfill their family obligations and their market demands. However, another portion of my respondents 23.3% are unable to reconciliate between their house responsibilities and their work outside.

Table 64. Women's Reconciliation between Informal Work and Housework

	Frequency	Percentage
No	70	23.3%
Yes	230	76.7%
Total	300	100%

Source: Fieldwork Results

The above statistics reveal that an important challenge facing the majority of respondents is the reconciliation between domestic responsibilities and work activities. The data show that this issue, on many occasions, tends to decrease the enthusiasm of many workers in the city under investigation and increase their vulnerability. Nevertheless, some interviewees pinpoint various strategies to address this issue. For example, they allocate Fridays for their families, especially to their children in order to be with them, to do different activities or take them in visits to their families, etc. Moreover, they would train their children to help them with the house chores, prepare meals for the family members at night or in the early morning.

Furthermore, this category of my respondents reveals that they are able to create harmony between reproductive and productive work. An interviewee commented on her ability to be a housewife, to raise her children and to perform her work as follows: 'I do not neglect my housework and children because I manage my time. I always create a balance between my time for my work and my time for my family responsibilities. I do not want to do harm to anyone.' From this statement, it might be concluded that if she is a full-time worker, a mother, a housewife, she would have family problems and might hurt her children who are likely to be subject to abnormal childhood and unhealthy parental care. Additionally, this is a very revealing point, which might be considered as a sign of strong attachment to social and cultural beliefs and stereotypes. They may have greater influence on women's decisions about their economic activities. They may even have negative impacts on their personality as they may feel guilty because of allocating much time to their work.

In this respect, one may assume that this type of women does a double work. They are extremely torn between their traditional gender roles and productive activities. In this regard, Commaille argue that women's reconciliation between domestic and economic work is done at the expense of their physical comfort and eventually absorbs a wide space of their free time (1993: 87). Consequently, many women resort to certain strategies to create equilibrium between their double duties. Some interviewees provided different reconciliatory strategies such as: following a daily schedule, time management, and the division of tasks on the days of the week, among many others.

Conclusion

In sum, the political and social participation of women in associations and cooperatives is behind their emancipation. Moreover, understanding the different domestic tasks of women within their private spheres is of paramount significance to understand the vulnerability of this category of workers. One may further deduce that the third hypothesis, which stipulates that the participation of women in the informal sector will not allow them to be active participants in politics and social activism but it will help them to judge themselves favorably, is confirmed. Indeed, women workers as self-employed in the informal sector show low interest in participating in politics as well as in adhering into cooperatives and associations. The absence of memberships and contribution in these fields entail their inability to be politically and socially empowered. The situation is aggravated by the burden of domestic work, as it is culturally and socially assumed to be their traditional gender roles.

Generally speaking, as working women forge in the twenty-first century, issues will continue to emerge in relation to both men's and women's conceptions and perceptions towards the division of labor. However, some of the constraints women face while they perform their economic activities are related to the decision making of tasks divisions. At the same time, findings have indicated that many women express their enjoyment of being workers in the informal sector. This type of work allows them to evaluate themselves favorably. This is mainly confirmed through their inclusion in social networks that allow the recognition of power, self-esteem, respect and more attainment of economic returns. Nevertheless, it can be mentioned that while the empowerment of women in the city of Fez is constrained by both the socio-cultural and the patriarchal features, the economic development is governed by other elements. This is the main objective of Chapter 6, which aims to present and discuss the challenges women may face up in their work and the different ways they deal with them.

CHAPTER 6

Difficulties and Perspectives of Women's Self-employment

ABSTRACT
In the previous chapter, it was shown how women's political and social development were restricted by various hindrances, namely the socio-cultural and the patriarchal aspects of the Moroccan society. There are two lines of development that constitute the base for the structure of the present chapter. The first line consists of a discussion of the major difficulties in self-employment. This section starts with the limitations that women face in their work. Then, an examination of their level of satisfaction regarding their participation in self-employed activities is tackled. The second line in the structuring of this chapter explores the opportunities offered to women to be a free business manager. It also provides an analysis of the data on women's intentions to expand their economic activities. The chapter ends up with a discussion of the various forms of assistance women require to develop their careers in the informal sector in particular and their situation as informal workers in general.

Difficulties of Women's Self-employment

Self-employed women in the city of Fez demonstrate their sufferings from various obstacles affecting the performance of their informal economic activities. The first sub-section attempts to discuss some problems reported by women which impede their development. The second one highlights the level of satisfaction of women concerning their working situation.

Limitations of Women's Work

The present research provides some of the positive aspects of women's participation in the informal sector activities. This sub-section tends, more particularly, to outline the negative aspects faced up by women in the self-employed activities. The respondents' replies are presented in Table 65 to summarize the main impediments women face in the performance of those activities. These obstacles are divided into formal and informal ones. The former is linked to the difficulties women face with respect to access to decent work and the unpredictable future that may threaten them. The latter is related to traditional principles and values, which are present in the social order and influence the self-employed women's participation in the labor market.

Table 65. Limitations Confronted by Self-employed Women

	Choice 1		Choice 2		Choice 3	
	Frequency	Percent	Frequency	Percent	Frequency	Percent
Occupational problems	119	39.7%	20	6.7%	39	13%
Too much hard work	36	12%	58	19.3%	20	6.7%
Lack of capital	19	6.3%	18	6%	2	0.7%
Unsatisfactory working environment	20	6.7%	36	12%	23	7.7%
Family and home responsibilities	24	8%	41	13.7%	41	13.7%
Lack of skills	7	2.3%	13	4.3%	10	3.3%
Difficulty in marketing	18	6%	44	14.7%	54	18%
Difficulty in transportation	5	1.7%	9	3%	10	3.3%
Unsatisfactory income	22	7.3%	37	12.3%	55	18.3%
Lack of work stability	28	9.3%	14	4.7%	37	12.3%
Others	2	0.7%	10	3.3%	9	3%
Total	300	100%	300	100%	300	100%

Source: Fieldwork Results

One of the disadvantages of the informal sector employment is related to occupational problems. For example, more than half of my respondents declare that stress is a prominent feature of these occupational constraints. Their work stresses them, especially when they are faced with a task that needs to be prepared on time. The following testimonies back up the statement made above:

'The negative aspects of working as self-employed are a factor of stress for me, especially when I promise my client to give them their products on time. In this case, I have to keep my promise and work hard' as pointed out by Karima, a crochet maker, 45 years old.

'Clients mostly control our lives. As embroiderers, we are left powerless and vulnerable. This is clear because clients decide in most cases about the wage of the piece to be embroidered, the time to handle the piece made, this is aggravated by the absence of legislation that could protect us from unfair treatment by the potential clients or the middlemen' as expressed by Souad a married embroiderer in the city of Fez.

'Sometimes work stresses me, mainly in cases when the person who gave it to me does not like it when it is done. In this case, I am not able to get money as a pay for the work done. Besides, I am obliged to unweave the embroidery and redo the piece of work again,' as claimed by Zakia, a divorced embroiderer.

From the above testimonies, it can be concluded that the relationship between the self-employed worker, the potential clients and the wage issue is not clear enough. Workers in this form of informal employment are still exposed to exploitation. Wages are not prescribed and self-employed women have to depend on the good willingness of the clients. In this regard, payment in this kind of work might be low. In some cases, it may be anything from food to clothes, most often second hand in quality as declared by Siham, a widow and a 41-year-old button maker.

Based on the nature of their work, many of those women experience other types of occupational difficulties when they initially want to establish their businesses. Most importantly, access to financial resources and raw materials are the major limitations confronted by these workers. For example, interviewees who work as seamstresses declare that they face problems relative to the provision of raw materials such as sewing machines, thread, tissue, sewing accessories, to name but a few. Others women, especially those working in pastry or food industry require baking equipment, refrigerators to start or to continue the performance of their economic activities.

Qualitative data also reveal that there are other occupational problems women face up in their work. They can be summarized as follows: 1) difficulty of the production flow, 2) competition from similar production units, 3) ignorance of marketing channels and rules of the markets, 4) the nature of potential clients is low and irregular, 5) beneficiaries of such activities have mostly low and irregular income. Besides, formal opportunities are limited in this regard. 6) The invisibility and location of production present a limitation to the development of women's work in the informal sector. In this sense, it influences the level of production's demand. This is due to the fact that most activities do not dispose of a local, or they operate at home and therefore invisible. Consequently, product's demand remains restricted to a particular proportion of customers who know about the place mostly through social networking.

The final issue worth addressing here relates to the mode of payment. Most informal workers make payment facilities to maintain flexible marketing strategies in order to keep their clients. This has to do with competition. The latter is frequently pointed out as an obstacle that women face. It is mainly observed from big units, especially those which use computers to do their designs. In this connection, Mejjati explains the growth in competition as follows: 'cette exacerbation de la concurrence est révélatrice de la croissance extensive de l'emploi informel, d'une demultiplication et d'une prolifération des micro-unites de meme que la vulnérabilité de celle d'age existente, face à la saturation du secteur informel' (2006 : 431) [This increased competition is indicative of the extensive growth of informal employment, it is a multiplication and proliferation of micro-units of the same vulnerability of this age, facing the saturation of the informal sector]. Thus, one may assume that competition and poor marketing strategies, leading to exploitation by middlemen especially in the craft sector, placed many self-employed women in the informal sector in a precarious position.

However, some of the self-employed women in the informal sector are observed to be exploited by their clients, particularly women who purchase their products. The data collected from the individual interviews reveal that some women are often exploited by other women, and some even refuse to pay them, or they paid them less than the amount agreed on at the beginning or before starting the work. Safia, one of my respondents, rightly noted that:

> many times I was exploited by my clients. They either refuse to pay me or pay me less than the price we agreed on when they asked for my services. Most of the time, I am forced to accept the money because I need it. However, sometimes I am obliged to argue for more because the work was hard and necessitated a lot of time for me.

A suitable justification for women's exploitation in the informal labor employment may be relative to the fact that women actors in this sector are not organized and do not work collectively. Their economic operations are individualistic and self-executed. They are not regulated by any common law. Moreover, there is a lack of the common criteria for setting prices for their activities. The goods and services they provide are informal, they are not recognized. Since there is no organized body of device or a mechanism to set a particular price for the product, most informal self-employed women are left at their clients' mercies. Therefore, most of their estimates to set a price; for instance, are confronted with bargaining strategies on the part of the client.

Informal workers in the area under investigation are subject to problems related to the excess of work and insufficient time for leisure. The findings are mainly available among married, divorced and widowed women with their children at home. Only the category of women who have no children cherish some time of leisure. This might be justified by their double responsibilities. Indeed, they have to manage their time and schedule it based on the amount of productive and reproductive tasks they have to perform. In general, most women with both domestic and work responsibilities do not have enough time to devote for leisure purposes.

Complexity in marketing goods and services produced by self-employed women remains another difficulty facing 38.7% of the respondents in the city of Fez. Thus, sometimes the problem is not attributed to the lack of marketing products, but to the lack of information on ways of marketing. In this respect, lack of marketing skills and training was found out in the research area to be another serious impediment of business development for those self-employed women.

Another difficulty encountered in this investigation relates to marketing, which is due to the absence of a local or a visible workplace. Indeed, Table 65 shows the various percentages of respondents who declare that the unsatisfactory working environmental conditions are crucial impediments limiting their development, the visibility of women's work and the regular selling of products. As a result, self-employed women tend to have very low revenues, which are associated with the low marketing procedures. This result is similar to the findings by Chen and Doane who claimed that informal workers, especially own account workers, who turn their homes to their main workplace, where their most informal work operations take place, are subject to a number of constraints:

> among the benefits of working in one's own home, one which is often mentioned by women is the ability to simultaneously do paid work and watch children, care for the elderly, or undertake other household tasks. TAlso, multi-tasking, which may be seen as a 'benefit' in terms of enabling women to fulfill multiple expectations, imposes concrete costs in terms of interruptions to work, lowering productivity and hence income. When a home-based worker has to stop her work in order to look after a child or to cook a meal, both her productivity and her earnings are affected. (2008: 18)

As a consequence, one may deduce that the unsatisfactory working environment has negative impacts on women's economic activities. It also increases their vulnerability within the family and market, as a self-employed woman worker might be less visible and less likely to be organized as a worker. She is likely to lose opportunities to get access to revenues for developing her skills. More importantly, she is hardly reached by organizations that are organizing workers. Therefore, the absence of a convenient local of work decreases women's chances to upgrade their personal identity. Besides, this has to do with social ties outside the family if compared with the other self-employed women who work in a workplace outside the home.

Moreover, women working in public spaces or shops are faced with different barriers. Indeed, these workers have negative costs of their activities as well as customers. Taking into account the costs of operating informally, some women pay their activities' registrations by paying the site licenses.

However, they often have to pay the costs of regularization, and they give their time and money, which are too high if compared to the small size of the business and income they are earning.

Another obstacle faced by women workers in self-employment in the informal sector is linked to their double work responsibilities. Self-employed women suffer from a dual burden. All of them agreed that they never get rid of their domestic work responsibilities and their traditional gender-based roles. This is emphasized by the following statement by Latifa who said: 'even though women and men in the informal employment may suffer from the same financial, institutional as well as other formal barriers, women are subject to additional constraints relative to domestic responsibilities.' In this respect, self-employed women's activities do not change their sexual division of labor at home. The same woman further added:

> Even though women have a greater participation in the market and a crucial contribution to the household income, this would not change their images of wives, mothers and housekeepers. In our case, our work is endless because when we finish the work, we go to our household responsibilities … A woman in our situation is considered as someone who reproduces but does not create reality. An urgent need to change the mentality is highly required in our society.

Naima, a carpet maker, gives the following view of her double responsibilities:

> The one big limitation and pressure I face as a woman is the burden of my productive and reproductive roles. I have three children and all of them need my assistance and help. I do not have a place where I can keep them. I have to walk long distances each day to take them to my mother before I go to the cooperative where I spend the whole day working. Additionally, I have to take care of the household chores when I come back home. Consequently, I suffer from many health problems because of the multiple duties and the heavy loads.

Karima, another respondent working as a traditional clothes maker narrated her story. She gave the various health outcomes that are caused by doing both productive and reproductive work:

> I get up in the early morning at about 5 a.m. I start with my household tasks, then I start work at almost 10 a.m. Sometimes, I work until midnight. Working after sunset is very tiring as the lack of sufficient light and the nature of the embroidery work

> makes my eyes aching me. I also get a headache on almost all day, which makes me feel unable to continue working. In addition, sitting on the floor causes me pain in my back.

Analyzing the data presented above reveals that most households are characterized by the availability of children. This indicates that the correlation between work in the informal sector and households with children is crucial and is taken for granted. Indeed, their availability within the house substantially increases women's double responsibilities. The explanation may be that women devote more time for their children within the household. Therefore, their economic performance remains low.

In this regard, the combination of work and household responsibilities, especially when children are young, represents a double burden for the women. Those women's situations may be in part due to widely shared beliefs that women are responsible for child-rearing and are innately better than other persons at looking after children. Consequently, as it was argued by Bernadette, Allegra and Correll that both men and women may believe that any sacrifices in their careers for the sake of family benefits and the focus on the family's demands should primarily be made by mothers, especially to the extent that they associate women and family.[1] Thus, a mother of young children may feel that she is not an adequate mother and opts to work less to have more time for her children. However, expectations that mothers should stay at home to take care of their children, as well as the traditional view that women are more responsible for child care than men, may lead to decisions such as to lessen their work time or to leave their productive work although a continuous employment history would develop women's earning opportunities and increase their potential and work progress.

Additionally, apart from being the sole individuals having the responsibility for child care, women in the city of Fez seem to be also burdened with the household chores. This study shows that married women spend

1 Bernadette Park, Allegra J. Smith and Joshua Correll. 'The Persistence of Implicit Behavioral Associations for Moms and Dads.' *Journal of Experimental Social Psychology*, Vol. 46, No. 5 (2010): 809–815.

an interesting part of their daily time on tasks such as housework, food preparation, clean up, and shopping for the household. Moreover, this unpaid work is more likely to negatively affect their ability to work. Improving their businesses is not very likely in these circumstances. Consequently, the family responsibility perpetuates the socio-cultural roles of females in the family. The majority of married women state that their husbands do not help them with domestic work as previously discussed in Chapter 5. Nearly all participants agree that they perform their productive work after they finish their domestic work. Few cases report that they may not do all the housework without the presence of a maid or a daughter who helps them in the house chores. It follows from all these findings that these women do not have much free time, let alone a leisure time.

The unpaid labor represents a crucial key element in the analysis of the employment and poverty reduction from a gender perspective. These activities, which belong to the unpaid labor, are extensively debated, and they are not related to the monetary logic. This is because they satisfy the needs of individuals and are the victors of social protection within the household. Domestic labor, in the present research in this region of Morocco, represents a constraint to many women informal workers as it limits the development of their activities and restricts their time of production.

Long working days, which are allocated to traditional gender-based roles, constrain their best performance of labor. At the same time, women's long and non-stop time cause harm to their health. This also means that due to the greater domestic demands, their efforts to reconciliate between domestic labor and market labor can be stressful with high level of marital and personal distress. Therefore, both their personal and marital lives negatively affect their market oriented labor. As a result, a more balanced division of household labor should actually have a greater positive influence on women's psychological and emotional well-being as well as their relationships with their husbands and other family members. In this respect, they commonly declare that they give priority to their children and domestic tasks before their economic activities. For example, Rahma, an interviewee who is working as a traditional button maker and a seamstress, stated:

> In the morning, I woke up the first one in order to help my children get ready for their schools and do my housework. This includes serving breakfast, changing the clothes for the younger ones, and making the lunch before I would get myself ready for work … As for my husband, he takes the child to school in the morning on his way to work, but he cannot bring him back at lunch time. So I am obliged to do it myself. The afternoon, I am free to concentrate on my work except in times when I receive guests. When the children and the husband are back, I would prepare dinner, wash the dishes, and come back to my activity until I fall asleep.

Soumia, another participant, narrated her experience as follows:

> Everyday, I begin by getting up at 7 a.m. with my child and take care of her immediate needs. Then, we will leave the house together to take her to school. I would later on go to the *souk* (public market) to buy the necessities. I come back home to prepare our lunch and dinner at the same time while my child is at school for the whole day. Directly, I go to my corner in the salon, take my sewing machine and start working until I feel tired. I would wait for my husband until he picks my daughter up from school and comes back to have a late lunch altogether. She plays, my husband reads or goes to the café while I come back to my activity until it is time for dinner.

It is worth emphasizing the strong impact of the social and cultural stereotypes that strongly affect women's decision not to be full time workers. In this respect, some of my respondents claim that if they are working and having a greater participation in the market, it would not change their traditional gender roles as wives and mothers. Amina, a young respondent who works as an embroiderer, pointed out that: 'women's tasks inside the home never end. I have to start my day doing my house chores, preparing the kids for school, cooking, and then going to do my needlework.' Thus, one can deduce that statistically such women are doubly discriminated against. On the one hand, their domestic responsibilities as wives and mothers are not treated as a recognized work. On the other hand, their income earning activities performed mostly in the home are not recorded, and they are very often unregistered.

The existence of customers and indeed access to markets are the key ingredients to a successful business venture. Women in the city of Fez reveal that their unsatisfactory working environments remain a crucial constraint to the development of their businesses. A woman's place of work in the home creates a special barrier to labor-force participation. Consequently, a larger part of women's vulnerability is mainly a result of their isolation that their home bound work involves. In the same respect, many women's options of development are limited because they are involved in those forms of work that are mostly performed from home. Thus, this greatly reduces their bargaining power.

Most importantly, women often point to their own lack of adequate financial resources to manage their activities as a major barrier to their success. Rachida whose age is 45 years old declares that: 'without the help of my husband, I couldn't finance my business and buy the materials needed for the production of goods.' Similarly, Saadia, a single mother, whose age is 26 years old states that: 'I had to struggle on my own to get money to start up my business and work to secure my living.' As a result, informal self-employed workers are forced to use hand-driven tools and outdated machinery. Consequently, it keeps their productivity low. Many interviewees argue that due to the lack of working capital, they cannot purchase raw materials in bulk at lower prices and take their goods to market where they can attract better prices.

Moreover, most findings show that there are weak relations between producers and banks due to the huge demand of papers. Most women show the limits they encounter when they want to get formal credits. The impossibility to benefit from formal credits is linked to its stiffness and lack of adaptation (collateral requirement, cost of procedures, terms and binding at the repayment). Therefore, their main recommendation relative to the productivity is to improve their efficiency and provide the working capital.

The quantitative data in Table 65 identifies the lack of skills as a problem and a constraint facing self-employed women in the city of Fez. This manifests itself in the inability to the development of their business opportunities. Moreover, the low educational attainment has influenced the development of the worker's culture, rather than self-employment. Therefore, from the above discussion on the various limitations women face in their performance of self-employed activities in the informal sector, one may doubt the level of satisfaction of those women. This is an issue that will be discussed at length in the subsequent sub-section.

Level of Satisfaction

Satisfaction of women from their informal activities is a considerable factor of their inclusion in development and empowerment. Based on Table 66, the statistics reveal that the distribution of women according to their level of satisfaction shows that the highest percentage 57.7% is accorded to those who feel satisfied about being workers in the informal sector in its self-employed form. It is observed that most women in this region of Morocco are satisfied with their work for many reasons. Firstly, women are aware of their crucial contributions to family expenditure as well as the national economy. For example, women who are own account workers are the most satisfied with their work. They are aware of how they manage productive and reproductive responsibilities. This is confirmed by Fatima who happily said: 'I love my job as a weaver, and I like it more than any other.' Secondly, other participants indicate that their businesses are often ways of self-development. As a vivid example, Samira, who owns a shop of clothes, declared: 'regardless of the fact that my work is my only source of income and livelihood for my family, it is also a source of self-satisfaction. This is because it allows me to be financially independent, to gain self-confidence and to be my own boss.' Similarly, other women in the sample often have a daily work plan and a clearly defined schedule of their private sphere roles. This means that they are able to manage their time between work and domestic life as effectively as possible. In this respect, Ilham, a 36-year-old *mâalma* of traditional clothes, shared her experience as follows:

> I have many responsibilities each day. I want to have it all settled. For this reason, I have to plan everything; otherwise, it will slip between your hands. For me, my day is a vintage day. I have to invest time and energy in my work. However, I also have personally invested a lot to take care of my family responsibilities. I am careful about balancing my time between work and home.

Thus, one might deduce from the above statements that women create their own strategies to reflect on their work and domestic life balance. Indeed, it is remarkable that they define goals, which allow them to reconciliate between what they have to do in their daily responsibilities. Because work is crucial for most of them and relate to their personality development, personal and work goals strategies are set as being the same. Of particular importance are participants' levels of satisfaction of increased self-efficacy. For example, their possibility to achieve their goals, the ability to meet the needs of their families, and the opportunity to influence their lives. The highly important examples are shown in the following statements:

- Meriam, a *makrami* and a crocket maker, states: 'I believe that things I planned for my family are good and now I can make them work.'
- Samira, a traditional dress maker and a *maâlma* in the field, points out: 'My work is more direct. I scheduled and planned steps successfully which I need to follow to get where I'm going.'
- Karima who is a widow, a mother of three children and a traditional dress maker, narrates her story as follows: 'before I started my current job, I was very depressed because of the loss of my husband in a traffic accident. I suffered from lack of money to care about my children. I decided to make use of the skills I learned from my mother who is a tailor. Then I started sewing jellabas and caftans to my family members, friends and relatives. I have succeeded to rent a shop and expand my activity. Now, things have changed and my children and I have everything we needed. This makes me feel satisfied and good about myself. I have faced all the obstacles to accomplish the set of goals I set for myself.'
- Hassania, an embroiderer who makes *Terz El-Fassi*, points out that: 'My work allows me to feel better and satisfied about it. However, I need to add other services, which may guarantee better self-esteem and more independence.'

Along with the above explanations, the data collected from the qualitative research revealed other things that women gain from work apart from income. In other words, work represents for women an opportunity to enlarge social networks beyond the family and neighbors. It clarifies personal identity. Other respondents who indicated that they feel satisfied while working in the informal sector are better reported improvements. For example, they have more respect from family members, achievements of their goals, and less stress. Some women also reported feeling like a role model for their children. Along the same line of reasoning, these examples by my respondents and interviewees confirm the conclusion made by Jahoda in the prominent work of Strangleman and Warren, as he said: 'work is [...] the very essence of being alive' (2008: 255).

Table 66. Level of Satisfaction

	Frequency	Percentage
Satisfied with work	173	57.7%
Not satisfied with the work	127	42.3%
Total	300	100%

Source: Fieldwork Results

In contrast, 42.3% of my respondents reveal their dissatisfaction from being workers in the informal sector. This portion maintains that self-employment cannot allow them to escape from the traditional view of women as a subordinate group. Sometimes, the work turns to be a burden rather than a source of happiness. These are some statements by women who do not find satisfaction in their daily self-employed activities:

- 'I would be very satisfied if I could be a housewife and my husband would be able to earn enough to support the family,' as pointed out by Sofia, 37 years old and a married woman.
- 'I will be happy if one day I have the means to have my own shop in the market. I want to develop my job, and why not to expand it to the international market,' as noted by Karima, 39 years old and a divorced respondent.
- 'If I have the capital, I would change my economic activity and start a small business in the commercial sector. The current one is not stable and its income is irregular,' as declared by Rajae, 27 years old and a single respondent.
- 'I started to think that I rather stay at home where I could take care of my children, rather than spending the whole day working as a bath attendant. I do not feel good about all types of psychological violence, but I am obliged to work because I do not have a man at home,' as claimed by Khadija, 34 years old and a divorced woman.

To conclude, although the level of work satisfaction is difficult to measure in mixed method study, differences in self-employed women's experiences are noticeable. The more successful women are in their business, the higher their level of satisfaction is granted. Work as a main source of livelihood, varied among respondents. This is clearly shown in the following table:

Table 67. Work Solely as a Source of Living

	Frequency	Percentage
No	108	36%
Yes	192	64%
Total	300	100%

Source: Fieldwork Results

The above statistics show that most respondents regard their informal work activities as sources of income. 64% of my respondents in the city of Fez regard their revenues relatively as a source of living. This is because they consider it as a crucial factor for poverty reduction and in achieving growth in their economic and social status. In this perspective, informal employment remains crucial, persistent and often even rising opportunities of the sole sources of living. In contrast, 36% of the respondents in the same sample in the area under investigation declare that their income opportunities do not allow them to secure their needs. Therefore, they do not consider their work as a sole source of living. They maintain that they either benefit from the family financial help, or they have other members working and sharing their incomes with workers in the city of Fez. For example, Halima claimed: 'I don't consider it a source of living because my father is the main breadwinner.'

Opposing this discussion, Table 68 shows that 75% of respondents in the research declare that their work is a means of economic and social independence while 24.3% claim that their work in the informal employment does not allow them to gain a social and economic independence within the family.

Table 68. Work as a Source of Economic and Social Independence within the Family and Society

	Frequency	Percentage
No	73	24.3%
Yes	227	75.7%
Total	300	100%

Source: Fieldwork Results

Results presented above demonstrate that opportunities to work in the informal sector are crucial initiatives to empower women at many levels. Indeed, Meagher also refers to the point of view developed by economists who argued that: 'the informal economic participation offers women a sphere of economic and social empowerment as well as contributing to greater poverty alleviation at the household level (2010: 473). Some women note that their engagement in informal economic activities is so important to their social situation. They confirm that their participation is instrumental to increase women's status in the home regardless of the patriarchal system that surrounds them.

Moreover, women's roles noticed a little change from the performance of the traditional gender-based roles in the practice of activities in public life. As an example, Halima who is a member of embroidery cooperative states that: 'a woman's work gives her status in the family and society as her gender roles change. Moreover, work provides her with a personal income, which secures her financial independence.' This means that this segment of workers becomes able to engage in various income-generating activities, which enable them to earn a living for themselves and their household members as well as gain self-recognition. Work has thus become another basis for determining status because of the social respect that goes along with it.

Consequently, women have changed the traditionally adopted practice of heading the household to the male figure, which has created an imbalance in the household power structure. Some women are granted the right to work and to be the main providers of income. They start to feel that their status is not threatened by men who are much bound with the household headership. The following statement by Fatiha serves as a prominent example in this case: 'my work enables me to exist and to be respected by others in my small and larger family. I successfully changed the traditional stereotype of the man as the responsible for others in the household. I am now the head of the household and the chief income earner.'

However, 24.3% of my respondents in the research area see that women's participation in the informal sector is not a source of securing an economic and social position in society. They conceive that women's daily work being nonsense. It fails to deliver empowerment for them due to the following factors. Some participants argue that along with emancipation, particularly the right to have decent work, has sprung an increase in domestic violence and oppression of women by men. In this respect, Houria points that: my work is not only a source of living, but also a source of my subordination and humiliation. More than that, it does not give me a status in my family and society at large.' Thus, it has led to the presence of much wife abandonment, which relatively puts a heavier material and psychological double burden on female household heads and makes many of them suffer more and be vulnerable.

Other participants confirm that men have relinquished their responsibility to provide for their households that has increased the burden of household management on women. The data revealed that some women are the first breadwinners within the household, and they are not getting any help in household management. Moreover, informal employment activities do not contribute to women's empowerment because they do not give them power compared to men. Some of my participants argue that regardless of women's participation in the increase of their income and search for financial independence, they do not challenge the socially and culturally set structures of a woman as a mother, a good wife and housekeeper. Consequently, women are kept in their subordinate positions and are conceived as second citizens.

Perspectives of Women's Self-employment

The current research reveals that most respondents have an optimistic and positive attitudes towards their units of production. As new opportunities arise, women become able to quickly take advantage of them and increase their output so as to meet the market demand. This sub-section tends to reveal the main perspectives of the development of women's participation in the informal sector. It focuses on the discussion of the reactions concerning women's freedom to manage their businesses. It then provides their intentions to develop their economic activities. Afterwards, it gives an overview about the main forms of assistance women need to develop their goods and services performed in the informal sector.

Women's Freedom to Manage the Business

Contrary to my expectations, as shown in Table 69, 72% of the respondents have the freedom to independently manage their own businesses. In other words, these self-employed women in this study area acknowledge that they are free to do their own jobs. They feel responsible for the choices they make in their economic activities, and they accept the outcomes. Accordingly, women have the freedom to deal with their incomes, and they are not influenced by power in the household. They assert that their husbands or fathers do not intervene in their property investment. Thus, this allows most of them the autonomy, mainly in their jobs, control over their earnings for personal consumption, savings and investment.

Most women who have the freedom to manage their own businesses such as the piece-rate laborers and own account workers report that they have full control over their economic activities and their outcomes. Therefore, autonomy equals the opportunity of being able to freely select and fulfill tasks. Halima pointed out that: 'I have the freedom to manage my own business. I spend most of my time in my shop. My husband does interfere neither in my work nor in my income spending.' From this quote, it is not hard to make a definitive relationship between freedom of business management and women's autonomy. Nevertheless, it appears that this allows women to translate their work into increased control and autonomy over their work and earnings.

Table 69. Women's Freedom to Manage the Business

	Frequency	Percent
No	84	28%
Yes	216	72%
Total	300	100%

Source: Fieldwork Results

However, only 28% of the respondents report that they cannot easily manage their own businesses without the interference of others. Salwa, a shop owner who sells clothes argues: 'I do not have the freedom to manage my own activity because I am obliged to follow my dominant business partner, who is also my father.' She further expresses that she tries to be autonomous, but she could not continue to achieve her goals in life because of the cultural perspective that a daughter should follow her father's orders. Conversely, one may assume that this lack of freedom to deal conclusively with one's business is influenced by the benefit fathers and husbands may gain from the investments of daughters and wives. This is also influenced by the social constraints. In this respect, Sadiqi said:

> The codes of honor and morality have been institutionalized by record history and religion and are inculcated in the family through everyday behavior. These codes, which consist in reserving all the family public reputation as well as the socially accepted conduct, unfortunately, rest upon women's good conduct, chastity, good upbringing and obedience, etc. (2003: 69)

Given this general pattern, it may appear that having the freedom to manage the business translates into increased control and autonomy over earnings and expenditures while lack of freedom to deal with their businesses and earnings leads to low control. However, a closer look suggests that such a conclusion is highly simplistic and that many intervening factors come into play. Sometimes, women are subject to various social and cultural impediments, which compel them to relegate to a second position and, eventually, entrust the male figure in the family, be it a husband, a father or even a brother in some cases, with all their possessions. Nevertheless, women participants in the sample in the city of Fez show their optimism to trespass all the hindrances. The subsequent section deals with their intentions to develop their work.

Women's Intentions to Develop the Work

Women in the research area understand that their self-employment activities have advantages for themselves as well as their families. Indeed, they discover that their employment is of positive outcome for their self-evaluation, attainment of financial sources, respect, independence, and power. In this perspective, 62.3% of the respondents declare that they have intentions to develop their economic activities. The findings of the present research suggest that these intentions may reflect these women's expectations of an accord between satisfying their employment objectives and their family responsibilities. They, therefore, expect to take action and develop their economic activities via different means.[2] At the same time, these women anticipated to find solutions that would likely jeopardize the development of their work but do not interfere with their families even though many of the participants planned on attaining new skills. A case in point is the following statement by Karima:

> my work as a self-employed producer contributes to learning new things. My daily interactions with different clients forced me in some way to gain new abilities. However, this did not stop me from searching for other ways to learn and develop my knowledge, capacities, and skills if I want my business to function for long periods.

Meanwhile, Sofia who works as a seamstress points out that:

> working in the craft sector is always updated. I have to acquire new skills each day to keep my production updated and following the fashion. For this reason, I have to improve my knowledge about activities on the market, planning and other craftsmen's productions.

2 See Table 71.

From these statements, one may conclude that self-employment has a crucial impact on enlarging women's enthusiasm to search for work development. Indeed, this potential might both convert to tangible plans and become a source of power in the field. Although from its economic side, the most important factor is the availability of financial resources. Their willingness to enlarge their scope of learning and skills acquisition might contribute to get economic capital, which also entails gaining a power in the structure of the field. Nevertheless, despite the common point shared by most respondents about their optimism concerning their future careers and lives, they are all convinced of the necessity to have government assistance. They also reveal that they can produce more output if they are provided with different types of help.

Table 70. Women's Intentions to Develop the Work

	Frequency	Percentage
No	113	37.7%
Yes	187	62.3%
Total	300	100%

Source: Fieldwork Results

These findings confirm the choice of 37.7% women who do not have intentions to develop their economic activities. Indeed, this is an annoying situation as only these women can produce more if the market demands dictate and if they are provided with help. Moreover, many women anticipate a pertaining inequality in their future lives, which obliges them to refrain from any development in their activities. This is also emphasized by the structural and the patriarchal systems. In other words, women show absence of strategies to develop their careers because they do not expect much societal movement toward a suitable place for women and gender equality. This interpretation is consistent with the absence of recognition of the informal sector and workers in the Moroccan laws. Therefore, I guess a challenge for feminists and human rights advocates, who wish to further achieve gender equality in different disciplines, is to consider the status of women informal workers and to revive in young women the belief that equality is a desirable and attainable objective. However, such beliefs are impossible to be on the ground without the participation of the concerned segments of society.

Table 71 demonstrates the main potentials for upgrading the economic activities of self-employed women in the research area. It emerges that 38.7% of women want to develop their product, up from 17.3% want to improve the design of their products. To have a stable place of work in the market is a prominent source of work development for 14.7% respondents in the research area while 12.7% of workers want to have locals outside the city of Fez and to sell their products in other places than the current ones. In order to develop their outputs, 6.7% of women want to add other services, others 4.7% want to buy extra materials needed for work to achieve this objective. Moreover, 3.3% of women reveal that they needed to participate in exhibitions, another 2.3% from the same sample want to have their own label on the market and only 0.7% of respondents want to create a cooperative. This means that women are more zealous to produce new products that just increase output, which indicates satisfactory potential for the informal sector to help diversify the economy of the city.

Table 71. Types of Work Development[3]

	Yes		No			
	Frequency	Percentage	Frequency	Percentage	Total	Percentage
Develop the product/service	116	38.7%	71	23.7%	187	62.4%
Sell the products/ services outside Fez	38	12.7%	149	49.7%	187	62.4%
Improve the design	52	17.3%	135	45%	187	62.3%
Addition of other services	20	6.7%	167	55.7%	187	62.4%

3 These statistics are concerned with 187 women who showed interest in developing their work activities (62.3%).

	Yes		No			
	Frequency	Percentage	Frequency	Percentage	Total	Percentage
Creation of a cooperative	2	0.7%	185	61.7%	187	62.4%
Buy extra materials needed for Work	14	4.7%	173	57.7%	187	62.4%
To have a personal shop in the market	44	14.7%	143	47.7%	187	62.4%
Participation in exhibitions	10	3.3%	177	59%	187	62.3%
To have my own label	7	2.3%	180	60%	187	62.3%

Source: Fieldwork Results

The above data reveal that there are two major forms of development of the economic activity. Firstly, women have potentials to either develop their goods and services or augment their marketing strategies. For example, women perform small-scale businesses within most cases as one person (the owner), but they have intentions to develop their products, which entails their plans to expand their activities by introducing new goods and services, improving the design, and creating their own label, etc. Moreover, respondents are aware of the importance of enlarging their networks as well as their sources of marketing the products. In this respect, they share a common point of having a stable workplace in the market. This would give them much visibility and accessibility to meet the market demands. Thus, it might be concluded from their answers that the participation of women in the labor market in its informal form needs an urgent assistance from different actors to uplift their situations. For example, Khadija states that: 'I am not satisfied about work because of the financial crisis and its impact on the marketing of our products. In addition, there is the absence of government encouragement to women who are working in their houses and who are not obvious to customers in the street.' The next cluster of results demonstrates the major propositions provided by self-employed women workers in the informal sector in the city of Fez.

Women and Forms of Assistance

Table 72. Women and Forms of Assistance

	Help Choice 1		Help Choice 2		Help Choice 3	
	Frequency	Percent	Frequency	Percent	Frequency	Percent
Provision of a fixed workplace	156	52%	24	8%	17	5.7%
Improvement of access to raw materials	24	8%	36	12%	15	5%
Take advantage of modern technologies	30	10%	35	11.7%	26	8.7%
Benefit from training and formations	9	3%	44	14.7%	24	8%
Assistance in marketing products	20	6.7%	78	26%	65	21.7%
Formalize the informal sector	42	14%	65	21.7%	103	34.3%
Access to education	16	5.3%	16	5.3%	45	15%
Others	3	1%	2	0.7%	5	1.7%
Total	300	100%	300	100%	300	100%

Source: Fieldwork Results

Given the various difficulties women encounter during their work in the informal sector, they express their wishes to be significantly assisted in their activities. For instance, the first help mentioned by 52% of the respondents in the city of Fez is to have a fixed local. This desire is part of the logic of own account workers to reinforce their productive capacities. Hence, to improve their competitive position in the markets. Allocating a place of work for workers can enhance productivity of the informal sector. Providing this facility is important for the integration of informal sector workers in the rest of the national economy. Most workers in this region of Morocco use their houses as their place of work. Their need to get a workshop located in public spaces would give them more visibility, improve their productivity and allow their products to be purchased widely. Some of the participants provide the following justifications:

- Karima, a married embroiderer, points out: 'I do not have a stable place to work, every day I have to choose a corner in my house and put my stuff.'
- Fatima, a widow pastry maker, pinpoints: 'It is difficult to ensure durability because I do not have a place of work. Availability of a local will be easier because the production and marketing will be easier.'
- Fatiha, a crochet and *makerami* maker, said: 'The big problem is that I need a place to produce and sell my products. I do not have any proper and own place to sell my produced items.'

As for members of cooperatives who already have a stable workplace, they demonstrate their need to have encouragement and support from the government to facilitate their formation by directing assistance. One of the members of the embroidery cooperative states: 'the government should take care of informal workers who are working in cooperatives because they are the only Jounoud Alkhafae (secret soldiers).' This is to be achieved through credit provision and training. Many respondents claim that the formalization of their activities is crucial to their reorganization in the world of labor market. Undeniably, it is important to understand that the formalization of informal segments and workers has various meanings for different activities and types of workers. Along the same line of reasoning, Chen provided information regarding the self-employed workers in the informal sector and formalization of their activities:

> for the self-employed, formalization should not mean just obtaining a license, registering their accounts, and paying taxes: these represent, to them, the costs of entry into the formal economy. What they would like is to receive the benefits of operating formally in return for paying these costs, including: enforceable commercial contracts; legal ownership of their place of business and means of production; tax breaks and incentive packages to increase their competitiveness; membership in trade associations; protection against creditors and clear bankruptcy rules; and social protection. (August 2012: 15)

From the quotation above, one can deduce that formalization is not a one-step process of legalizing the activity through registration and paying taxes enjoyed by formal enterprises and workers. Policy makers and government actors should also take into consideration that the formalization of the informal sector is an on-going process of extending the advantages and benefits of the formal sector to the informal workers.[4] Almost all respondents in the city of Fez agree on the fact that they have to reduce their barriers within the informal sector for the sake of participation in formal activities. Here, several suggestions aiming at stimulating informal sector formalization should be provided based on the questionnaire answers. A credible one is the creation of a law which includes everyone, whether workers in formal or informal sectors of the economy. Women should have the legal status of their economic activities performed informally. This way, they may ensure their legal empowerment.

Furthermore, the empirical evidence seems to suggest that licenses can be used as a tool securing inclusion or exclusion. In this standpoint, licensing self-employed workers gives informal women the right to operate. If women are able to have a securer of livelihood and they are able to invest in their economic activities, security of tenure is critical. One may deduce that being able to secure a work license as well as locals are key mechanisms in the better development of the work. The critical issue, however, is how many licenses as a proportion of the total number of women informal workers are issued?

Other respondents provide other options to develop their economic activities. For example, some women operating as self-employed workers in the informal sector have severe working conditions. They are exploited since they have loads of work because they work continuously without holidays and weekly breaks. For this reason, women demonstrate an urgency to regulate their work and provide laws to protect them and their activities.

A significant number of the respondents in the research study conducted in the city of Fez demonstrate their need to be assisted in marketing their products. They need programs to be designed to augment their abilities of meeting the market demand and developing their selling strategies. As a consequence, these programs may allow the contribution to the economy by encouraging innovation in the labor market and stimulating economic activity. The encouragement of the economic flow of these activities may

4 See Chen (2012), op. cit., 16 for an example of an approach to formalize informal enterprises and informal workers.

encourage women to expand their activities, and hence help the development of the national economy by creating jobs for additional employees as well as developing their careers that may generate sufficient income to support their families.

Training, as one of the help options, is requested by many respondents in the research study. They report their need for training skills to support them develop their work and enhance their productivity in the informal sector. For example, business and marketing trainings are regarded to be the main required ones in order to provide women with information and skills to successfully operate an economic activity. Additionally, training may focus on the provision of basic and adequate information on business management, self-esteem training, as well as personal financial management. One may assume that these trainings would be subject to program creation by government or civil-society actors to offer this type of assistance to informal workers for a specified period. There is also the obligation of the evolutionary process as well as follow up sessions with the beneficiaries.

Overall, the data reveal that most workers lack educational attainment and professional skills. Many of them did not either receive formal education because they came from low educated and poor families who find it difficult to send their daughters to school for either economic or cultural reasons. Therefore, they end up working in informal activities at a young age to support themselves and their families. Soumia narrated her life story as follows:

> I work as an embroiderer and I am responsible for my three children and parents. I look after them all. I really want to further my education at least to help my children with their homework. I couldn't do that before because my parents were too poor to keep me in school. But now since I have a source of income and I can finance my own education, I want to further my studies and go beyond where I am now.

For this reason, adult literacy and professional training represent a crucial form of assistance to be guaranteed to self-employed women, especially in places where informal workers live. Hence, instead of the allocation of resources by women, the government should encourage the civil society to provide training programs. The latter should be geared mainly towards labor market requirement. Respondents' choices range from responses of the 74 respondents who select the training choice as an option. For instance, findings of the present research indicate the management training by 14.7%, as well as marketing trainings 14.3%, which gained the highest rates of women's choices, followed by the technical training 7% and the financial training 6.7%. These trainings are in a way or another suitable for informal workers. Therefore, they help them to secure an economic success. Thus, training is deemed essential to women's economic success.

Another segment of women workers in this sample claim that the lack of access to credits affects their performance in the informal sector. Indeed, they view credits as a constraint on the informal sector, which keeps their productivity low and its development stagnant. Barriers to credits do not only hamper the work of informal workers, but as explained by Heintz and Valodia, there are other factors that contribute to the aggravation of this situation. They summarized them as follows: 'large interest rate spreads, poor information systems, the asset portfolio of banks (including reserves), and high transaction costs, in some cases linked to inadequate information' (2008: 22). As a result, some women resolve to use traditional and informal ways to support their activities while others consider peer lending as a model of financing since most women have no assets to serve as collateral. In this respect, there is a need to consider loan services, which may help participants set economic, personal and family goals. In addition, it may resolve circumstances that may stand as an obstacle in front of their success as small-scale workers and hinder their progress towards economic development and self-sufficiency.

In this regard, one may conclude that a number of support initiatives can help break women out of the vicious cycle of poverty and the hardness of working in the informal sector. Support dedicated for self-employed women in the informal sector indicates the extent to which they are in need of being incorporated into urban plans. For instance, these women need to have stable places of work. Moreover, some of these measures would encompass trainings and access to technologies for capacity building of female entrepreneurs in the informal self-employed activities, strengthening women's rights, access to social protection rights as well as engendering micro-finance and its policies of acquisition, as well as build their education and skill capacities. Such initiatives would help women change their conditions within the informal sector, and break the poverty cycle.

Conclusion

In sum, based on the findings of the research, my participants' work experiences suggest that self-employed women workers in the informal sector can be protected and promoted through public interventions and policies. Most notably, of course, direct assistance has been of interest to most respondents in the study area. Not just micro-financial services but also other forms of direct assistance.[5] More importantly, this category of workers shows an urgent need to be integrated into macroeconomic, sectoral and regulatory policies. In this respect, the present investigation demonstrates several types of needed assistance revealed by respondents to protect and promote self-employed producers and informal workers in general.

A number of interventions are declared by my participants to be important for the formalization of informal activities. On the one hand, they affirmed the need to act at the macro-level. For example, to create a stable macroeconomic environment, to promote growth, to ensure property rights and legal security,to provide a social protection system, and to secure the possibility of workers to benefit from public services and infrastructure. On the other hand, they confirmed the importance of intervening at the micro-level. That is to say to provide a number of support mechanisms (i.e. business development services, micro-finance services, skills training for informal workers, capacity building and encouragement of their participation in self-help organizations as a way to promote public participation in the shaping of policies). All this represents the benchmark for the formalization of the informal sector and provides an impetus for pursuing own interests and rights within the informal sector.

Most importantly, self-employment proves to be a crucial form of employment in the informal sector that remains of a large share of the total national economy. The production of its workers takes place in different types of operations. They range between micro and small units, family businesses, or single person operations. Women working in all these

5 See Table 72.

types of jobs face various barriers and at the same time show optimism for the future. In this regard, this chapter focused on the discussion of these two main points. It traced the various barriers women confront in their self-employment. When it comes to the future of self-employed women in the city of Fez and Morocco. results revealed that it has a good aspect. That stands behind many women's choice of this form of informal employment.

Conclusion and Recommendations

The main objective of the present investigation was to examine the participation of women in the shadow segments of work and its role in the household poverty reduction in the city of Fez. In fact, this book has focused on the self-employed activities as components of the economy, which allow many women to secure a source of income. Thus, this conclusion summarizes and synthesizes the findings of the foregoing discussions. It ends up with a number of recommendations and suggestions.

The first chapter of the present book focused on providing a theoretical understanding of the main concepts. It particularly concentrated on various previous studies about the informal sector, gender and poverty reduction. The purpose is to pave the way to a comprehensive reading, interpretation and analysis of the data collected in the city of Fez. The second chapter provided the main methodological framework followed in the collection of the data. It was basically based on a double tool approach using both quantitative and qualitative methods. In this respect, the mixed methods approach, using both the questionnaires and the interviews, served as an important means to generate some findings and to come out with scientific results. The latter were analyzed using statistical and ethnographic methods of analysis in order to reach the conclusions.

The third, fourth, fifth and sixth chapters were devoted to data analysis. While the third chapter examined the situation of women in self-employed activities, mainly focusing on the personal and professional characteristics, as well as on women's main reasons and motivations behind their participation in informal work. The fourth chapter dealt with the contribution of women's work in poverty reduction within the household. Chapter 5 focused on the relationship between women's work in informal activities and their emancipation. In the sixth chapter, the focus was shifted to a discussion of the various difficulties women are confronted with in their work as well as their main perspectives and potentials in the future. The book provides a number of findings and conclusions.

Despite of the non-representation of women in statistics on the labor force, the present study revealed that the active participation of women especially in self-employed activities. The analysis of the data indicated that the informal sector in the city of Fez is regarded as one of the components of a set of economic activities, which motivates many women to secure a source of income in the whole country. By examining the lives of self-employed workers, this investigation sheds light on the 'unseen' or 'invisible' women whose profiles are determined by their socio-demographic situation (i.e. their socioeconomic belonging, educational attainment, marital status, presence of children, to name but a few).

Within the present form of employment in the informal sector in the city of Fez, women are generally found to operate in activities which barely guarantee a source of survival. They are likely to be of causal or seasonal nature. They often do not require an educational level and skills. They are physically demanding, with long hours of work, lower productivity and little opportunity to expand in a formal context. Additional characteristics of these shadow activities may be relative to the lack of opportunities to upward mobility, and improve skills. Thus, the self-employed producers perform various activities that take many forms, but which in the present research are mostly manifested in crafts, services, trade and to a lesser extent textile informal activities. Most of these activities are carried out within the context of own-account ownership. They are invisible both within state official statistics and within individual's perceptions. This means that women's activities are seen as an extension of their traditional gender-based roles, and hence they are not formally perceived as a job.

Despite the fact that most activities performed by women in the target group are invisible, they enable the vast majority to gain money to live on and to survive. However, the data showed that most economic activities are exercised in non preferable places of work and employment status. Thus, in the field survey in the city of Fez, most female informal workers are not declared to the local authorities. This means that they do not have any local authorization to exercise their activities. At the same time, those who are employed have no salaried worker contracts with their employers.

Consequently, the findings showed that the condition of women in the informal segments of the labor market differed markedly from those who work at home, those who scavenge without locals, those who produce products on a family basis, as well as those who sell their goods and services in the market. However, all the female self-employed workers in the informal sector in the city of Fez have one thing in common, which is linked to their absence from the legal regulations and their lack of benefit from the social security.

Apart from the demographic and socioeconomic factors, the results revealed the presence of other elements behind women's choice of self-employment. These include flexible schedules, family related reasons, presence of children at home, among others. These represent the other principal reasons why women choose self-employment over wage employment. Moreover, they show that activities within the informal sector are prominent because they provide a considerable source of income and employment for women in the research area, where formal employment opportunities are restricted and social-security is almost absent. The findings of this study also revealed that the disqualification of women in the city of Fez to join the formal sector leads them to practice money providing activities as an option to help guarantee a survival. In other words, many women opted for self-employment opportunities in the informal sector to improve their living standards, to achieve social and economic inclusion in their personal environment as well as in society at large. This means that this sector is not likely to disappear soon.

The findings demonstrated that the income, derived from informal activities to some extent, albeit limited sustain the expenses of the women's families and the household members in general. In other words, the income generated via working as self-employed workers allows women to meet the basic daily needs of their families. However, women's economic activities are important to the national economy and to the households, and as such deserve further research and documentation on either the role of women in the informal economy or on the nature of employment in Morocco.

As the data from the questionnaires emphasized, the informal sector activities are fragmented ones, in which activities range from indoors to outdoors in order to contribute to the family members' needs. The presence of women heads or members of cooperatives and professional associations, as found in the study survey, was shown to be another indicator of the role played by the informal sector in the city of Fez. It was stated to be as a means of subsistence and self-sufficiency for a large proportion of women. The meetings with some women during the fieldwork indicated that most of them practice their economic activities in domains such as: food making, clothes making, and trading sectors as a way to meet their personal needs as well as those of their family members. In general, one may conclude that the informal sector of the economy directly contributes to the economic as well the social fabric of the family, in particular, and the city of Fez and Morocco in general.

Chapter 5 concluded that the participation of women workers in self-employed activities in political and community-based activism is limited. For instance, the data showed their absence from the political arena, which is constrained by many factors among which we can cite: trust in the Moroccan political system, corruption, events of oppression, fear of the past, the negative perceptions of the world of politics, the patriarchal structure of society, and the nature of the political sphere, among others. However, few women who find a place in politics are encouraged to join this field either because of their educational attainment or by the availability of a relative within these political institutions. Furthermore, the shallow presence of women in social activism proved to be omnipresent in the research area. The data revealed that women's cooperative involvement and associative participation are mediocre. In this respect, the low presence is related to the structure of the Moroccan society as it is characterized by male domination in most fields.

Generally speaking, women's absence from the political scene and the social based activism is explained by various factors. Indeed, the burden of the socio-cultural barriers and patriarchy prove to be significant in this context. They weaken their opportunities to be active participants. Hence, their weak participation limits their full integration in sustainable development and their political emancipation. This situation is aggravated by the domestic labor responsibilities allocated to women based on their gender. As a result, the empowerment of the female workers in the informal sector in the city of Fez is mostly limited by both the socio-cultural and the patriarchal features. Therefore, it enhances their social exclusion.

Findings on the basis of the data analyzed in the sixth chapter revealed that the informal female workers face various impediments that hinder their full participation in the labor market. Indeed, they are divided into formal and informal barriers. On the one hand, the formal obstacles were related to the inability to have access to decent work, to good working conditions as well as to their ignorance about the future of their activities, which for most respondents is unclear. On the other hand, the informal obstacles were shown to be linked to the traditional principles and values, which are present in the social order, and they influence the participation of women in the labor force. Moreover, the level of women's satisfaction showed variation due to the strategies followed. For instance, women who created their own ways to manage and balance between the responsibilities of daily life demonstrated high levels of satisfaction, which allowed them to achieve their goals and to meet their needs. In contrast, others regarded that their dissatisfaction with work in the informal sector is linked to their traditional gender-based stereotypes. These allocate women to subordinate positions. They are considered as second citizens and only helpers as far as financial provisions to the household are concerned. Chapter 6 also focused on the main perspectives and potentials to develop women's careers within the informal sector, in particular, and their situations as workers in general. The data revealed that most respondents have an optimistic and positive future about their units of production. Such futuristic image of the development of their careers will certainly lead many women to evaluate themselves favorably. Moreover, as maintained via the interviewees' reactions, the optimism of women is a way to anticipate greater psychological goodness, as well as attain respect, self-esteem and power within the household and society at large.

The socio-demographic and the economic trends indicated that the self-employed activities in the informal sector are on the increase, thus self-employment is a reality that is unlikely to fade away. Indeed, the present research demonstrated that women represent a crucial proportion of informal workers. Their participation in this form of the economy enables them to generate revenues, which are more likely to be spent on their livelihood. Additionally, the data have proven that the participation of women in the city of Fez to their household expenditure allows them a position within the family. In fact, they become able to cherish a certain level of assertiveness, confidence and autonomy though sometimes restricted by cultural and traditional behaviors. Moreover, from the economic perspective, although the individual's income is often low, cumulatively these activities contribution to households and to local economies is considerable. In view of the major findings and conclusions derived above, the subsequent section provides recommendations for policy.

Confronted with these data, the sector of the informal self-employment, like other live sectors, is witnessing ups and downs due to the economic changes. Moreover, women's participation in the economic activities within this sector has got into a new stage symbolized by its source of survival. Therefore, the informal sector in its self-employment form is called to do its utmost to ensure a continuous contribution to employment. This will be achieved, through a developmental plan. This latter aims to integrate the sector in its formal economic milieu and make it strong enough to face the obstacles of formality as well as the world competitiveness, which characterize today's national economy. Accordingly, the following are some recommendations policy makers and stakeholders should take into account while dealing with the issue:

- There is a need to develop strategies to uplift the conditions of the informal female workforce. On the one hand, this may happen through the adoption of social labor standards to boost women's situation in this sector. These may include fighting all forms of discrimination towards women, getting access to education and vocational training, improving the working conditions as they prove to be priorities of human development. On the other hand, the development of women's situation is possible via the establishment of a social protection law for labor at a lower cost.
- The findings of this study demonstrated that the lack of start-up capital was among the most crucial factors affecting women's performance of self-employed activities in the city of Fez. To offset this situation, there is a need for both government and other stakeholders to ensure that self-employed women in Morocco should be provided with credits and loans from banks.

- Education and training have a crucial role to play in developing women's situation in the informal sector. For this reason, women's participation would be more effective if policy and legal frameworks of the informal sector are more supportive of women's concerns. In this respect, there is an urgent need to develop programs to focus not only on the economic aspect of women's self-employment but also on other women's broader concerns (i.e. health, education, and community development). Moreover, there is an urgent need for promoting equal and active participation of women in management training, upgrading their financial services, and teaching marketing skills, to name but a few. Additionally, women necessitate to develop their participation in political and community-based services to empower and provide them with a place in their communities and society at large.
- Training designed to acquire technical and professional knowledge is of great importance to increase productivity. In other words, if self-employed women benefit from developed technical knowledge and practical skills, they will definitely be able to develop the quality and to advance the means of production. The support of the state should be manifested at this level via the development of short trainings, taking into consideration its appropriation to sectors of activity and workers themselves. Moreover, these state' trainings must be conducted in the workplace and/or in a familial work environment. Its content must be related to the market demand. In this respect, the product or the service performed by informal workers must be well defined. To achieve these potential strategies, the state has to coordinate with NGOs to implement the training activities with efficiency. This is an initiative to help self-employed women get a possibility to identify their problems, evaluate the efforts required to implement solutions that are at the same time realistic and collectively controllable.
- Self-employed producers suffer, in the present state of things, from different impediments. They include mostly isolation, exclusion and lack of organization. Because they operate their activities outside regulations they are also denied access to formal credits, vocational training and encouragement to investment profits. Moreover, these women should benefit from all their rights (i.e. economic rights).

Moreover, the self-employment activities are exercised in a world where orientations tend to be individualistic. For this reason, there is a necessity to develop projects in order to increase the ability of producers, to develop group strategies, and create associative networks to support higher production and marketing with a high collective profitability.

- The participation of women in the informal sector is wide and crucial. However, it is greatly underestimated and not recognized in national economic statistics. In this regard, the government statistics should be revised in order to include women labor force for the sake of having credible statistics of women in total labor force. This would oblige the government to acknowledge the existence of the informal sector, its contribution to the formal economy and its workers. Thus, If the government is interested in formalizing the informal sector, it must expand protection rules available for the formal workers to the informal ones.

Having summarized the findings of the present research and suggested some recommendations to cope with persistent hindrances to the promotion of women's situation and integration, it is highly relevant to make some suggestions for further research. Since the present study was conducted in the city of Fez, it seems impossible to generalize the results to all regions in Morocco. This study needs, therefore, to be replicated in different regions, including both urban and rural areas. This will provide the opportunity to do a comparative study and to provide development opportunities to those in need.

A major limitation of the study is that it focuses only on one form of employment in the informal sector. Indications are that covering only self-employment in the city of Fez may portray a significantly different picture in terms of the situation of women workers in different informal activities. Thus, future studies would need to include other forms of informal employment and enlarge the research area. Other studies on women should not be limited only to gender as a social construct. They must be open to investigate other variables that intersect with the gender component to frame the various perceptions of the gender roles. For instance, future research should include age, social class, educational attainment, ethnicity as well as regional belonging of the sample of the study.

It is important to compare the participation of both males and females in the informal sector to approach the concept of gender with more precision. This would in the future provide a reference point for many policy makers and stakeholders to develop policies and programs to promote the situations of the invisible workers in the shadow segments of work. Further research should also focus on the vital role of women dwellers in rural areas and their work in the informal sector. In fact, considerable research is available about this category of women, but little is known about their situation as far as work is concerned, considering the different social variables such as age, level of education, social class and others. In this perspective, it is high time that these women speak for themselves and reveal their situation instead of having others to unveil their situations and speak for them from a distant angle.

Bibliography

Abzhad, Mohamed, and Abdessalam Labchir. 'Emploi dans le Secteur Informel.' *Population et Développement au Maroc*. Rabat: Centre d'études et de Recherche Démographiques, 1998: 355–364.

Akesbi, Azeddine. 'Analysis of the Labor Market in Morocco: A Segmented Approach,' Centre d'orientation et de planification de l'Education Morocco, 3 September 2000, available from <http://www.erf.org.eg/html/blabor1.pdf> (accessed 23 September 2014).

Akorsu, Angela D. 'Labour Standards Application in the Informal Economy of Ghana: the Patterns and Pressures.' *Economic Annals*, Vol. LVIII, No. 196 (2013): 157–175.

Aksikas, Jaafar. 'Prisoners of Globalization: Marginality, Community and the New Informal Economy in Morocco.' *Mediteranean Politics*, Vol. 12, No. 2 (2007): 249–262.

Babbie, Earl. *The practice of Social Research* (13th Edn). Austria: Wadsworth Cengage Learning, 2013.

Banerjee, Nirmala, and Sachetana Kolkata. 'Unravelling the Informal Sector.' *Labor, Capital and Society*, No. 37 (2004): 22–45.

Baxter, Janeen. 'Barriers to Equality: Men's and Women's Attitudes to Workplace Entitlements in Australia.' *Journal of Sociology*, Vol. 36, No. 1 (2000): 12–29.

Becker, Gary. 'Human Capital, Effort, and the Sexual Division of Labor.' *Journal of Labor and Economics*, Vol. 3, No. 1 (1985): 533–558.

Belarbi, Aicha. 'Salariat Féminin et Division Sexuelle du Travail dans la Famille: Cas de la Femme Fonctionnaire.' Fatima Mernissi, ed. *Femmes Partagées: Famille-Travail*. Casablanca: Le Fennec, 1988: 79–98.

Beneria, Lourdes. *Gender, Development and Globalization: Economics as if All People Mattered*. New York: Routledge, 2003.

Beneria, Lourdes, and Martha Roldan. *The Crossroads of Class and Gender: Industrial Home work, Subcontracting and Household Dynamics in Mexico City*. Chicago: University of Chicago Press, 1987.

Benjelloun, Therese. *Femme, Culture, Entreprise au Maroc*. Casablanca: Wallada, 1993.

Biadillah, Maryem. *Women in the Moroccan Economy: Employees, Self-Employed*. Ifran: Al-Akhawayn University Press, 2002.

Bielby, William T., and James N. Baron. 'A Woman's Place is with other Women. Sex Segregation within Organizations.' Barbara F. Reskin, ed. *Sex Segregation in the Workplace*. Washington, DC: National Academy Press, 1984.

Bourqia, Rahma, et al. *Femmes, culture et société au Maghreb: Culture, femmes et famille*. Casablanca: Afrique Orient, 1996.

Bradshaw, Sarah. *Gendered Poverties and Power Relations: Looking Inside Communities and Households*. Managua: ICD, 2002.

Bradshaw, Sarah, and Brian Linneker. *Challenging Women's Poverty: Perspectives on Gender and Poverty Reduction Strategies from Nicaragua and Honduras*. London: Catholic Institute of International Relations, 2003.

Browne, Jude. *Sex Segregation and Inequality in the Modern Labor Market*. Bristol: Policy Press, 2006.

Bryman, Alan. *Social Science Methods* (3rd Edn). Oxford: Oxford University Press, 2008.

Budig, Michelle. 'Gender, Self-Employment, and Earnings: the Interlocking Structures of Family and Professional Status.' *Gender and Society*, Vol. 20, No. 6 (2006): 725–753.

Cagatay, Nilufer. *Trade, Gender and Poverty*. New York: United Nations Development Programme, Social Development and Poverty Elimination Division, 2001.

———. *Gender and Poverty*, Working Paper 5, New York: United Nations Development Programme, Social Development and Poverty Elimination Division, 1998.

Cairoli, Laelitia M. 'Garment Factory Workers in the City of Fez.' *Middle East Journal*, Vol. 53, No. 1 (Winter, 1999): 28–43.

Castells, Manuel, and Alejandro Portes. 'World Underneath: The Origins, Dynamics, and Effects of the Informal Economy.' Portes, Alejandro, Manuel Castells, and Lauren Benton, eds. *The Informal Economy: Studies in Advanced and Less Developed Countries*. Baltimore MD: Johns Hopkins University Press (1989): 11–37.

Chant, Sylvia. 'Gendered Poverty Across Space and Time: Introduction and Overview.' In Chant, Sylvia, ed. *The International Handbook of Gender and Poverty: Concepts, Research, Policy*. Cheltenham: Edward Elgar Publishing Limited (2010a): 1–26.

———. 'Towards a (re) Conceptualization of the 'Feminization of Poverty: Reflections on Gender Differentiated Poverty from Gambia, Philippines and Costa Rica.' Chant, Sylvia, ed. *The International Handbook of Gender and Poverty: Concepts, Research, Policy*. Cheltenham: Edward Elgar Publishing Limited (2010b): 111–116.

———. 'The Feminization of Poverty and the 'Feminization' of Anti Poverty Programmes: Room for Revision.' *Journal of Development Studies*, Vol. 44, No. 2 (2008): 165–197.

———. *Gender, Generation and Poverty: Exploring the 'Feminisation of Poverty' in Africa, Asia and Latin America*. Cheltenham: Edward Elgar Publishing, 2007.

———. *Women Headed Households. Diversity and Dynamics in the Developing World*, London: Palgrave Macmillan Press, 1997a.

———. 'Women-headed Households: Poorest of the Poor? Perspectives from Mexico, Costa Rica and the Philippines.' *IDS Bulletin*. Vol. 28, No. 3 (1997b): 26–48.

Charmes, Jacque. 'Trends in Informal Sector Employment in the Middle East.' Hakimian, Hassan and Jeffry Nugent. *Trade Policy and Economy Integration in the Middle East and North Africa: Economic Boundaries in Flux*. London: Routledge (2004): 166–183.

———. 'Emplois et Revenus dans l'Informel (non agricol) au Maghreb.' Bernard, Chantal. *Nouvelles Logiques Marchandes au Maghreb: l'informel dans les Années 80*. Paris: Centre National de la Recherche Scientifique (1991): 41–59.

Chen, Martha. *The Informal Economy: Definitions, Theories and Policies*. Working Paper 1, Cambridge: WIEGO, August 2012.

———. 'Informality and Social Protection: Theories and Realities', *Institute of Development Studies*, Vol. 39, No. 2 (2008): 18–27.

Chen, Martha, and Donna Doane. *Informality in South Asia: A Review*, Working Paper 4. Cambridge: WEIGO, September 2008.

Chen, Martha, Joann Vanek and Marilyn Carr. *Mainstreaming Informal Employment and Gender in Poverty Reduction: A Handbook for Policy-Makers and Other Stakeholders*. London: The Commonwealth Secretariat, 2004.

Chen, Martha, Joann Vanek and James Heintz. 'Informality, Gender and Poverty: A Global Picture.' *Economic and Political Weekly* (2006): 2131–2139.

Chen, Martha, et al. *Progress of the World's Women: Women, Work and Poverty*. New York: UNIFEM, 2005.

Chikhaoui, Isabelle B. 'The Invisible Economy at the Edges of the Medina of Tunisia.' In Richard, Lobban, ed. *Middle Eastern Women and the Invisible Economy*. Gainesville: University Press of Florida, 1998: 215–230.

Code de la Famille. Collection Textes et Documents, N°. 126, 1ere édition. Publications de la Revue Marocaine d'Administration Local et de Développement, Casablanca : Imprimerie Al Maarif – Al Jadida, 2004.

Commaille, Jacque. *Les Stratégies des Femmes: Travail, Famille et Politique*. Paris: La Découverte, 1993.

Creswell, John. W. *Research Design: Qualitative, Quantitative, and Mixed Approaches* (2nd Edn). Thousand Oaks, CA: Sage Publications, 2003.

Creswell, John W., Vicki L. and Plano Clark. *Designing and Conducting Mixed Methods Research* (2nd Edn), Thousand Oaks, CA: Sage Publications, 2011.

Cross, John C., and Bruce D. Johnson. 'Expanding Dual Labour Market Theory: Crack Dealers and the Informal Sector.' *International Journal of Sociology and Social Policy*, Vol. 20, No. 1/2 (2000): 96–134.

De Soto, Hernando. *The Other Path: The Economic Answer to Terrorism*. New York: Harper Collins, 1989.

De Vaus, David. *Surveys in Social Research* (5th edn). London: Routledge, 2002.

Dieter, Cassel., and Cichy Ernst Ulrich. 'Explaining the Growing Shadow Economy in East and West: a Comparative Systems Approach.' *Comparative Economic Studies*, Vol. 28, No. 1 (1986): 20–41.

Dilnot, A., and Morris, C. 'What we Know about the Black Economy in the United Kingdom?' *Fiscal Studies*, No. 2 (March 1981): 163–179.

Direction de la Statisque. *La Femme Marocaine en Chiffres: Tendences d'Evolution des Charactéristiques Démographiques et Socioprofessionnelles*. Rabat: Haut Commissariat au Plan, 2013.

———. *La Femme Marocaine en Chiffre: Tendances d'Evolution des Charactériqtiques Démographiques et Socioprofessionelles*. Rabat: Haut Commissariat au Plan, 2008.

———. *Enquête National sur le Secteur Informel 2006–2007*. Rabat: Haut Commissariat au Plan, 2007.

———. *Enquète National sur le Secteur Informel, 1999/2000*. Rabat: Haut Commissariat au Plan, 2003.

Direction des Etudes et des Prèvisions Financiers. *Bilan du Programe d'Ajustement Structurel*. Rabat: Ministère de l'Economie et des Finance, 1995.

Doeringer, Peter B., and Michael J. Piore. *Internal Labor Markets and Manpower Analysis*, Lexington, MA: Heath, 1971.

Dubey, Amaresh, Gangopadhyay Shubhashis and Wilima Wadhwa. 'Occupational Structure and Incidence of Poverty in Indian Towns of Different Sizes.' *Review of Development Economics*, Vol. 5, No. 1 (2001): 49–59.

Ennaji, Moha. 'Women's NGOs and Social Change in Morocco.' *Femmes Méditerranéennes et leurs Droits. Travaux du Colloque International: 28, 29, 30 Avril*. Mohamadia: Fédala Press, 2005.

Ennaji, Moha, and Fatima Sadiqi. *Migration and Gender in Morocco: the Impact of Migration on the Women left Behind*. Trenton, NJ: Red Sea Press, 2008.

Fejjal, Ali. 'Le Secteur Informel: Concept et Mesure.' *Annales Marocaines d'Economie*, No.4 (Spring 1993): 29–38.

Ferman, Patricia, and Ferman, Louis. 'The Structural Underpinning of the Irregular Economy.' *Poverty and Human Resources Abstracts*. Vol. 8 (1973): 3–17.

Floro, Maria Sagrario. 'Women's Well Being, Poverty, and Work Intensity.' *Feminist Economics*, Vol. 1, No. 3 (1995): 1–25.

Folbre, Nancy. 'Hearts and Spades: Paradigms of Household Economics.' *World Development*, Vol. 14, No. 2 (1986): 245–255.

Frey, Bruno S., Hannelore Weck and Werner W. Pommerehne. 'Has the Shadow Economy Grown in Germany? An Exploratory Study.' *Review of World Economics*, No. 118, (1982): 499–524.

Gallaway, Julia, and Alexendra Bernasek. 'Gender and Informal Sector Employment in Indonesia.' *Journal of Economic Issues*, Vol. 36, No. 2 (2002): 313–321.

Ghebremichael, Berhane. 'The Role of Cooperatives in Empowering Women.' *Journal of Business Management and Social Sciences Research*, Vol. 2, No. 5 (2013): 51–54.

Gilbert, Alan, and Josef Gugler. *Cities, Poverty, and Development: Urbanization in the Third World*. New York: Oxford University Press, 1982.

Gray, David E. *Doing Research in the Real World* (2nd edn). London: Sage Publications, 2009.

Guerraoui, Driss. *Femmes Fonctionnaires du Maroc : Enquête et Témoignages*. Casablanca: Editions Toubkal, 2002.

Guillermo, Perry, et al. *Informality: Exit and Exclusion*. Washington, DC: The World Bank, 2007.

Gutmann, Peter. 'The Subterranean Economy.' *Financial Analysis Journal*, Vol. 33, No. 6 (November-December, 1977): 26–34.

Hart, Keith. 'Informal Income Opportunities and Urban Employment in Ghana.' *The Journal of Modern African Studies*, Vol. 11, N. 1 (1973): 61–89.

Heintz, James. 'Women's Employment, Economic Risk and Poverty.' in Chant, Sylvia. *The International Handbook of Gender and Poverty: Concepts, Research, Policy*. Cheltenham: Edward Elgar, 2010: 434–439.

Heintz, James, and Imraan Valodia. *Informality in Africa: A Review. Working paper No. 3*. Cambridge: WEIGO, 2008.

Hesse-Biber, Sharlene. 'Qualitative Approaches to Mixed Methods Practice.' *Qualitative Inquiry*, Vol. 16, No. 6 (2010): 455–468.

Houston, Joel. 'The Underground Economy: a Troubling Issue for Policymakers.' *Business Review Federal Reserve Bank of Philadelphia* (September-October, 1987): 3–12.

Hoyman, Michele. 'Female Participation in the Informal Economy: A Neglected Issue.' *Annals of the American Academy of Political and Social Science*, No. 493 (1987): 64–82.

Humm, Magie. *The Dictionary of Feminist Theory*. New York: Harvester Whedsheaf, 1989.

ILO. *Global Employment Trends for Women*. Geneva: International Labor Office, 2004.

———. *Defining Strategies for Improving Working and Employment: Conditions in Micro and Small Entreprises and the Informal Economy: Overview of the ILO Learning and Research Agenda*. Geneva: International Labor Office, 2003.

———. *Women and Men in the Informal Economy: a Statistical Picture*. Geneva: International Labor Office, 2002.

———. *All Women are Working Women: The Feminization of Poverty*. Geneva: International Labor Office, 1996.

———. *Employment, Incomes and Equality: A Strategy for Increasing Productive Employment in Kenya*. Geneva: International Labour Office, 1972.

Kantor, Paula. 'A Gendered Analysis of Decent Work Deficits in India's Urban Informal Economy: Case Study Perspectives from Surat.' In Chant, Sylvia. *The International Handbook for Gender and Poverty*. Cheltenham: Edward Elgar Publishing, 2010: 478–483.

Khan, Tasnim, and Rana Ejaz Ali Khan. 'Urban Informal Sector: How Much Women Are Struggling for Family Survival.' *The Pakistan Development Review*, Vol. 48, No. 1 (2009): 67–95.

Labor Code, No. 65–99, promulgated by Dahir No. 1–03-194 dated 11 September 2003.

Layachi, Azzedine. 'Reform and the Politics of Inclusion in the Maghrib.' *Journal of North African Studies*, Vol. 5, No. 3 (2001): 15–42.

Leech, Nancy L., and Anthony J. Onwuegbuzie. 'A typology of mixed methods research designs.' *Springer Science*, Vol. 43 (2009): 265–275.

Lister, Ruth. *Poverty*. Cambridge: Polity Press, 2004.

Loayza, Norman, and Jamel Rigolini. 'Informal Employment: Safety Net or Growth Engine?' *World Development*, Vol. 39, No. 9 (2011): 1503–1515.

Losby, Jan L., et al. *Informal Economy Literature Review*. Institute for Social and Economic Development. 2002. Available online: <http://www.kingslowassoc.com/images/Informal_Economy_Lit_Review.pdf> (accessed: 8 September 2013).

McCrohan, Kevin, James D. Smith and Terry K. Adams. 'Consumer Purchases in Informal Markets: Estimates for the 1980s, Prospects for the 1990s.' *Journal for the Retailing*, Vol, 67, No. 1 (1991): 22–50.

McCrohan, Kevin, and Timothy F. Sugrue. 'An Empirical Analysis of Informal Markets Participation.' *Social Science Quarterly*, Vol. 79, No. 1 (March 1998): 212–226.

MacEwen, Scott. 'Informal Sector or Female Sector? Gender Bias in Urban Labour Market Models'. In Elson, D. *Male Bias in the Development Process*. Manchester: Manchester University Press, 1995.

Maloney, William. 'Informality Revisited.' *World Development*, Vol. 32, No. 7 (2004): 1159–1178.

Mason, Jennifer. *Qualitative Researching* (2nd Edn). London: Sage Publications, 2002.

Mazumdar, Dipack. 'The Theory of Urban Underemployment in Less Developed Countries. World Bank Staff Working Paper.' *World Bank*, No. 198 (1975): 1–39. Retrieved from: <http://documents.worldbank.org/curated/en/1975/02/1555237/theory-urban-underemployment-less-developed-countries> (accessed 20 July 2012).

Meagher, Kate. 'The empowerment Trap: Gender, Poverty and the Informal Economy in Sub-Saharan Africa.' In Chant, Sylvia. *The International Handbook for Gender and Poverty*. Cheltenham: Edward Elgar Publishing (2010): 472–477.

Mechouat, Karima. Urban Women and Work: a Case Study of Women in the City of Fez. Unpublished doctorate dissertation. Faculty of Letters and Human Sciences Dhar Mehraz-Fez, 2009.

Medeiros, Marcelo, and Joana, Costa. 'The Feminization of Poverty: a Widespread Phenomenon?' In Chant, Sylvia, ed. *The International Handbook of Poverty and Gender: Concepts, Research and Policy*. Cheltenham: Edward Edgar Publishing (2010): 95–100.

———. *Poverty among Women in Latin America: Feminization or Over representation? Working Paper* 20, Brazil: International Poverty Center – UNDP, 2006.

Mehra, Rekha, Esim Simel, and Margaret Simms. *Fulfilling the Beijing Commitment: Reducing Poverty, Enhancing Women's Economic Options*. Washington, DC: International Center For Research on Women, 2000.

Mejjati Alami, Rajaa. 'le Secteur Informel au Maroc: 1956–2004.' *50 ans de Développement Humains au Maroc et Perspèctives en 2025* (2006): 419–435. Available online: <http://europemaroc.com/files/Secteur%20informel.pdf> (accessed 10 April 2011).

Meknassi, Filali Rachid. *Femmes et Travail*. Casablanca: Editions Fennec, 1994.

Mernissi, Fatima. *Beyond the Veil: Male-Female Dynamics in Modern Muslim Society*. Bloomington: Indiana University Press, 1987.

Minot, Nicholas, et al. 'Agriculture, Trade, and Poverty in Morocco.' In Nicholas Minot, et al. *Trade Liberalization and Poverty*. Washington, DC: International Food Policy Research Institute (2010): 165–180.

Moghadam, Valentine. 'The Feminization of Poverty: Notes on a Concept and Trend.' Occasional Paper. Vol. Normal IL, No. 2: Illinois State University, Women's Studies Program, 1997.

Moser, Caroline. 'The Informal Sector Revisited: Viability and Vulnerability in Urban Development.' *Regional. Development Dialogue*, Vol. 5 (1984): 135–178.

———. 'Informal Sector or Petty Commodity Production: Dualism or Independence in Urban Development.' *World Development*, Vol. 6, No. 9 (1978): 1041–1064.

Neuman, Lawrence. W. *Social Research Methods: Qualitative and Quantitative Approaches* (6th Edn). Boston, MA: University of Wisconsin at Whitewater, 2006.

Park, Bernadette, Allegria J. Smith and Joshua Correll. 'The persistence of Implicit Behavioral Associations for Moms and Dads.' *Journal of Experimental Social Psychology*, Vol. 46, No. 5 (2010): 809–815.

Pearce, Diana. 'Welfare is not for Women: Why the War on Poverty cannot Conquer the Feminization of Poverty.' In Linda Gordon, ed. *Women, the State, and Welfare*, London: University of Wisconsin Press (1990): 265–279.

———. 'The Feminization of Poverty: Women, Work and Welfare.' *Urban and Social Change Review*, (1978): 28–36.

Peterson, Janice, and Margaret Lewis. *The Elgar Companion to Feminist Economics*. Gloucester: Edward Elgar Publishing, 1999.

Raijman, Rebecca. 'Mexican Immigrants and Informal Self-Employment: a Case study in the city of Chicago.' *Human Organization*, Vol. 60, No. 1 (2001): 47–45.

Rassam, Amal. 'The Silent Workers: Women and Craft Production in Morocco.' Patricia L. Fiske, W. R. Pickering and Ralph S. Yohe, eds. *From the Far West: Carpets and Textiles of Morocco*. Washington, DC: The Textile Museum (1980): 65–71.

Sadiqi, Fatima. *Moroccan Feminist Discourses*. New York: Palgrave Macmillan, 2014.

———. *Women, Gender* and *Language in Morocco*. Leiden: Brill, 2003.

Saginak, Kelli A., and M. Alan Saginak. 'Balancing Work and Family: Equity, Gender and Marital Satisfaction.' *The Family Journal*, Vol. 13, No. 2 (2005): 162–166.

Salime, Zakia. *Between Feminism and Islam: Human Rights and Sharia Law in Morocco*. Minneapolis: University of Minnesota Press, 2011.

Schaefer Davis, Susan. 'Women Weavers OnLine: Rural Moroccan Women on the Internet' in *Gender Technology and Development*. New Delhi: Sage Publications, Vol. 8, No.1, 2004.

Sebti, Mohammed. 'Les Métiers de l'Informel, une Insertion par le Bas' in Sebti, Mohammed, et al. *Gens de Marrakech: Géo-démographie de la Ville Rouge*. Paris: Martine Rousso Rossmann (2009): 149–172.

Sedjari, Ali D. 'Quelle Intégration du Secteur Informel Urbain au Maroc.' *Le Devenir de la Ville*. Paris: L'Harmattan, 1999.

Sen, Amartya. *Development as Freedom*. Oxford: Oxford University Press, 1999.

Sethuraman, Salem V. 'The Urban Informal Sector: Concepts, Measurement and Policy.' *International Labour Review*, Vol. 114, No. 1 (January 1976): 69–81.

Simon, Carl P., and Ann D. Witte. *Beating the System – The Underground Economy*. Boston, MA: Auburn House Publishing Compay, 1982.

Skalli, Loubna. 'Women and Poverty in Morocco: the Many Faces of Social Exclusion.' *Feminist Review*, No. 69 (2001): 73–89.

Slaoui, Souad. 'How much Digital Activism Plays a Role in Political Activism: A Case Study of Morocco's February 20th Movement.' *Journalism and Mass Communication*, Vol. 4, N° 3, March 2014, 163–171.

Standing, Guy. 'Global Feminization through Flexible Labor.' *World Development*, Vol. 17, No. 7 (1989): 1077–1095.

Strangleman, Tim, and Tracey Warren. *Work and Society: Sociological Approaches: Themes and Methods*. New York: Routledge, 2008.

Tanzi, Vito. 'Uses and Abuses of Estimates of the Underground Economy.' *The Economic Journal*. Vol. 109, No. 456 (June, 1999): 338–347.

Tesfay, Aregawi, and Haileslasie Tadele. 'The Role of Cooperatives in Promoting Socio-economic Empowerment of Women: Evidence from Multipurpose Cooperative Societies in South-Eastern Zone of Tigray, Ethiopia.' *International Journal of Community Development*, Vol. 1, No. 1 (2013): 1–11.

Todaro, Michael. 'A Model of Labor Migration and Urban Unemployment in Less Developed Countries.' *American Economic Review*. No. 59 (1969): 138–148.

Tokman, Victor E. 'Policies for a Heterogeneous Informal Sector in Latin America.' *World Development*, Vol. 17, No. 7 (1989): 1067–1076.

Vinary, Paola. 'Family Life Cycle and the Informal Economy in Central Italy.' *International Journal of Urban and Regional Research*, Vol. 9, No. 1 (1985): 89–98.

Wellington, Alison J. 'Self-Employment: the New Solution for Balancing Family and Career?' *Labour Economics*, Vol. 13 (2006): 357–386.

West, Candace, and Don H. Zimmerman. 'Doing Gender'. In Jackson, Stevi, and Sue Scott. *Gender: a Sociological Reader*. London: Routledge (2002): 42–47.

World Bank. *Gender Equality and the Millennium Development Goals. Gender and Development Group*. World Bank, 2001.

Websites

<http://www.hcp.ma/Taux-d-accroissement-de-la-population-du-Maroc-en-par-periode-et-milieu-de-residence-1960-2050_a683.html> (accessed 10 November 2013).

<http://www.alamana.org.ma/> (accessed 12 April 2014).

<http://www.zakourafondation.org/> (accessed 12 April 2014).

<http://www.albaraka.ma/fr/> (accessed 12 April 2014).

Index

Appendix

Questionnaire

Researcher: Souad BELHORMA
Date:
Place:
Hour:

Axis I: General Information about the surveyed woman

1) How old are you?
20–30 ☐ 30–45 ☐ 45–60 ☐ Above 60 ☐

2) What is your geographic belonging?
Urban ☐ rural ☐
- Place of Birth ....

3) What is your marital status?
Single ☐ Married ☐ One of the wives ☐ Single mother ☐
Divorced ☐ Widow ☐ Abandoned Woman ☐
- For married women:
  1) Does your husband work?
  Unemployed Husband ☐ Employed Husband ☐ Others ☐
  2) Does your husband have revenue?
  Stable ☐ not stable ☐
  3) How old is your Husband?
  20–30 ☐ 30–45 ☐ 45–60 ☐ Above 60 ☐
  4) What is the educational level of your husband?
  Illiterate ☐ Illiteracy courses ☐
  Primary school level ☐ Secondary school level ☐
  High school level ☐ University level ☐
  Others ....

4) What is your educational level?

Illiterate ☐ Illiteracy courses ☐
Complete Primary school level ☐
Incomplete Primary school level ☐ Secondary school level ☐
High school level ☐ University level ☐
Others ....

5) Do you have children?

Yes ☐ NO ☐

6) What is the number, age, sex and the educational level of your children?

Number of Children		Age (from older to younger)	Sex		Education	
			Male	Female	Yes	No
One child						
Two children						
Three children						
Four children						
Five children						
Six children						
Above six children						

7) Did you get a professional training?

Yes ☐ NO ☐

- If the answer is yes, in which area? ....
....
....

8) What is the type of your house?

Independent ☐ Housing with others ☐ Others........................

9) What is the nature of your house?

Ownership ☐ Rent ☐ Mortgage ☐ Others ....

Axis II: Women and Work in the Informal Sector

10) What is the type of your work in the informal sector?

....

11) What is the nature of your current work?
Stable ☐ Permanent ☐ Periodic ☐

12) What is the nature of your work's ownership?
Personal ownership ☐ Familial ownership ☐
Partnership ☐ Cooperative ☐
Others ....

13) What is your employment status?
Employer in an informal enterprise ☐ Own account worker ☐
Family unpaid worker ☐ Member of a cooperative ☐

14) Where do you practice your work?
Home ☐ Open areas ☐
Market ☐ Street vendor ☐
Shop ☐ Cooperative ☐
Others..

15) How many co-workers do you have?

....

16) How old were you when first started working in this activity?
Before 15 years old ☐ before 20 years old ☐ others ....

17) How did you start your activity? (You can choose more than one answer)
Familial tradition (Profession passed from one generation to another) ☐
Personal choice ☐ Habit ☐ Husband's job ☐
Socio-economic conditions ☐ Others...

18) What are the motivational aspects behind your work in the informal sector?

In response to the challenges of modern society ☐
In response to the modern aspirations ☐
In response to traditions ☐
In response to family needs ☐
Search for financial independence ☐
Livelihood source ☐
Flexibility in work ☐
Possibility of exercising work from home ☐
Others ……………………………………………………………………………………

19) Is work authorized or registered at the local authorities?
Yes ☐ NO ☐

20) What are your material sources to start your business?

Own money saving ☐ Bank loan ☐
Micro- credit ☐ Loan from family/relative ☐
Sales of property ☐ No need ☐
Others ……………………………………………………………………………………

21) What are the three main difficulties that affect your work (arrange the answers in order of importance: 1-more important, 3- less important)

Answers	Classification
Occupational Problems	
A lot of hard work	
Absence of capital	
Inadequacy of work environment	
Responsibilities of family and household	
Lack of competences	
Difficulties in marketing	
Difficulties in transportation	
Inadequacy of revenue	
Lack of work's stability	
Others	

Axis III: The participation of women in poverty reduction

22) How many months do you work during the year?

....

- If the number is less than 12 months, what are the reasons? (You can choose more than one answer).

Seasonal reasons ☐ my activity is new ☐ Lack of raw material ☐
High cost of raw materials ☐ lack of financial assistance ☐
Others ....

23) How many days do you work per week?

....

What are they?

....

24) How many hours do you work per day?
Less than 8 hours ☐ 8 hours ☐
More than 8 hours ☐ Others ....

25) How many rest days do you have?

....

What are they? ....

26) Where do you market your products? (You can choose more than one answer.)
Among relatives and friends ☐ in the market ☐ In open areas ☐
At home ☐ export ☐ Cooperatives ☐
Others ....

27) To whom you sell most of your products? (You can choose more than one answer.)
Individuals ☐ Cooperatives ☐ Brokers ☐ Stores ☐
Organized markets ☐ Weekly markets ☐ Passers in streets ☐
Others ....

28) What is the way of getting your income?

Daily	☐	Weekly	☐	Each 15 days	☐
Monthly	☐	By piece	☐	Others......................	

29) How much is your weekly income?

Less than 300 Dhs	☐	Between 300 and 500 dhs	☐
Between 500 and 1000 dhs	☐	Above 1000 dhs	☐

30) Are you the first breadwinner of the family?
Yes ☐ No ☐

31) Do you contribute in bearing the daily expenses of the family?
Yes ☐ No ☐

32) Where do you spend your income? (You can choose more than one answer.)

Nutrition costs		Health and medicines costs	
Clothes costs	☐	Shelter costs	☐
School supplies costs	☐	Purchase of household equipment	☐
Transportation costs	☐	others	

33) Are you obliged to contribute to the household expenses?
Yes ☐ NO ☐
Please explain..
....

34) Do you have the freedom to use your income?
Yes ☐ NO ☐
Please explain ....
....

35) Do you spend part of your income on yourself?
Yes ☐ NO ☐

- If your answer is yes, state where do you spend it? (You can choose more than one answer.)
  Personal care ☐ Excursions ☐

Visits to the parents ☐ Purchase of Jewelries ☐
Others ....

36) Do you save part of your income?
Yes ☐ NO ☐

- If your answer is yes, how much do you save from your income?
  Less than 100 dhs ☐ between 100 and 300 dhs ☐
  Between 300 and 500 dhs ☐ Above 500dhs ☐

37) Where do you save the amount of money?

Bank account	☐	Post account	☐
Micro-credits	☐	Group saving schemes (Daret)	☐
Purchase of jewelries	☐	Others	☐

Axis IV: The Contribution of women's work to their emancipation

38) Are you a member of a political party?
Yes ☐ NO ☐

- If your answer is yes,
  - What is its name?..
  - Why?..
- If your answer is No,
  - Why?..

39) What is your role inside the political party?
Member ☐ Board member ☐ Others.................................

40) Are you a member of a feminist or a Human rights' association?
Yes ☐ NO ☐

- If your answer is yes,
  - What is its name?..
  - Why?..
- If your answer is No,
  - Why?..

41) Are you a member of a cooperative?
Yes ☐ NO ☐

- If your answer is yes,
  - What is its name?..
  - Why?..
  - What is its activity?...
- If your answer is No,
  Why?..

42) If you have a capital or an economic project, do you have the freedom of its management without the intervention of a family member?
Yes ☐ NO ☐
Please explain
....
....
....

43) What are the three forms of aid required for your work? (Organize your answer in order of importance: 1- more important, 3- less important.)

Answers	Organization
Provision of a stable workplace	
Improve access to raw materials	
Benefit from new technologies	
Benefit from trainings	
Assistance in marketing products	
Formalization of the informal sector	
Completion of education	
Others	

44) In case your choice is training, what type training would you like to benefit from? (There is a possibility to choose more than one answer.)
Financial training ☐ Technical training ☐
Training in management ☐ Training in marketing ☐
Others...

45) Are you satisfied from your work?
Satisfied about my work ☐ Not satisfied about my work ☐
Please explain

……………………………………………………………………………………

……………………………………………………………………………………

46) Do you consider your work as a source of survival?
Yes ☐ NO ☐
Please explain

……………………………………………………………………………………

……………………………………………………………………………………

47) Can your business help you to achieve economic and social independence within family and society?
Yes ☐ NO ☐
Please explain

……………………………………………………………………………………

48) Do you intentions to increase the level of your work via the development of your products/ services?
Yes ☐ No ☐
If the answer is yes, what are the products/ services you want to develop?

– –
– –
– –

49) Do you do housework in parallel with your work in the informal sector?
Yes ☐ No ☐

50) Do you have a maid helping you in your housework?
Yes ☐ No ☐

51) Does your husband help you in bearing the burden of household chores?
Yes ☐ No ☐

52) What do you think of the cultural and social heritage which urges that doing household chores and child rearing is the first responsibility of women?

Agree ☐ Disagree ☐ I don't know ☐

Please explain

……………………………………………………………………………………………

……………………………………………………………………………………………

53) Are you able to do reconciliation between your work in the informal sector and your household responsibilities?

Yes ☐ No ☐

If your answer is no, what do you suggest as a solution?

……………………………………………………………………………………………

……………………………………………………………………………………………

54) How do you see yourself in 10 years?

……………………………………………………………………………………………

……………………………………………………………………………………………

55) Do you have other things you want to add about the themes we talked about?

……………………………………………………………………………………………

……………………………………………………………………………………………

Thank you

Interview Guide

Name of the Interviewee:
Date of the Interview:
Time of the Interview:

Respondent's Profile

1- What is your current work?

** Now, let us talk more precisely about your informal activity. I would like to know more details and as much as I can about your work. (Note: if a person performs more than one activity in the informal sector, the respondent is requested to talk first about the informal activity that she considers to be the primary one because other questions will be asked later on concerning the other work.)

2- What kind of work do/did you do?
3- Is/was this the first informal work that you have done?
4- How did you first start out working informally in this line of work?
5- How long have you done this particular activity?
6- For how many hours on average do you work per day?
7- In a particular week, how many hours do/did you work informally?
8- How many years do/ did you work for yourself?
9- Who are/were your primary customers/ clients?
10- Do/did you advertise, is it by word-of-mouth, or do people approach you?
11- How are/were you paid?
*** Are you paid in cash, by check, or through other arrangements?

Benefits and Motivational Reasons for the Informal Work

12- What aspects about working informally do you like?
13- What are the greatest benefits about working informally?
14- What aspects about working informally do you like least?

15- What are the biggest problems about working informally?
16- What led you to seek informal work?
17- How did you first get started working informally?
18- Do you imagine yourself earning income through informal work in the future?
19- What would need to happen for you to stop working in the informal work and have full time wage employment?

Respondent's Other Informal Work

20- We have just talked about your primary informal work and you mentioned previously that you do/did other informal activities, tell me about your other informal work?
21- How many hours do you work per a typical week for this informal job?
22- How much do you earn in a typical week from this other informal work?

Demographic Questions

Before we end, I just have a few personal questions to ask you. These questions help me get a picture of who works informally. Again, everything you share will be kept confidential.

23- What is your age?
24- Where are you from?
25- Where do you live?
26- What is your current marital situation?
27- How many children do you have?
28- How much education have you had?
29- What is your income per day, per week, per month?
30- Do you have any query or additions that can enrich one of the themes raised above or is there a subject you would like to speak about?

Africa in Development

Series Editor: Jeggan C. Senghor
Institute of Commonwealth Studies, University of London

While African development remains a preoccupation, policy craftsmen and a multiplicity of domestic and international actors have been engaged in the quest for solutions to the myriad problems associated with poverty and underdevelopment. Academic and scholarly responses have built on traditional and non-traditional analytical frameworks and promoted a multidimensional discourse on, for example, conflict management, peace and security systems, HIV/AIDS, democratic governance, and the implications of globalization.

This series is designed to encourage innovative thinking on a broad range of development issues. Thus its remit extends to all fields of intellectual inquiry with the aim of highlighting the advantages of a synergistic interdisciplinary perspective on the challenges of and opportunities for development in the continent. Of particular interest are studies with a heavy empirical content which also have a bearing on policy debates and those that question theoretical orthodoxies while being grounded on concrete developmental concerns.

The series welcomes proposals for collected papers as well as monographs from recent PhDs no less than from established scholars.

Book proposals should be sent to oxford@peterlang.com.

Volume 1 Jeggan C. Senghor: The Politics of Senegambian Integration, 1958–1994. 335 pages. 2008.

Volume 2 Finex Ndhlovu: The Politics of Language and Nation Building in Zimbabwe. 243 pages. 2009.

Volume 3 Sabelo J. Ndlovu-Gatsheni: Do 'Zimbabweans' Exist? Trajectories of Nationalism, National Identity Formation and Crisis in a Postcolonial State. 426 pages. 2009.

Volume 4 Suzanne Mulligan: Confronting the Challenge: Poverty, Gender and HIV in South Africa. 207 pages. 2010.

Volume 5 Johnson W. Makoba: Rethinking Development Strategies in Africa: The Triple Partnership as an Alternative Approach – The Case of Uganda. 287 pages. 2011.

Vols 6–8 Forthcoming

Volume 9 Edward Cavanagh: The Griqua Past and the Limits of South African History, 1902–1994. 152 pages. 2011.

Volume 10 Ayokunle Olumuyiwa Omobowale: The *Tokunbo* Phenomenon and the Second-Hand Economy in Nigeria. 216 pages. 2013.

Volume 11 Titus O. Pacho: Critical and Creative Education for the New Africa. 213 pages. 2013.

Volume 12 Kehinde Olabimtan: Samuel Johnson of Yorubaland, 1846–1901: Identity, Change and the Making of the Mission Agent. 363 pages. 2013.

Volume 13 Emefiena Ezeani: Cooperative Collegial Democracy for Africa and Multi-ethnic Societies: Democracy without Tears. 215 pages. 2013.

Volume 14 John Idriss Lahai: Gender in Practice: Culture, Politics and Society in Sierra Leone. 290 pages. 2016.

Volume 15 Anthony Victor Obeng: Decolonizing Africa and African Development: The Twenty-First-Century Pan-Africanist Challenge. 300 pages. 2017.

Volume 16 Souad Belhorma: Women in the Informal Sector and Poverty Reduction in Morocco: the city of Fez as a case study. 332 pages. 2019.

Made in United States
North Haven, CT
20 October 2026

20740128R00183